To Laura & David
with my best wishes

By Yannis Andricopoulos

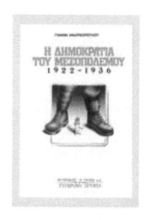

i

This is an immensely readable work which goes on a fresh and challenging exploration of historical events and ideas. The message is strengthened by Yannis' personal perspective and style. I am left touched, educated and reflective.

Malcolm Stern, co-founder of 'Alternatives', London

An insightfully and eloquently written personal story that fuses movingly together politics, history and ideas.

Michael Eales, Leadership Consultant

Through this erudite memoir, Yannis brings once again his incisive gaze to crucial issues of our time. His illuminating analysis carries its own solution: to revitalise our civil society we need also to look more deeply into our own selves. His journey is an inspiration.

Crysse Morrison, writer, journalist

A fascinating book interlinking Yannis' personal story with Greece's history and wider cultural developments in a way that is often both surprising and entertaining. It is a 'biography with a difference' that ends with the conclusion that the political rests in the personal.

Silke Ziehl, Entelia Institute, Munich & London

History, Politics and Dreams

by

Yannis Andricopoulos

Grosvenor House
Publishing Limited

The right of Yannis Andricopoulos to be identified as the author of this
work has been asserted by him in accordance with Section 78
of the Copyright, Designs and Patents Act 1988

The book cover picture is copyright to Yannis Andricopoulos

This book is published by
Grosvenor House Publishing Ltd
28-30 High Street, Guildford, Surrey, GU1 3EL.
www.grosvenorhousepublishing.co.uk

A CIP record for this book
is available from the British Library

ISBN 978-1-78148-370-1

Contents

1

On History's Shores

Sunday morning, December the 3rd. In the sparkling sunshine the world looks like a newborn baby on suavity's breast. The pomegranates in the garden are beaming, the creatures of the earth have abandoned their daily tasks and enjoy the multicoloured filigrees of air, the hearty good mornings of the neighbours give wings to their singing thoughts.

The day is tingling with joy. Nothing in it to indicate the sun is shining in vain. Nothing to suggest the hours are pregnant with disaster.

I put on my best clothes, chat with my friends about that bully, the one who lives up the road, and then make the move for my appointment with the day's big event: the huge demonstration in central Athens in support of the National Liberation Front (EAM).

On the way, I come across a British soldier guarding the German Evangelical church at the very top of Sina street. With a smile on his face and a Woodbine between his fingers, he offers me a bar of chocolate, the very first chocolate I had ever tasted. Ineffable delight.

In Panepistimiou Avenue the crowd is assembling: young and old, men and women, town and country folks. Most have scrawny figures, affably premature wrinkles and clothes Oxfam would regretfully be unable to accept. Four years of war, occupation, famine and malnutrition had left their incontestable mark. Nevertheless, looking forward to a break from human viciousness and holding flags or placards in their hands, they are all now cheery and playful. Flirtatious, too.

To see better what is going on I climb on a stool on the street's pavement just in front of the Agricultural Bank of Greece. Notaras, the short, bald owner of the basement beeraría, the pub next to the bank, had kindly given me a hand. Next to me is Yannis Manos, my best friend who later on developed the bad habit of outsmarting me in maths. I was, however, able to take it as, I told myself, he was a whole six months older than me.

Soon the crowds – a quarter of a million people – start parading in front of us towards Syntagma square chanting rhythmically E-A-M. I respond to these waves of intoxicating ebullience with my clenched palm at the end of an arm stretched up in the air and moving vigorously to the music of the slogans. I am chanting and singing with them, and many demonstrators, women in particular, wave back with a smile.

One of them teases me.

– 'Oh, what a beautiful voice.'

I blushed from neck to hairline in embarrassment.

But this is all there is in my book of memories as I was not even five at the time. The rest comes from stories verbalising an anguish desperately looking for clothes to conceal its wretched features. The demonstrators reached Syntagma square where, without provocation, they were fired upon by the security battalions, the extreme right wing gangs that had been armed and equipped by the German occupation forces to fight EAM.

This venal force had now been re-employed by the British whose army had been sent to Greece by prime minister Churchill, not to fight the Germans, but to ensure that after the latter's withdrawal the country would not be taken over by EAM.

– 'Is that so?', Mark Rutherford, a new acquaintance, asked rather unexpectedly when I was talking about it in a small group of people.

I do not know how we had got into this conversation. Just before that he had been explaining to me here, in the Isle of Wight, the Tao essence of the original intention.

The tone of incredulity in his voice, though elaborately low, did not pass unnoticed.

– 'I've just been watching', he carried on almost apologetically, 'some recently released digitized Pathe News footage from a historic cinema newsreel. The story was that Britain liberated Greece from the Germans'.

– 'Fiddlesticks', I retorted vehemently. 'The British troops had precise instructions not to engage militarily the Germans.'

Instantly reconnecting with my Greek excitability surprised me as after all these years in England I thought it had been watered down. But I should not have been surprised. Temper is not tempered by time.

– 'Well, OK', nonplussed, he responded. 'But what's exactly this EAM?'

His karmic energy had gone by then.

– 'EAM, the National Liberation Front', I said, 'represented the wartime Greek resistance movement. Though the communists had played a leading role in its formation, its aim was the liberation of the country from the occupying forces and, after the war, the restoration of the sovereign rights of the people. These rights had been denied to them by the prewar beastly regime, controlled by the King, the army and the fascists of Metaxas, the dictator, whom the old and pathetic political establishment was unwilling or unable to confront.'

The intention was to give him an answer as short and economical as mini-skirts. But I could not resist the temptation to expand. Without invitation I therefore carried on.

– 'EAM's appeal was almost by definition widespread. Its ranks had been joined by people from all walks of life whatever their profession, social class or previous political allegiances. They represented the best of their generation. This force, as the British themselves conceded, was "universally believed to be manned by patriots and democrats". It embodied the hopes and the aspirations of the nation.'

Yet, British prime minister Churchill was determined to annihilate it.

Not because EAM intended to grab and monopolise after the war the power that it already exerted in mainland Greece. Its intention, instead, was to work with the British and the puppet government-in-exile the latter had set up in Cairo but under two conditions. First, that King George, the British stooge in the throne of Greece and the power behind the pre-war Metaxas dictatorship, would not return unless the people decided in a referendum to bring him back. And, secondly, that the authoritarian army would be re-organised in tune with the democratic expectations of the people.

Having finished the thorough examination of his fingernails by the time I had finished with my answer, Mark proceeded then to inform me that they needed trimming.

– 'Good idea', I said as cheerily as I could. I almost added:

– 'But just make sure you leave enough length to scratch, if it ever itches, the skin of your curiosity.'

The same political discussion, I remember, I first had back in 1944, while talking with Idomeneas Stratigopoulos, a 20-year old member of EAM.

– 'What EAM wants is very reasonable', he told me while I was drawing a cat on paper. 'This is in everybody's interests.'

That was, I thought, as plain as the nose in his face.

Ido's views, despite the waving of his hands in the space above his head, contained nothing striking. I remember it nevertheless because he was talking to me the same way he would be talking to an adult which is not what a child can expect. Ido later on was hit by a bullet in the leg that caused a wound that never healed, and then frustrated at developments, he left Greece for good. He settled in Paris where he worked for the French media as a journalist. I reconnected with him after 1966.

But Churchill would not hear a word about it all.

For one thing, his preoccupation or, indeed, his obsession with Greece was phenomenal – even on D-Day he spent quite a lot of time dealing with developments on the Greek front. And for another, his thick-skinned stubbornness, the bullheadedness the British themselves were already so well acquainted with, would not allow the relaxation of the pertinacious pursuit of his goals.

Whatever the people's expectations, the king, a man as English as Yorkshire puddings, had to be restored to the throne and, together with the army, the same army that in 1935 had destroyed the democratic institutions, ensure that Greece remained within the British sphere of influence.

Politics, obviously, is just another word to describe the pursuit of self-interest.

Twenty-eight people dead and scores injured on that Sunday, the 3rd of December 1944. Next day, the Anglo-Greek war, i.e. the war between EAM and the 80,000 British troops despatched to Greece for that very purpose, began. It ended a few weeks later with the defeat, though not the annihilation, of EAM.

Thankfully, I captured only small fragments of this momentous and also tragic event. Still, the memory of those days remains affixed on me like a number branded with red-hot iron on the haunches of army horses.

I can still see EAM fighters calling the Athenians with home-made funnel-shaped horns to resist the British, the latter using their artillery from the Lycabettus hill against EAM units entrenched in parts of the city or, early in 1945, the hundreds of

EAM prisoners shepherded by the British into the cadets academy. They were shouting:

– 'Brits! Let us choose our own government!'

Their spirit was anything but broken. From my side of the barbed wire the picture looked, however, rather dismal. Defiance had lost its sparkly colour.

Yet, this was not the worst I had witnessed. The latter came the day, probably in January 1945, when, walking with my mother, Rinoula, we reached the National Garden on its Queen Sofia Avenue borders. A stone-silent crowd assembled there was observing the piling up in lorries of many, perhaps a hundred, naked dead bodies for removal and burial.

So used to death, I was not touched by the spectacle at the time and the only question, I remember, I asked my mother was:

– 'Why are these people naked?'

With equal simpleness, I could have asked her why women have breasts.

But the long term impact of what I had witnessed was traumatic. It touched all the four corners of my existence. The event had, however, nothing unique as the dead at the time seemed to outnumber the living.

Probably a month earlier, Alice, my five-year old girl friend, had been killed from a stray bullet in front of our house, in Apokavkon Street, and so had Marina, a twenty year-old girl and a member of my father's resistance group. When I knocked on her door in Daphnomelis Street, the neighbour told my father that she had gone. For good.

Death seemed to be hiding around every corner.

I did not hear what a hairdresser said in another instance, when my father stopped at his shop to ask him about one of his colleagues. But I remember his doleful eyes, the almost silent whispering in response to my father's question and what I sensed as a rueful attempt at humour.

Was I surprised? Certainly not.

To us, the kids, death looked as natural as TV ads look in our days and mourning just as normal as the civil servants' salaried routines. The boundaries between life and death had been blurred. The spirits of the dead and those of the living seemed to co-exist in one and the same world like soap bubbles roving in the screech of the wind.

In such a context, it did not even occur to me that kids under the age of five do not fire guns, as I did outside Athens when I visited the guerilla camp where my father, Mitsos, was stationed or that people do not play football with human skulls scattered in unbuilt parts of the city as I did a few years later with my friends.

The extraordinary acceptance of this world was in direct proportion to what we, the kids, perceived as normal life. Death looked like a custom people dutifully had to observe.

Life could be questioned, but only if you have experienced something different. But we could not do that. Our world was the only one we knew. We could not even imagine that life could appear in a different set of clothes or offer us alternatives and choices.

This, in a way, was not absolutely true as, according to my mother, I had repeatedly asked her:

– 'Mum, please, give me a piece of meat even if it's as small as my fingernail.'

She could not oblige.

There was one thing, however, that did not look to me like part of some preordained destiny.

It is what happened one afternoon, sometime in the first few months of 1945. Three armed men in some sort of uniform slid into our house like an eel into a rock. I am not sure what exactly happened while they were there as my mother sent me immediately to our neighbours, a Greek family that had arrived from Odessa as refugees the time the Bolsheviks took over.

What I know is that by the time I had finished the tea served from their hot samovar and practised a few more words in Russian before being asked to come back home all the expensive stock my father had brought from his shop to the house for safe keeping was no longer there.

– 'They've just gone', she managed to tell me with a reassuring voice in which one could easily detect something more than a soupçon of blind terror. The event left her with a psychological trauma from which she never really recovered.

To keep her silent, she told the neighbours later, the intruders had stuck a gun in her belly.

All this was, of course, a long time ago, when, as Hilary Mantel said while talking about Cromwell's time, 'life was simple and violent and usually brief'. It was the time my childhood was a resident of Greece's long wars that started when, first, Mussolini's Italy and then Hitler's Germany attacked Greece. The country was occupied, brutalised and forced to travel through a sea of suffering that nobody can recall without pain that makes even the blood in the veins ache. The famine alone killed as many as three hundred thousand people, most of them in Athens during the winter of 1941 – 1942.

I have memories of it all – the Germans patrolling Panepistimiou Avenue, the clandestine resistance networks my father was involved with and the diet of rotten green peas that turned me off green peas forever.

Time has moved swiftly since to keep its various appointments with progress – smartphones, genetically modified food, sperm-banks, drones, bankers' bonuses or anti-ageing treatments to turn back the clock. But this, a memory of pure flowing sadness, is not destined to go. What will never go either is the memory of the inexhaustible inner reserve of adaptive capability and the camaraderie that rescued us from spiritual annihilation.

In the battle against fear, pain or grief, the mother who had lost a son, the sick old lady around the corner, the orphan or the crippled young man were never on their own. We were there for each other, sometimes crying in each other's arms and often laughing at ourselves. In our very ordinary way, the way we were all before the market turned us into unique individuals indistinguishable from each other, this is how we succeeded in beating death.

Simple people, i.e. people who perspire, do not talk this way, and we never did. But that was the triumph of the human spirit over monstrous wickedness and primordial pain, the dance of the heart on the raging shores of history.

The legacy of these early experiences was not, therefore, that of fear caused by devastation and death. It was, instead, that of awe at the inexhaustible strength that enables man to rise above his rank and humiliate death, reverence for this tremendous power generated by the indestructible human spirit when the fire burns fiercely inside.

In the womb of mystery, where Thanatos and Eros are being reconciled, we had, strangely, found ourselves. The absolute, marching beyond the tumult of the time into the pledges of a future clothed with our desires, the new world of pristine freshness that was to be born, had given life the meaning denied by calculation, trades-off and compromises.

– 'Fascinating', an English acquaintance who looked like everyone else but even more so, commented over his fruit salad.

Those who lived through the Blitz, the time the UK was bombarded by nazi Germany, would have certainly given a different answer.

What sustained us was also the vision of a nicer world. It was all a dream.

The White Terror unleashed by the fascist gangs against the former EAM fighters turned gradually into a horror story. Between 1945 and 1946 the male population of entire villages was in some instances wiped out, thousands were murdered and many others were arrested and tortured.

One of them was Antonis Brillakis, one of the Left's leaders in later years, who, as he told me in Frankfurt in 1969, was dipped in the sea tied up in a bag full of cats, which, struggling for their lives, tore his flesh to the bone.

The Gestapo could not have been more innovative.

Almost incredibly, whereas in France, Italy or Yugoslavia the prisons were filled up with collaborators of the Nazis, in Greece they were flooded with ex-resistance fighters.

– 'Fair play', Menios, a friend who had spent years in a concentration camp, told me during our family's Easter meal I had invited him to, 'doesn't figure in reality's books. It exists only in gracious tales.'

'Driven by the winds and errors of the sea', as Dryden would have it, the Greek communists, despite Moscow's implicit refusal to support them, opted then for an armed insurrection.

– 'Could all this have been averted?', the Greeks ask themselves decades after this dreadful experience, when, like Adam, they sit down to recollect the time of their fall.

One answer one could give is:

– 'Yes, if the democratic forces had surrendered unconditionally to the Nazi gangs.'

Another one could be:

– 'Yes, if the British were not so bloody-minded.'

Clement Attlee, the Labour leader, had won the 1945 elections in Britain by a huge landslide, but the country's strategic interests had not changed. The cold war had already began and an ugly mood was sweeping across Europe.

In 1947 the Americans had, meanwhile, stepped into the British shoes. They did so in order to strengthen the West's security against the Soviet Union as, they believed, the collapse of Greece would threaten their own interests. The insouciant promiscuity of their sympathies and the corrupt and manipulative political establishment of the country ensured easily the latter's utter subservience. The task ahead, not all that easy, was to consolidate their domination through the military, which had its own priorities.

Yet, despite the difficulties, the US became in no time the super government of Greece. No decisions were taken without the Americans' approval. Governments, their vassals, were appointed and dismissed by them.

But, on the other hand, ministers, all those who despite their efforts still remain unremarkable, could still freely choose the brand of cigarettes they fancied.

The communist insurrection led inevitably to a full-scale and most destructive civil war. A few years later, in 1949, the US-backed extreme Right, victorious and savage, consolidated itself in power for a long time to come. More than one hundred thousand people, 'folk as simple as trees in sunlight', branded as communists, were either executed, tortured, imprisoned or deported to concentration camps. Millions were expelled from public life.

One of them was my father. He was arrested and kept in a draughty police cell in Athens where I met him under the cold yellow stare of the station's officers.

– 'When will you be back home?', I asked. 'Soon', he said with a voice devoid of any certainty.

He was released a month later but only after he had signed a 'declaration of repentance' by which he denounced communism and the 'traitorous' organisations under its spell.

My father had joined EAM but he was not a communist. Still signing such a statement under the threat of his being deported to a concentration camp was for him a humiliating experience that, he felt, he had to go through if my mother, myself and also my younger sister were not to be left abandoned to the mercy of our savage times.

I did not give this momentous event any thought at the time as, in the first place, I did not exactly know what was going on. Later on, when I became fully aware of it, I felt embarrassed by his action.

Doubts emerged only later, when I became a father myself.

– 'What would I have done in his position?'

I asked myself this question in my West Hampstead home while my children, Ari and Chloe, were opening their presents under the Christmas tree. 'Would I not have done the same to protect my family? One could give his life in the pursuit of a principle, but does the latter justify sacrificing for it also the life of his children?

– 'Children are real. Are principles as real?'

Sitting on the blade of such decisions is not like ensconcing yourself on a Le Corbusier leather chair. Thankfully, however, it all had to do with the past, which, lying on the sofa by the oval window, was nevertheless staring silently at me.

So, 'democracy had won', as Yannis Ritsos, the troubadour of modern Greece who spent several of his best years as a political prisoner in concentration camps, penned. But 'mouths were stuffed with silence', the patterned silence whose reverberations determined every day's figurations. The ghost of the 'ever victorious' army of liberation, the artifact of the Left's wishful thinking, was now strolling discomfitedly through the ruins of the future, mercilessly haunting the vibes of the present.

The dream had been crushed. The attempt to penetrate into the ideal future's omphalian zone had ended in tragedy. The cries of despair could be heard even by those who had not yet been born.

This vision was nothing but a chimaera, evidence, perhaps, of an irrepressible penchant for the grotesque, a bizarre representation of an imagined world dictated by the need to escape the hideousness of the time. Despite the growth of a powerful democratic movement during the years of the occupation, we had all ended up with a quasi-fascist regime established with Britain's help by the despised royalists, the remnants of the pre-war dictatorship and the collaborators of the Nazis.

But the next question was how we, the inheritors of so many misfortunes, could now come to terms with the meaninglessness of a past that had once meant so much to so many, the 'hissing lies dyed deeply in (my) country's blood', the harrowing realisation that history had been written by the betrayed, mislaid now and nobody's loss. 'So many bodies cast into the jaws of the sea, the jaws of the earth', George Seferis, the poet, lamented by Acheron, the river of sorrows, 'so many souls given over to the millstones, like wheat... so much life plunged into an abyss for an empty garment'. All in vain. Everything for nothing, the voice of the void, the sign of absurdity.

The sea, as Márquez would have said, had grown larger with our tears just as the Nile had with Isis' tears.

– 'Where do you then take it from here?'

That was what we kept asking ourselves in the effort to make sense in a world that no longer did.

It was not a question a ten-year old boy needed to answer, particularly as this ten-year old boy had discovered a bookshop off Phillelinon Street, close to the first public library Pisistratos had established in Athens in BC540, where I could borrow books which introduced me to the world of literary fiction. The universe all of a sudden was painted with colours which only the imagination could see.

But meanwhile, in what was, perhaps, destiny's joke, the communists had buried their dead only to discover years later the dismal futility of the ultimate sacrifice. Unfortunately, those who had joined the communist party, men and women committed to ending capitalist injustice and repression, and ready, as the early Christians, to die for their beliefs, had never doubted or questioned their Bible's truth.

– 'These beliefs', Stathis Damianacos, a good old friend from the university days remarked, 'fill you with a mystic power that cannot be challenged.'

Stathis later on had a distinguished career in France in the field of cultural sociology. He died alone in his Paris flat in 2003.

These people who had 'gain'd no title and who lost no friend', had the strength to stand fearlessly before the firing squad, accept irrepressibly death, treat 'death to a raki served in their grandfathers' skulls', as Yannis Ritsos immortalised the mood in his verse. But, as if they were partially mute, they did not have the courage to question the commands of their party.

The phenomenon, not particularly Greek, could be understood, but only if one was willing to accept that the high party priests had turned socialism into religion.

The questions we all had to answer, blood-red in colour, were there, but what, thankfully, saved me from internal demolition was principally my age.

Being a member of the baby generation that had not really experienced either the German occupation, the horrors of the civil war or the worst brutalities of the quasi-fascist regime that emerged victorious from the carnage, my investment in all that makes the heart tick, the future, was not in blood.

In the pursuit of a dream, I had not paid the price the older generations had. Yet, just as a drop of blood on the white tablecloth, the impact of these events left an indelible mark on my life.

At that time at least, all this was, however, far too remote from the prosaic severity of my daily life. The civil war itself had not touched me as it was conducted in the countryside, far away from the capital, and the reports on its development, as they appeared in the heavily censored Athenian press, could not catch the interest of a very young boy. Besides, talk about the war could not burst the framework of our harrowing daily realities that a contemporary family cannot even conceive.

We lived in the neighbourhood of the unimaginable. The economy had been ruined, the country was bankrupt, farmland and villages had been devastated, and about a quarter of the population was homeless.

– 'The masses of people', Paul Porter, head of the first US mission to Greece, reported early in 1947, 'live on a bare subsistence'. Yet, 'traders, speculators and black marketers thrive in wealth and luxury.'

Ourselves, we had nothing to heat the house with in the cold winter days, when even the ghosts could be heard complaining, no refrigeration or proper cooking facilities, no hot water, no washing machine and no shower room. Baths were taken in a metal bucket.

But I never felt any discomfort about it all. Comfort was not our currency in those days. And the birds, after all, though they have even less, could still fly high.

Even so we were still pretty lucky as some of the families in the middle class neighbourhood where I used to live, had to endure life in a one room flat with the kitchen or the toilet across the communal yard. As bad looked to me the state of the only Jewish family in my neighbourhood with whom, however, we had no contact as we had been warned that Jews eat children.

Only a fool could ignore such a warning.

An even worse and lingering testament of those times' hardship was the slum called Kountouriotika, located behind the Panathinaikos FC stadium. I had to go through it daily on my way to school. Housing a few thousand refugees who came to Greece following the 1922 Asia Minor disaster, it looked exactly as it did when it was first established: a shantytown with people living in corrugated shacks without running water, heat or electricity.

Further, we had no toys, not even a ball, to play with in the neighbourhood's rugged streets, furrowed by the rainwater. Hence to amuse ourselves we had to improvise as when, in the forties, we used to place bullets on the rails of the tramway, which, once the tram went over, exploded and hit I never knew what.

– 'Bingo! One more German.'

Much more fun than fireworks.

The priest in a black cossock, who one day crossed our path while we were enjoying our game, did not seem to share our enthusiasm. We did not mind it, and, as the custom was and still is, we secretly touched our genitals. Seeing a priest in the morning is considered to be bad luck to be countered by making contact with our most vital organ.

Unfortunately, none of these instances could be documented photographically as cameras embodied aspirations far above their income. Nobody I knew had a camera. They were for everyone an unaffordable luxury.

Equal to that, if not more fun, were all the games with sexual undertones in which, educated far in advance of our years, we all indulged from a very early age. Unfortunately, in one instance, when I was ten and Theoni, a girl of similar age, tried to initiate me, not exactly in sex, but in its mystery, I ended up in trouble.

My mother saw us and, incensed, offered me a hint of discouragement by hitting me on the head with a frying pan.

This, I am sure, must have put God in a very difficult position.

But this did not really bother me as at the time other things on my list of worries had gained priority.

2

A Time Short On Doubts

Up until this point life had not shown much to recommend itself. All I had experienced was war, death, oppression, deprivation and pain. Having been caught in the cold draught of those days had left me with a lasting revulsion for almost everything that had invaded my life. It left its mark on me and in a subtle way it moulded my thinking.

Still, with the new decade, and as we all gradually started to grow out of the misery of the wars, I was nevertheless ready to travel beyond the past painful experiences.

But life was resolutely reluctant to oblige.

In 1953 the government devalued the drachma by a massive 50 per cent vis-a-vis the US dollar. Whatsoever its effect on the economy, the devaluation hit my father very hard as a large business loan he had secured the year before had instantly doubled in size because it had been made in gold sovereigns. The result was more hardship for us though my mother could still manage to get some food to our Russian neighbour, a nurse, Anna Prokopovna, who had escaped the bolsheviks in 1917 hoping to find a better life in Greece.

– 'Misfortune', someone said, 'is the mother of invention.'

It was not in my case. It marked, instead, the beginnings of a dreary time amply illustrated by that new and ludicrously long raincoat, the size of a horse blanket, I had been given and had, despite my protests, to wear.

– 'Don't worry', my mother re-assured me after wiping her hands on the edge of her apron. 'You'll grow up and one day it will fit you very nicely.'

Her argument never cut any ice. But I could do nothing. There were no laws against a family's long term economic planning. Or against long raincoats. If there were, I might have sued my parents later for not doing their best for me.

Remembering, perhaps, things that had never happened, a woman with a snowflake headband I met twenty or so years ago in a Hampstead teashop told me that she had actually done so. We enjoyed our tea, which, she said, she liked made with very wet water, but I never bothered to get the details of her venture. I was with her on listening rather than speaking terms.

In that same raincoat, in which I could never impress the girls I had just started to take an interest in, I had to go to school and also to part-time jobs. One of them involved the selling of Christmas decorations in street stalls in Aeolus Street, the old commercial part of Athens, during my school holidays.

The pressure this put me under was at times so high that once, during a French lesson at school, I burst into tears which bedewed my cheeks.

– 'I'm sorry', I told the young female teacher whose long, photogenic legs, amply displayed, illuminated the dark room we were sitting. 'I just cannot find the time to do my homework.'

That was half the truth. The other half was that selling was not something I could do. Some people can sell sunglasses to the blind or scarves at Isadora Duncan's funeral. I could not sell water to a thirsty fellow lost in the desert. I lacked the essential qualities required for the job.

Clients, when buying something, would as a rule ask for a discount, which I would offer without any discussion. I did not have it in me to argue that the price was just right as I could not engage them in a discussion of the kind a sales woman resorted to a century later in Antigua when offering me an alternative to what I was thinking of buying.

– 'It's not cheaper', she said, 'but it's less expensive.'

Money talk was just distasteful.

Trying to be clever, once I overcharged a smartly-dressed, middle-aged woman of transparent gentleness. The thinking behind it was that after the expected request for a discount, I would, for a change, end up with the right price. Except that she did not ask for a discount and after thanking me, she left.

I still feel guilty about it.

My business sense, if I ever had one, must have been mislaid somewhere, perhaps in a 'rats' alley where the dead men lost their bones'. Almost a lifetime later I came across William Thackeray's view that the selling of goods is:

– 'A shameful and infamous practice, meriting the contempt and scorn of all real gentlemen.'

I could under no circumstances lay claim to being a 'real gentleman' or even just a gentleman. But for some strange reason selling had turned out to be as unsettling as the reasons that forced me into it.

My life, I felt at that point, had been derailed. But this did not stop me having fun. I still relished the boisterous street games which, though immensely enjoyable, could instill terror into the heart of most parents of our days, swimming in the still unpolluted waters of Phaleron Bay, going to the church of Saint Isidore, in Lycabettus, where I used to attend the midnight Easter mass, attending the Karaghiozis shows by Mollas in Radar, the Alexandra Avenue open-air theatre, Fernandel's and later on the Jerry Lewis' films or the tunes of the earthy music of Tsitsanis.

Though I never had the pleasure of listening to Tsitsanis in a live performance, I addressed my goodbye to him when his springs of existence gave way in London in 1984.

I did also greatly enjoy the vivacity of our neighbourhood relations. They flourished particularly in the hot summer evenings when we all gathered on the steps of our street houses to indulge in a bit of gossip and discuss the events of the day. We laughed a lot, too, as when my neighbour kyrios Spyros, a tall, skinny, loquacious man, walked in his pyjamas to the police station, half a mile away, to protest at something another neighbour had done.

– 'You forgot your tie', Koula Hourmouzis, another neighbor and a second mother to me, teased him, while rolling her eyes up in disbelief.

– 'Don't you worry about it', he retorted with the same fury that guided his steps.

Koula, last time I saw her, in her eighties, had fine lines crinkled around her lively eyes. But nothing was alive in the cloisters of her memory. Dementia had completely drained her out.

Played out in the streets rather than on television screens, life was not infected as yet by the virus that has hit our contemporary societies: loneliness, euphemistically called 'independence'. People were not lonely like trees in a forest. 'No tree in a forest', Hermann Hesse, the Swiss poet, said, 'knows his neighbour. Each is alone'.

We were, instead, a closely-knit community sharing willingly and sometimes unwillingly our likes and dislikes as well as our closely guarded secrets of which, of course, everybody was fully aware.

Many of my neighbours were also quite interesting people. One of them, Philippos Nakas, turned later into the founder of a chain of shops selling musical instruments and of the Athens-based Nakas conservatory, and another one, Aspasia Kalodiki, was married later to Nikiphoros Mandilaras, an outstanding lawyer who was killed by the military junta in 1967.

Another neighbour, Elias Demetracopoulos, turned into a journalist with a formidable cache of key diplomatic and political contacts. As a lobbyist in Washington during the Greek dictatorship, he became a thorn in the side of president Nixon and then 'a target of destruction' by his administration.

I renewed my connection with him in Washington in 1972, when I was researching the State Department's archives on pre-war Greece.

Despite the spiritual joy offered by all the simple pleasures of life, something had nevertheless shifted in me following my father's bankruptcy.

I could no longer take anything for granted. Life, all of a sudden, looked incomprehensible, confusing, and rudderless. The days of celestial innocence were, obviously, over. The time to start forging practical dreams seemed to be coming fast.

Together with it came a hidden anxiety that kept fluttering its wings ominously in the tranquillity of the night. It was reflected in my perceptions of myself – my behaviour and my daily routines and habits. It looked as if the parameters of what I should expect in my future, circumscribed life had been drawn.

I felt as if I was destined to be part of a crowd that was never going to travel first class or, unless I sold one of my kidneys, sit for a cocktail at Zonars, the fancy patisserie near Syntagma Square favoured by seemingly opulent American visitors. Rather than thinking I could go with Jules Verne on a trip around the world in eighty days or fly to tropical St Lucia and enjoy a drink with a celebrity as I did later with Amy Winehouse, the English singer songwriter, I had to settle for a job.

– 'Perhaps, a door-to-door salesman to keep you off the streets', a conceited schoolmate helpfully suggested.

My answer came in words not realised.

Alternatively, and if lucky enough, I might, perhaps, be seated on the other side of the door I was looking at as a boy while standing stock still in front of the National Bank of Greece. But by then, I might have even convinced myself that seated there as the bank's employee was the result of my unbiased free will and discriminating judgment.

School had never encouraged us to plan for something different, to have ambitions and work hard for their realisation. Such topics were never raised in our league. They would not fit our station. But even if ambitions were there, they were pulverised in the blender of survival. On the other hand, the possibility of becoming a bank or a state employee was abhorrent to me. As viewed from my dreams' open windows the prospect was just too abysmal.

As far as I was concerned, middle-class security implied on the one hand, a centrally-heated existence but, on the other, withdrawal into a tenebrous non-existence, absorption into ordinariness. A life insipid and indescribable. It meant disengagement from life and engagement with details beyond the boundaries of meaning.

This may sound absurd in our days, but certainly there are other absurdities of greater consequence.

In any case, a job in the public sector was out of the question. To get such a job, even as a municipal road-sweeper, one needed a certificate of loyalty to the post-civil war regime, which more than half the population would have never been supplied with by the state security apparatus. Fortunately, for the time being, I did not, however, have to look for a job. If nothing else, I was too young for it.

Though underpinned by the understanding that life had made no commitments to me to be honoured whatever the circumstances, the craving for meaning was, meanwhile, taking me in an entirely different direction. More than anything else, I felt, I had to honour my political inheritance and join the march into the future.

Loyal to lost causes, I did not, therefore, care about 'success' in professional terms. I did not care about possessions either. Neither in those times nor at any other time up to our days has either of them lured me by their spell. What mattered was our common future.

I was, of course, fully aware that, politically speaking, we were 'out at sea with broken oars'. But that was of minor importance. What mattered was the future, which, incidentally, was being shaped in ways that were not even vaguely discernible to me.

Valentina, a 1950 song by Yorgos Mitsakis, had already tuned into it.

– 'Hi Valentina', it went on, 'you've now got a car and drive wherever you fancy. Soon, as it goes, we'll also see you in trousers.'

Knitting, which was hitherto regarded, just like breasts, as a female sex characteristic had lost its importance. Our past was being threatened and so were our prejudices on whose shoulders our macho self-image happily rested. But I was not exactly aware of it all as our focus was different: politics.

Politics at the time was for us not the marketplace where one could open a shop and trade in promises. It was, instead, the arena in which the future, a force much more powerful than any personal considerations, would be dancing to the frenzied tunes of our heart. The approach was of course romantic, totally alien to the professional nature of politics. Yet, it had to be that way because the commitment made was to an idea which had to be free from lesser calculations.

This was what I passionately believed in though I scarcely knew what the 'idea' really was. Its skin was alluring, just as Mary's, the daughter of our milkman, but all else, as in Mary's case, was subject to our imagination.

I did, however, know that the Left, this heroic and now destitute grouping of ordinary, decent people, was my tribe whose traditions and practices had to be fastidiously observed. This was the legacy of the resistance against the Nazis, which, despite the ferocious attack on it by the post-civil war regime, refused stubbornly to disappear into the mists of history. It had been immortalised.

It is still alive and kicking in contemporary Greece.

Rather than weaken, this legacy was, meanwhile, being strengthened during the turbulent times the country was still going through. The actions of the country's corrupt and brutal regime, totally immune to accusations of civility or even common sense, had made sure of it. The statement, this 'grandiloquous nonsense', made by government minister Panayotis Kanellopoulos, which he himself greatly regretted later on, typified it all.

He described the hellish concentration camps where more than twenty thousand left-wingers were being held and tortured as Greece's 'New Parthenon'.

Many others had during the same period been executed by firing squad. Among the latter were four communists, including the communist leader Nicos Beloyannis, 'the man with the carnation' as immortalised in a sketch by Pablo Picasso. They were executed in 1952 as 'Soviet spies'. And this was while the centrist government of Nikolaos Plastiras was in office, a 'government' that nevertheless had zero power in its hands as all power rested with the extreme right wing establishment. The latter, represented by both the palace and the military, remained committed to extra-parliamentary solutions averted only thanks to US opposition.

I had, incidentally, taken a glimpse of Plastiras when in August 1952 he visited the Virgin Mary's church in Tinos island, perhaps in order to do a bulk confession for the whole nation. I had gone there with my mother who wanted to pray in this island's 'miraculous' church for a cure to the effects of the shock she had received during the 1945 armed robbery in our house.

Plastiras, with one foot in Charon's ferry to the other world, was waving to the crowd with an uncertain smile on his face.

He died a year later poor as a church mouse.

God was, however, nowhere to be seen either in the Virgin Mary's church or in Athens. I was told He had moved abroad.

Two years later the state did also execute Nicos Ploumpides, one of the most tragic figures of the Greek communist movement. He was shot while singing the communist international with the divine brightness of a last smile on his face, and this when the party's Secretary General Nicos Zachariades, a Stalinist as hard as baked clay, had denounced him for his own reasons as an agent of the security police.

The party, just like the British troops and officers in the First World War, had ended up as a group of 'lions led by donkeys'.

At the same time, the state's secret service fabricated a despicable case against twenty 'communist' air force officers, which collapsed completely a few years later, but not before it had given the extreme right all it needed to undermine the few moderate elements in government.

This affair had somehow touched me personally.

I just happened to pass outside the Averoff prison, close to my school, where those officers were being held and where at the moment there was a small crowd of people. I joined them out of curiosity, but then a photo of that crowd of which I was a part was published in the next day's newspapers. The caption in one of them referred to that crowd as 'communist sympathisers'.

I was one of them though I did not at the time have a clue as to what it was all about.

– 'Don't ask me why I was there', I told Mr Beldaos, my teacher of classics, a man who would begin every single sentence with the idiorythmic and totally meaningless word 'namke'. 'Ask the Fates!'

The word 'namke' was apparently the password he needed to open the gate to the chamber of his thoughts.

Communism, as an ideal, for reasons that I cannot exactly put my finger on, was, meanwhile, winning me over.

Perhaps the actions of the terrorist state, hitting me at an emotional level, was the catalyst to my radicalisation. Perhaps I was also fed up with my school's moronic 'patriotic' references to ancient Greece, destined to make us feel secure in our history, or the lessons in compliance offered daily to us by our headmaster, a man conceited as a sultan and mentally alert as an iron gate.

More likely, I needed, like many of the people I knew, to believe in a future very different to what we were being forced to accept.

Like them, I also needed to keep my unaudited dream as represented by the Soviet Union intact as nothing else seemed to provide stimulation.

That had nothing to do with the Gulag Archipelago. It was, instead, the dream of a world providing security of existence to everyone and also the conditions for the free development of each individual as the prerequisite for the free development of all.

Looking back at those times, I have no reason to question the nobility of this dream, which, like a candle dancing in our hands, guided us through the dark, wretched alleys of our daily life.

The same dream of a fair world had guided numerous generations before ours and was and still is the source of inspiration for the Occupy Movement from Madrid's Plaza de las Cortes and Athens' Syntagma Square to Manhattan's Zuccotti Park and London's St Paul's cathedral.

In all these cases, people, disenchanted with the system that had flourished to the benefit of the top 'one per cent' and feeling betrayed by their politicians, revolted and asked for an end to it all.

It was not all that different for me in the fifties except that my fancy, impregnated by illusions, had wrongly identified this dream with the Soviet Union.

But that was a time short on doubts and confusions and rich in certainties which looked as good as a heavy jacket in a cold winter night. Doubts, if any, knew at the time their place.

Hence, when in 1953 I heard on the radio that Stalin had been liberated from his worldly presence, I froze as if a cold finger-tip had touched my heart. The father figure had gone and we had all been left alone, like orphans, to face the winds of fate. Soon after, a few of my schoolmates met to honour his memory.

– 'The heart of the great wartime leader who led the country to victory against the nazis', the speaker said, 'has stopped beating. But his legacy will live forever.'

Even the basil on the window seal seemed to have been touched by the occasion. On the other hand, unimpressed, the cat just managed to swallow back a yawn.

The eulogy was inspired not so much by the 'triumph' of socialism in one country, but by the defeat of the Nazis in Moscow and Stalingrad. Yet the dream of a different world was ever present. Attached to the same dream as outlined by Vladimir Lenin, the leader of the Russian October revolution, only a few years later I lectured on his life with quotations from his Materialism and Empiriocriticism, a lousy book, according to Umberto Eco's irreverent convictions.

But, as Eco added with some understanding of the human condition, that was just inevitable if you screwed Krupskaya all the time.

It could not be anything else for me considering all the comforting certainties I had wrapped myself in.

I can, however, take today some comfort at the thought that the blame for this rested not with me but with the universe which has apparently decreed that when young you have the answer to everything. Questions appear only later, as you grow older, when you find yourself swimming, to quote a contemporary, in certain uncertainties and uncertain certainties, and when your questions exceed by far the answers you can confidently give.

It is then that, as Yeats might say, 'the key is turned on our uncertainty' and you realise that the bridge to the future may be excellent, if it is, but far too short.

Remarkably, however, I had at the same time refused to join the illegal communist party.

The idea was put to me by an older party member, a man looking like an elderly spinster, while we sauntered from Asclepius Street to Plaka in 1958. It was late afternoon but still very hot and the reverberation of the church bell seemed hushed in the smouldering serenity of the sunset hour.

On the way, we stopped for a pirozhki in a small eating place run by a Pontian Greek next to the Anglican church in Philellinon Street. Soon after I told him, albeit with a twinge of uneasiness but as respectfully as I had been schooled to treat my elders, that I could not do it. I just could not see the point of joining the party partly because I did not need to, but mainly because I could make no connection with it and its exiled leadership. The latter, so detached from my realities, seemed just like a ghost looking for a home to haunt. But I had joined the pro-communist EDA, the United Democratic Left.

Strangely enough, it was at the same time that the first doubts of my undocumented dreamworld had began to emerge in the form of questions which could not be answered during the long night chats with my friends under the star-lit Athenian sky.

– 'How come', I wondered together, for example, with Babis Theodoridis, a good friend who from the vegetable market he was working to support himself as a student rose to the leadership of the reformist communist party, 'the Soviet politburo enjoyed such a unanimity on every single occasion when we had to deal daily with such a divergent sets of views?'

That was a mystery as deep as the construction of the Great Pyramid of Cheops, built before the invention of the wheel. Even the cleverest of us could not work this out. Thankfully, however, working things out in those times was not in our job description.

Relieved, we would then walk out to satisfy our inner yearning with a cream bougatsa with lots of cinnamon.

But, far more seriously, how could we explain the Hungarian uprising of 1956, which the Soviets had denounced as the work of 'Fascist, Hitlerite, reactionary, counter-revolutionary hooligans financed by the imperialist west which took advantage of the unrest to stage a counterrevolution?'

I remember the discomfort everyone experienced when talking about it in the offices of the EDA. Yet, as we all knew what things needed to be left unsaid, nobody really challenged the official Soviet version. Our reservations were there, but we all kept them to ourselves before, conveniently, letting them fade into oblivion.

Basically, I think now, subconsciously we did not want to acknowledge the sheer cussedness of our reality because by doing so we would also have to say goodbye to the dream which sustained our lives. Our sense of reality, so acromegalic, resembled the arms of the Persian king Artaxerxes – the one was longer than the other.

Yet doubts had left their fingerprints all over the ongoing mental structures.

But in my early years, the days people did not mind looking old, I could neither travel beyond the boundaries of my current circumstances nor trade in doubts. Neither of them were the currency of those times. Besides, in the situation we had found ourselves in nothing could trim our wings.

The great enemy of truth, US president John Kennedy had once stated, is very often not the lie, but the myth, persistent, persuasive and unrealistic. Even the Soviet leader Nikita Khrushchev's 1956 report to the Soviet party's congress on the atrocities of the Stalinist era made hardly any difference. It led instantly to the dismissal of Zachariades, the Secretary General of the Greek Communist party, and his exile to Siberia where in 1973 he either died following a heart attack, was killed by the KGB or, when his depression was radicalised, committed suicide.

But where I was, in Athens, the event did not make headlines in my generation's thinking. Its footprints, on sand, had gone by the next wind. Just like Silenus, the earth-born Satyr, who, usually as drunk as a cardinal, could not distinguish truth from falsehood, we could not tell day from night.

Alternatively, some things had to be believed to be seen.

Even more remote was at the time the thinking of the New Left, which, influenced particularly by the publication of Marx's Philosophical Manuscripts, focused on the humanistic outlook of Marxism in a political, moral, social and even in an aesthetic context.

All I had heard of was Roger Garaudy, the darling of the French intellectual society, whose socialist 'reservations' were nevertheless dismissed by the 'wise' in the party. As they said with ineffable delight evident in the tone of their voice:

– 'You cannot expect anything else from an intellectual.'

Garaudy, incidentally, was expelled from the French communist party after he denounced the 1968 Soviet invasion in Czechoslovakia, converted later to Islam and then dismissed the Holocaust as a myth. He vindicated, Odysseus Elytis, the Greek poet, might have said, 'the claims of the unexpected'.

Meanwhile, the Greek economy had come to a standstill as the government, according to Paul Porter, the American emissary to Greece in the post-WWII era, cuddled only 'the interests of a clique of merchants and banksters'.

Some things never seem to change. The water is always wet.

And this when the Marshall plan had over a four year period poured into Greece $700 millions while the country was still playing host to the primordial pain ten years of war and also the earlier misfortunes had left behind.

As queen Frederica, an arrogant, autocratic and small-minded woman, the pillar of the American domination of Greece, explained disdainfully to George Marshall, the US secretary of state after whom the Marshall plan was named, the nation's political leadership was 'hopeless'.

Frederica, incidentally, when a girl, was a member of the Hitler youth and later on, after the war, she had reportedly defended Nazi Germany. Three of her brothers had also served in the Wehrmacht.

Nevertheless, she was right in her assessment of the politicians. She was their custodian.

3

Ph.D. in Effervescence

As the years went on, the leaves of the civil war spirit were gradually turning yellow, and the future, despite the defeat's tragic consequences, remained as seductive as the fragrance of the lemon trees in springtime Athens. It was what denied legitimacy to the present and pointed towards the fulfilment of the dream.

The repressive regime could imprison us, but it could not arrest our aspirations.

The focus of our activities had, however, shifted. Socialism had emigrated to 'the dim and distant future' as, to quote T S Eliot, 'between the idea and the reality, between the motion and the act falls the shadow'. You cannot after all fly without wings. The goal was, instead, a new political equilibrium that would end the monolithic power of the Right and bring in a democratic order that respected the rights of its citizens, responded to their needs and fulfilled their aspirations.

I think this represented a genuine acceptance by the Left of the new realities and an equally sincere commitment to the democratic process which might, or might not, lead to a socialist world. It was also the protection of the country's national interests against the overwhelming pressures of the great Powers.

That seemed to me to be the spirit of the times in 1956, the year I entered university, the Panteion University of Social and

Political Sciences, as it is called today. And me and the other members of the first post-civil war generation embodied it and advanced it. Not in the lecture halls, which I did my best to avoid, but outside them.

Those years, my university years, have been a part of my life I have never really thought very much about. Something in it was, and still is, baffling.

To begin with, I did not go to university in order to get a degree on the strength of which I could later apply for a job. I had neither ambitions of this sort nor was I empowered by the spirit of routine that enables most people to get through in life. The passion for the ordinary, the lumpy, enervating mundane, was missing.

I did not join it either because I wanted to learn something. The thirst for knowledge, sometimes associated with the medieval polymath Robert Grosseteste, was not there. The goal, instead, was to pass the exams and get a degree that, I knew, would only open for me the doors to a vacuous nowhere. Specialising later on as a solicitor was an afterthought.

So I am asking myself today:

– 'Why, on earth, did I go to university?'

And the only answer I can think of is:

– 'I didn't know what else to do.'

My motivation as a student was, therefore, zero and my aspirations utterly irrelevant to my student status. Either, I had not grown up as yet, or, perhaps, I was destined to become a politician.

For this fecklessness I have certainly to take responsibility. But the general picture, when looked at from a distance, was also disturbing. There was no encouragement at school or college to move beyond the mundanity of life, expand our horizons, realise our potential, aim high and conquer the distant high peaks.

Nothing to inspire, motivate, stimulate us to be the creators of our destiny, dream the undreamable and go for the seemingly impossible.

A mixture of the comic, the pathetic and the grotesque, we were guided by fate to our final destination, the slaughterhouse of the soulless salaried routines. There were, of course, exemptions to this rule, but the vast majority, caught in the stultifying doldrums of our culture, was just content to memorise what was to be forgotten the day after the exams.

On the other hand, none of us had, indeed, arrived on earth expecting it to be a soul-fulfilling place.

Rather than a thriving intellectual centre, the university in these conditions was, thus, a world depopulated of ideas. Although we had a few decent teachers, people like Michalis Stasinopoulos, later in 1974 -1975 interim president of the Greek Republic, international law professor George Tenekides or constitutional law professor George Daskalakis, debates on the broad subjects they raised were as rare as snowballs in hell.

We were simply not interested in what we viewed as dehydrated mental concepts. The focus was on necessity, which, as Milan Kundera, the Czech novelist put it, was inextricably bound with weight and value, for only necessity is heavy, and only what is heavy has value. And necessity was associated with the struggle for a humane society, which, among other things, would, incongruously, enable people to develop their potential to the full.

The idea was certainly noble, but like Odysseus, whose legs were short in proportion to his body, looked nobler sitting rather than standing. But the university life had another side, too, a life in tune with the politics of the day. It was that that opened up for me an entirely new world and forced me to work out my inchoate ideas and articulate and adjust them to our realities.

In the process, I had to engage in public discussions and develop skills I did not possess, study the art of persuasion, elaborate plans of action and organise events that stretched their legs to the outer suburbs of my experiences. All the sudden, I found myself negotiating political deals within the university's student movement context, leading election campaigns, organising demonstrations, and participating in many other political activities.

It was what enabled me to look at my fears in the eye and turned me into the leader of the university's large Left-leaning student movement.

And this was what validated my time as a student and eventually rewarded me with a Ph.D. in effervescence.

Very often I also addressed crowds of as many as one hundred thousand people during the election campaigns of EDA. In the latter events I was not a speaker but the enthusiastic young man reading slogans carefully prepared by the party officials, who had assessed that my stirring voice was what they needed to raise the heat down in the square.

Sofia Recliti, a very good friend, certainly agreed with them.

– 'Wonders are many on earth' she said misquoting mischievously Sophocles, 'and the greatest of these is you.'

Sofia came to London in the early sixties to pursue her postgraduate studies, was hit by a bus, which like all other vehicles in this country was driving on the wrong side of the road, was seriously injured and eventually forced to return to Greece.

During the same time, I also translated from Russian a book on Turkey that, summarised, was published in three parts in the daily pro-communist newspaper *Avghi*. It was my very first contact with that newspaper which later on employed me as a member of its staff. The 'Turkish' story had been approved by Stathis Efstathiades, the newspaper's international editor, who later settled in New York.

When I met him there in 1972, he was kind enough to take me on a guided tour of the UN headquarters, home of indecision.

My Russian, unfortunately, not used for decades after those days, abandoned me in revenge.

The police state, meanwhile, was ever present in the everyday life of the university. I made my acquaintance with its brutality in 1956, when Cyprus, still a British colony, was a focal point of our activities.

The struggle against the British colonial rule had already started and the Greeks wanted their government to give the Cypriots its full support, which was never offered. A policy of disentanglement instigated by king Paul, the British fifth column in Greece, was, instead, the preferred option.

The implication was that opposition to it in support of Enosis, the union of Cyprus with Greece, as manifested in frequent massive demonstrations, had to be crushed.

The state was unable to stand up to its foreign protectors while at the same time not prepared to tolerate dissent at home.

I made my acquaintance with its power in 1956, the year Archbishop Makarios was exiled by the British to Seychelles, and Athens was rocked by anti-British and anti-government demonstrations. In one of them I was arrested together with Manos Faltaits, founder in 1964 of the Faltaits folk museum in Skyros island, and beaten up by police in plain clothes before taken to their notorious headquarters in Bouboulina Street.

The road had been named after Laskarina Bouboulina, a naval commander and a heroine of the 1821 Greek war of independence. But Bouboulina Street in my time was associated, not with the leading lady, but with the security police headquarters from where people had often been defenestrated.

In this awful place where the spirit of evil peered from every corner, I was received by Karahalios, its chief, a middle aged man in a three-piece suit and hair, brylcreemed, neatly brushed back. He scrutinized me with his knifelike gaze and then he offered me a bit of 'parental' advice.

– 'It's all pointless', he said. 'Leave politics on the side and take care of yourself.'

At least, he did not charge for his advice.

Incidentally, the first phase of the Cyprus dispute ended with the 1959 Zurich agreement between the UK, Greece and Turkey that established the independent state of Cyprus. Archbishop Makarios, a man whom king Paul avoided like 'poison', under pressure, endorsed it.

Yet state violence could not force concessions despised by our conscience. It could not break our spirit, either. It only galvanised it. And the unequal battle for civil and human rights was not just carried on. It was also gathering momentum.

This was evident in the many other conflicts over, for example, educational reforms or the introduction of student public transport fares. Eventually, in the 1958 national elections, held less than ten years after the end of the civil war, EDA, the pro-communist party, won nearly the 25 per cent of the vote.

Although we had somehow detected the new mood sweeping Greece, we could hardly believe the figures. Our reality had been taken by surprise. As surprised and also alarmed, the Right counter-attacked.

Of the various new fascist groups employed for the purpose, the most important was EKOF, whose terrorist tactics resembled those of Hitler's Sturmabteilung. Its members, thugs, had set as their task to patrol the university campuses and the streets of Athens and terrorise anybody they could identify as a left-winger. One of them, Hermes Evangelidis, a good friend, attacked by a crowd of bullies in Panepistimiou street, was trying, albeit unsuccessfully, to defend himself with his umbrella.

Hermes was killed nearly two decades later when his plane crashed in a South American country, where he had been dispatched as the Greek embassy's press attaché. In another similar event which could make no excuse for its occurrence, in Hippocrates Street, I lost a tooth.

The worst came on a late April 1960 night, when thousands of EKOFites surrounded a theatre in Athens where a left-wing student gathering was taking place. About one hundred of them were present inside the theatre.

The inevitable explosion was ignited when one of them cheered for Adolf Eichmann, the German Nazi SS-Obersturmbannführer and one of the major organizers of the Holocaust. Eichmann, captured by Mossad operatives in Argentina, was at the time standing trial in Israel – he was executed in 1962.

After the inevitable battle that wrecked the theatre, the students, forced by the police, left in groups of three to be ruthlessly chased in the dark streets of Athens, all those with great, splendiferous names, by the neo-fascist thugs. I can still hear their incoherent shouts and hissing threats.

– 'Bulgars, tonight you'll die.'

– 'You dirty dogs, you'll all die tonight.'

– 'Commies, your end has come.'

Hundreds of students were viciously attacked and injured, though, thankfully, nobody died. It was a night of pure terror, St Bartholomew's night.

A source of their indefinite depth of virulency, albeit minor at the time, was Costas Plevris, a man ideologically on the right of Hitler, a Holocaust denier and later the leader of a fascist party and author of numerous hate books. Plevris, a man badly in need of sedatives because of his ill-tempered nature, once, in a damp, drizzly November day, threatened me with a gun.

– 'Are you out of your mind?, I asked him almost as shocked as the day I saw the strikingly beautiful girl I fancied holding hands with the university's sprinter champion.

– 'No', he replied with a chilling smile, exteriorizing his inner certainties and the strength of his convictions. 'And you better be careful.'

Later on, when I started work as a journalist, he offered to provide me with information about the activities of other fascist groups in exchange for my presenting him as the main threat to the democratic institutions.

The time the military junta grabbed power he was placed in charge of the 'national' education of the Greek armed forces and the police. Leading members of EKOF, people like Lukas Papangelis, with whom I had clashed repeatedly during the university years, and many others, were also appointed members of the military government.

Soon after the St Batholomew's night I had another experience with the EKOF gangs, in Hippocrates Street.

Led by one of them we called the 'kiosk' because of his size, about thirty of their members were about to attack our group of ten, including myself. My own reaction, impervious to discouragement, was at that point almost suicidal. Knowing that on the other side of the road were about thirty builders, all EDA members led by my friend Christos Reclitis, I challenged the 'kiosk' to attack me.

With my finger on his belly, I shouted at him

– 'Come on! Hit me if you have the balls.'

It was quite a challenge I still cannot believe I went for.

He laughed nervously, surveyed the entire scene, eyeing in particular the builders, and then took his group and walked away. My winged prayers had, obviously, reached Zeus in good time. I think that was the very first time EKOF had been forced to retreat.

Had it not, I would have ended up in hospital.

The event enhanced, of course, my reputation as a gutsy fellow, and reputation, as A.E. Housman, the lyrical and epigrammatic English poet,put it, is something like a mattress interposed between you and the hard ground. It did not look like that as the ground instead got harder.

The campaign of terror was carried on, and in the 1961 national elections, the 'elections of violence and fraud', Konstantinos Karamanlis, the leader of the Right, won his third successive victory to be challenged by George Papandreou, the leader of the Centre Union party. Papandreou's 'relentless struggle' won him the majority of the votes in 1963.

Life was not, however, all about problems, agony and struggle. There was a lot to enjoy, too: the time in Plaka, the old historical neighbourhood of Athens under the Acropolis, where we would go to have a few glasses of retsina and sing the rebetika of Tsitsanis, Hiotis, Vamvakaris and many others, the all-night parties, the excursions to Parnitha, the densely forested mountain north of Athens, and to the Athenian sea resorts, Brigitte Bardot, Jacques Tati, Jeanne Moreau and all the rest of the French La Nouvelle Vague plus Jane Russell, Marilyn Monroe, the girls and the love affairs.

The cash in our pocket was still just enough for fares and a cheese pie. Shrimps cooked in dolphin's milk would have to wait for a while. Holidays, the inalienable right of the consumer since the 1966 introduction by Freddie Laker of the no frills flights, was, likewise, beyond our operational budget.

We could not even dream of a week-long break on the beach. Still we were better off that many others, the hundreds of thousands who had moved from the countryside to Athens and Thessaloniki. They were all struggling to put food on their plates.

Yet, in 1960 I found myself travelling for the first time a few miles beyond the spot I was born, holidaying on the island of Rhodes. Invited to do so by a wealthy uncle from the US and his two daughters, I could not wait for the day to arrive. One of my assumptions was, however, wrong-footed. He had paid for my fares and I had, of course, taken it for granted that he would cover all the other expenses, too.

I discovered my mistake only on arrival, the moment he asked:

– 'We're staying in this hotel.' And then circumspectly, as if he did not want to be indiscreet, he carried on: 'Where are you staying?'

I told him I had already made some arrangements. While starving, I then spent the first two nights in the historical Muslim cemetery of the city and the third on the beach before I contacted the local members of EDA, who generously offered me all the help I needed.

Just like the splendour of some of our failures which half-price guarantees had failed to avert, this was certainly the kind of stuff that makes a holiday truly unforgettable.

Despite my adventures and the politically virtuous life I was leading, I was, however, still unsettled.

I was, I felt, part of a crowd which was making a contribution to a better world, but had nothing to say that had not yet been said and nothing new to impart. It was not that thoughts were viewed as purposeless as the exhorting of the waves. It was, instead, that the need to think had never made itself felt. Unlike the old Athenians, who, as Thucydides said, were addicted to innovation, we were not there to break new ground.

Soldiers after all are not required to think.

A part of me was, as a result, in a territory that did not feel like home. I was getting on with my life but with a sense of discomfort that kept whispering something to my ear except that it was in a language I was not familiar with.

Unable to work things out I, thus, kept taking my thinking-avoidance pills. The girl in the painting on my kitchen wall did not seem thrilled. But she continued resting with her head on her arm and her palm upon her golden treasure.

One day, however, the message was deciphered, or so I thought, and the hereafter came to consciousness. All I had to do was give myself to the study of Marxism. Having done so, I could then make our case from a new angle and in some new unknown colours.

Thankfully, my friend Babis Theodoridis dissuaded me from doing so.

– 'Don't be stupid', he cut me short before swallowing another of these roasted chestnuts we had bought while walking in Zappeion.

He would have reacted the same if I had told him I was planning to unionise the spirits of the dead. I listened to what he said and rather than pursue the matter further I did, instead, have another chestnut while watching the pigeons washing themselves, naked, in the fountain of the park.

Intelligence seemed to have re-opened her eyes.

As time, like tide, could wait for no man, I had, meanwhile, been taken to another chapter for my future autobiography. In October 1961 I joined the army as a conscript.

It was just weeks before the national elections that became known in Greece's political history as the elections of 'violence and fraud'. I knew exactly what to expect.

But even if I did not, the inscription above the camp's gate that read 'abandon hope all you who enter here', albeit evasive to the eye, would have told me. The army's sickening brutality hit me instantly in the face.

That was in Corinth, in the Peloponnese. Just a few days after my arrival, I was summoned by the camp's military intelligence chief to his office, where I had to stand in attention in front of him, next to a wood burning stove, and listen to his menacing talk while being burnt. Yet I did not move. Determined not to cower under his threats, I wanted to show him that he could not break me even if at the end I would need hospitalisation for the treatment of my burnt body.

He got the message, particularly after I refused to sign a document renouncing communism and its scions.

– 'Sign this document', he kept saying menacingly.

– 'No', I kept repeating. 'My convictions are not the army's business.'

Unfortunately, I failed to convince him. If I had any doubt, the searing pain in my ribs, the bruises on my face and the taste of blood in my mouth I took with me when I left his office made certain of it. As a result of my contumacy and dogged self-assertion I had become a 'dangerous communist'. In northern Greece, later on, I shared this honour with Yorgos Votsis, a media star in later years.

The pressure from then on was relentless. Not because the career officers thought they could one day break my spirit, but because, I think, they were afraid that I might resort to acts of sabotage to further my 'cause'. That was nothing less than a cretinous assumption as was the reasoning behind their decision to confiscate my radio so that I would not get subversive instructions from 'Free Greece', the Greek communist radio station based in Bucharest.

As if someone would bother to listen to it.

As foolish was their refusal to send me to a city-based unit after my six month training, as was the unbroken rule, but, for security reasons, to keep me in the same unit where I received the six months long training no less than four times. Their communist had ended up as one of the very best-trained soldiers in the whole division, an expert in the handling of a number of weapons and with sufficient skills to serve with the Greek Special Air Service.

My resolve during this time was, however, tested several times. One of them was in November 1963, the day after John Kennedy, the US president, was killed.

– 'The communists have killed him', the colonel in charge of our unit announced with the pompous certainty of his rank and, perhaps, while still recovering from the kisses of his wife. 'And they will pay for it.'

Communists would have to die if we were to protect our 'free' world.

Conveniently, they could perhaps commit suicide – with this in mind I had already left letters in Athens that I had no such intention. Equally well, they could be killed during military exercises with live ammunition – a small number of fatalities, we had been informed, could easily be explained.

Should that happen, I wondered whether the state would pay the costs of my funeral.

The uncertainty as to whether I would emerge from my military service alive, gave me, however, something I still treasure: the belief that, if fear is not overfeared, man can overcome it and master his own fate whatever the circumstances. Death is not the yardstick. If Plato was right, the fear of death is only the pretence of wisdom, not real wisdom.

Defying the odds is after all what shows, as Joseph Conrad might say once again:

– 'The inner worth of a man, the edge of his temper, and the fibre of his stuff.'

It is what, in effect, turned me from a teenager into a man.

Refusing to succumb to the violence of the state was a matter of principle and also honour. As Nicos Kazantzakis, this wholly Greek writer, said, even if you know you will never win, sometimes you have just to battle for your own sake, your own integrity and self-respect. But, of course, never is a very long time.

Regardless, submission to violence is the only thing worse than violence for both the individual and the institutions, far more destructive than resistance to it. Pride would not let me, either, give in to it. I would have equally well refused to denounce, if someone had tried to force me to, even what I despised and hated.

Pride, foolish pride, may take one to his own or other people's destruction. But in certain circumstances it can also underpin virtue by turning into the unyielding wharf on which the fiery waves of repression can be crushed. The world, I thought, would be saved, if it could be, only by the unsubmissive, the salt of the earth, those who, as novelist André Gide said, 'must achieve God'.

In this, I was not far out of tune with the rhythms of life at the time.

My standing up against all the pressures and inevitably becoming a representative of the heroic era we were going through or, alternatively, having opted for a career in heroism at a time when heroism was valued much more than excellence in any particular area such as cosmetic surgery or bond trading, awarded me, incidentally, a good marriage prospect.

– 'My family', one of the fellows in my company told me confidentially, 'would certainly be interested in the possibility'.

Just to make sure I took him seriously enough, he added:

– 'Her dowry will be four hundred sheep.'

The thought of asking him, just for the fun of it, to make it five hundred was never externalised.

My time in the army awarded me with one more insight. It dispelled for good the naive belief I had always held that people on the Left of the political spectrum were good, honest, responsible characters as opposed to those on the Right who, I believed, were unprincipled, selfish and ultimately unconcerned.

Political convictions, I discovered, are as relevant in terms of a person's character as high winds or heavy rain.

People, whether on the Right or the Left, give only too easily precedence to the pursuit of self-interest often amply displayed in the company of irresponsibility, stupidity, intolerance, dishonesty, greed, envy, vanity, vindictiveness, cruelty and so on.

Evil, colourless and odourless, is of no fixed address. It resides in 'them', but also in 'us'.

This was an understanding, which, transcending my personal boundaries, moved me into a world beyond common assumptions.

Meanwhile, by the time I left the army, twenty-seven months later, popular revulsion at the terrorist nature of the state had reached such a point that the February 1964 elections brought triumphantly to power the centrist George Papandreou. Konstantinos Karamanlis, the authoritarian right-wing prime minister since 1955, was out.

His departure became almost inevitable following the 'unrelenting struggle' against the government launched by George Papandreou on account of the 1961 fraudulent elections, the 1963 murder by fascist thugs of Grigoris Lambrakis, a left-wing deputy, and also his funeral that brought nearly one million people out on the streets of Athens.

Following that, the Lambrakis Youth, a powerful left wing movement, established under the presidency of Mikis Theodorakis, the composer, challenged further the right wing monopoly of power. Karamanlis' departure was further hastened by his clash with the palace which wanted to keep ruling the country the way absolute monarchs had done since the time of the Pharaohs.

Better days with plenty of honey and walnuts in their basket were obviously on the way.

4

Unlicensed Expectations

My generation, the first post-civil war generation, had, as the elders said, given a historic battle that challenged successfully the regime built since the 1935 Kondylis dictatorship. I was never aware of it in these terms, for the youngsters do not think in terms of generations. They see life that begins at about the time they enter it. But we were, indeed, the first such generation and at the time we all felt good about it.

It was good for me personally, too, as this experience took me off the streets of dysphoria I used to frequent in my early teens and altered, albeit not fully, my polluted self-perceptions.

It taught me I can stand my ground, guard my integrity and fight for my beliefs. Perhaps, I would never be able to enjoy a Daiquiri Mulata in Antigua's Coral Reef or associate with ladies wearing stilettos, an angora sweater and a pencil skirt. But, on the other hand, it would be me rather than the winds of fate that would determine my path in life.

I would be the architect of my own fortune.

Fate is not something absolute. It always gives us a choice between our managed realities and those our soul craves for. It is up to us, as Aeschylus said, to make the right choice.

The latter, the 'right' choice, usually identified with loyalty to lost causes, does not, however, come with a passport to the land of happiness.

47

This was, anyhow, what I liked to believe in 'words fertilised with intent'. Nevertheless, the trauma in my adolescence had not fully healed, self-confidence in my dealings with people was still malnourished and my petit-bourgeois background discouraged any intrepid inklings of my imagination. Living only in a small fragment of my being, I had no ambitions or aspirations to become one day something like a successful lawyer, athlete, entrepreneur or whatever. I was not driven like the professionals of our days.

My life had been and looked likely to remain unhampered by achievement. The latter looks a luxury when you are conditioned to think only of survival.

I was reminded of it in May 2014, while talking in the café of the Athens Archaeological Museum with my friend Astero Christodoulidi, a journalist of long standing, struggling now to survive on a pension that guarantees starvation.

– 'Achievement?', she repeated with incredulity after she folded her newspaper noisily, like a pelican folding its wings. 'The only achievement I could aspire to is paying my bills.'

Yet, though I knew that a degree in 'political science' was a millstone rather than a stepping stone, I had not even worked out what I was going to do with my life. What I needed at that point was a lucky break. But luck, if Palladas, the 4th century AD Alexandrian poet, was right, 'follows her own blind course, kind to the criminal, trampling on the just'.

Thankfully, in this instance he was wrong.

Soon after I finished my time in the army, I was introduced by Yorgos Votsis, my army friend, to the editor of *Avghi*, the pro-communist daily, and offered a job as a member of its high-powered journalistic team. It was a turning point in my life from every point of view. If nothing else, I was at last somebody, and my name on the newspaper provided the doubters with all the necessary documentation.

– 'Oh yes, I'm a journalist', I would tell with exaggerated casualness anyone who would ask while my chest, filled with a breathless excitement, kept sending intoxicating fumes to my head.

Girls were definitely impressed.

The job enabled me to upgrade my self-confidence and self-respect, and pursue, for the first time in my life, the achievement of excellence.

Also, as importantly, gainfully employed for a change, I would now be working in a most interesting field, challenged daily by events and growing on every single occasion.

Incidentally, the job made necessary the instalment of a telephone line at home, missing until then. Telephones were a luxury in those days that only the well-off could afford. Even a prime minister, Nikolaos Plastiras, did not have one. As he had famously said back in 1952:

– 'Greece is poor and you're asking me to have a telephone?'

But even if they had a telephone, those who wanted to chat would do so over a coffee or a glass of wine. 'Civilisation' had not as yet obliterated the past. The past was both lived and still alive.

The time was momentous, as apart from politics, life in Athens was changing fast.

It had all started in the late fifties, the time the Karamanlis' government had embarked on heavy investment in infrastructure, promotion of tourism and the modernisation of agricultural and industrial production. The time was also marked by massive unemployment that forced the emigration particularly to West Germany, Australia and Belgium of hundreds of thousands of workers.

One of them was my uncle, Yannis Delfinis, who joined the mining community in Belgium where he eventually died after a crippling mining accident.

Living and working in Belgium was a choice for him, but not a free choice. Hence his melancholic, dreaming eyes that always invited an arm around his shoulders and some reassuring words.

– 'Don't worry. You'll retire one day on an island, grill the red mullets you fished yourself and enjoy them with a glass of wine.' He never did.

The rapid development of the economy that matched that of West Germany was accelerated after 1962, when Greece joined the EEC.

It was underpinned by the influx of large amounts of foreign private capital, the rise of tourism, the expansion of shipping activity and the emigrants remittances which all had a positive effect on the balance of payments. A large structural shift from agriculture towards industry, benefiting particularly the textile and chemical sectors and also metallurgy, did also help the rapid growth.

Further, although half the country still lacked electricity, a robust construction industry had started to change the face of the cities with paramount economic and social consequences.

Athens in the sixties was an entirely different proposition to the city of the previous decade. Its pre-war face, still intact in the fifties, was now receiving a massive facelift, not only physically, but also culturally.

A new, autonomous and very dynamic cultural renewal with summer in its blood had challenged vigorously the rigid mental structures of the previous generations. It was led by Mikis Theodorakis whose concerts electrified their audience and whose songs gave an outlet to the anger that had flooded our brain at the excesses of the ruling class. The sobbing music of the fifties was replaced by the hopeful, effervescent and spirited music of the new times.

Many other composers made a similar contribution, including the great Manos Hadjidakis, Stavros Xarhakos, Dionysis

Savopoulos, with whom I shared an apple when I first met him in his flat, Manos Loizos, who visited me a number of years later in Skyros, Yannis Markopoulos, my university colleague, and many others.

Many of them based their songs on lyrics by some of Greece's greatest poets, including Yannis Ritsos, a friend of Mikis since the days they were both held in the Makronisos concentration camp, George Seferis and also Odyseas Elytis, a poet said to have been nourished, like Pindar, by bees with honey instead of milk.

–'Poetry', I told my friend Katerina Plassara without any feelings of embarrassment for the admission, 'is the voice of our soul'.

Katerina has since published a few novels. The few poems, which I had written, were subsequently misplaced and lost.

We do not see much of this in our contemporary mean-spirited time. Drone strikes in Afghanistan have not produced a single song or poem and novels about the Iraq war are mostly military adventure sagas for armchair warriors. Rather than write poetry, we tweet.

All this was reinforced by the revival of rebetiko, the rebels' songs, which had been looked down on by the 'good' society and banned by the state-run radio. The rebetiko with musicians such as Tsitsanis, Papaioannou, Vamvakaris and many others reached in the sixties its heyday.

The impact of all this on every other sphere of human activity, from food to fashion to which the girls, even those who, my religious education teacher would say again, have not sinned as yet, had subscribed unconditionally, and from entertainment to social rights was phenomenal.

And I was anything but immune to it.

Entering, albeit belatedly, into the twentieth century, I bought an electric fridge for the family home plus a record player and a few records. To the horror of just one generation behind mine, I danced to the tunes of rock 'n' roll, I was often seen in jeans, I spent now and then the early hours of the morning having drinks with some body in them and listening to Kostas Hatzis, an eccentric musician, or frequented restaurants in which working class people would never be seen.

In one of them, the waiter, apparently an old communist bent by time, having overheard my discussion with my friends, dismissively told us:

– 'If you are who you think you are, you would not be here.'

How wrong he was! He had not realised that the increased pressure for political change was fundamentally due to the rising middle class' impatient expectation to be an integral part of it all rather than its critic or a pathetic observer on the margins.

My time with *Avghi* started, strangely enough, with a totally unexpected assignment: to attend Saudi Arabian king Ibn Saud's press conference in Kavouri, one of the most exclusive seaside neighbourhoods of Athens.

I do not remember anything that was said during its course but I still remember I was dressed up to do justice to the chandeliers. I also remember the sumptuous buffet to which we were all invited to help ourselves.

The Saudi king, the wealthiest man in the world who wore his years with distinction, wanted obviously to please us, particularly as he liked Greece where he eventually retired until he was liberated from his worldly presence.

Soon after, I also got the first taste of corruption. The PR man of Santorini's local manufacturers, and later on the spokesman for the 1967 Greek military junta, attempted to bribe me in order to offer his clients support in their opposition to the extension of the national social insurance to their island the government had decided.

– 'What's this?', I asked him on the coach taking us back to Athens, pointing to the sealed envelope he had just handed me.

– 'Oh, it's just a little present', he said, obviously surprised at my question, while shifting uncomfortably his buttocks on the chair. I told him he ought to be ashamed of himself.

My area of responsibility was defined – I was the labour correspondent, assistant to Tasos Demou, a gentle, unassuming, intelligent man, who took me by the hand when I entered journalism, in March 1964, and patiently guided me step by step.

– 'When you write a story', his first lesson was, 'make sure you answer the questions "who, what, when and where". The "why", of fundamental importance, is usually subject to interpretations. Newspapers, in general, prefer to deal with the superficial "how".

But being assistant labour correspondent did not prevent me from getting involved in various other projects including a visit to northern Greece's coal mines, the Marathon peace marches or the trial of the Lambrakis murderers in Thessaloniki where I had gone as an assistant to Yannis Voultepsis, a 'born journalist' and the newspaper's star investigative reporter.

All this had helped me to meet lots of different people, open up to the world and expand my understandings and horizons.

My reality was in the meantime being re-defined in other ways, too. Something in my own world had already started shifting almost as soon as I entered journalism with *Avghi*. Encouraged by a few senior colleagues, and curious as cats, I had looked and discovered the disparity between the dream of a free world and the crudity of its consummation.

The crash course came in Bulgaria which I had visited for a few days in 1965 in what was my first ever trip abroad. People now see travelling abroad as their birth right, undeniable even before they can walk. In those days it was a privilege affordable only by a few.

The disagreeable odour of this trip hit me as soon as I found myself on the Bulgarian side of the frontier.

Whilst on the train, the passport control officer took a letter my editor had supplied me to the editor of a Bulgarian daily in which he was asking him to be of help to me, if I needed any. I grabbed it back from him. As amazed at my behaviour as I was when my cousin, Vasilis Morfopoulos, informed me the time I was a kid what it takes for a woman to get pregnant, he disappeared only to return a minute later with another six officers, who demanded I handed the letter over to them.

– 'Letters', they insisted, 'can only be sent through the post office.'

Perhaps, they needed a visa, too.

I had no choice but to comply. And that was the beginning of my misadventure in Bulgaria. The rest happened in Sofia.

Able at the time to speak decent Russian, I acquainted myself with several young and agreeable people, courageous enough to manage their fear of talking to someone from the capitalist world. From my point of view, these chats contained nothing the regime could perceive as a threat. Even in talking about my own country, Greece, all I was trying to do was dispel their illusions.

– 'Nothing is easy anywhere', I used to say with the same force I would offer the same piece of wisdom in our days. 'You just work, if you can find work, to earn a wage good enough to buy you bread.'

Yet, despite my connections with *Avghi*, I was being shadowed day and night by the Sofia security police and never met any of these young people for a second time. At the end, I had no alternative but leave the country. My conclusion was that the socialist splendid edifice was as real as the castle built for Aladdin by the Genie of the Lamp.

Euripides, I decided, was quite right when he said that:

– 'Things have one appearance when far away, and quite another when looked at closely.'

The few extra days from my annual leave were spent in Belgrade, where I arrived on New Year's eve. I picked a very nice hotel and joined the midnight dinner feast together, courtesy of the staff, with a single young Austrian.

At midnight, when the lights were switched off, a soft hand grabbed mine and held it until the lights were turned on again. It was the hand of a young female Serb from the table next to ours. I looked at her practically out of breath and she smiled serenely at me. With her 'soft, gentle, and low voice, an excellent thing in woman', as king Lear might say once again, she then invited me to join her family at the next table. We effortlessly consumed there a few bottles of wine before they all invited me to their home, in Novi Sad, where I spent the night.

What I still cannot understand is why on arrival the brother of the girl insisted that he had to wash my feet in a bucket in front of the chair in which I was seated.

Some form of hospitality, I suppose, deserving all my anglicised sympathies prescribed for those poor foreign people with unfamiliar or strange habits.

The dominant feature of the time was, however, the struggle between the new government of George Papandreou and the young king Constantine.

The latter, just like his father, king Paul and particularly his mother, queen Frederica, a vicious woman, was determined to control the government and, if not, to force it out of the picture. He eventually succeeded in doing so in July 1965, but not before Papandreou had managed to broadcast his stirring message asking the burning question:

– 'Who runs this country? The king or the people?'

Within just a couple of hours one million people were out in the streets denouncing the royal coup d'etat. The wrath of the nation at the blatant disregard of its wishes was expressed and crisply-articulated also in the subsequent massive daily demonstrations that shocked the establishment.

In one of them, Sotiris Petroulas, a university colleague, was killed. I went to his house, where thousands of people had arrived to demonstrate their sympathy with the family, and where, for some bizarre reason, I found myself helping two other men to dress up his dead body.

I did so despite the dreadful smell emanated from the chemicals used during the preceding autopsy. At the end, I took his hand into mine and wished him a good journey to what Pablo Neruda called 'the other shore of the sea which has no other shore'.

In another instance, I made it my job to protect Panayotis Kanellopoulos, the new leader of the Right, who had almost suicidally walked from parliament into the frenzied crowd.

– 'Sir', I told him as respectfully as I could, 'go back to the House. You're not safe here'.

In the state of mind he was, I do not think he even heard me.

But the burning question remained. We had triumphed and we would be victorious once again in the next elections except that the extreme Right, i.e. the palace and the military, would not, as we all knew, yield power whatever the election results might be. On the other hand, the Left together with the Centre were equally determined to change at last the course of history. In this, the latter had now the militant support of the working class rallied under the flag of the '115' alliance of unions.

Covering this area, labour relations, became, despite my lack of experience, my first senior responsibility fairly soon after I started work with *Avghi*.

This happened unexpectedly as the newspaper's labour editor, Tasos Demou, a brave journalist awarded in 1971 a gold medal by the International Union of Journalists for his services to democracy, had just been arrested and imprisoned for two years.

The charge was that in a speech he had delivered in a rally held by the Greek Union of Journalists of which he was the general secretary, he had incited people to violence.

What I recall he had said was that we should fight to avert the arrival of the coming dictatorship.

That year, 1966, was my last year in Greece. My job in the newspaper had meanwhile changed. I was now its parliamentary correspondent. That meant I was moving to the very centre of politics where I would be in contact with the makers of all policies and the thinking behind them.

– 'Very exciting', I thought.

It was not. The people who were making the headlines were usually absent, and the debates were dull, uninspiring, enervating, as if parliament was moving in a vacuum drained of purpose and importance. Everything looked flimsy and ephemeral.

Rightly so in some sense as everyone knew that the power games were being played elsewhere, in the palace, the barracks and the corridors of Langley, Virginia.

– 'Where are our representatives', I asked Yannis Pasalides, the octogenarian president of EDA, a medical doctor born in Odessa, later a member of parliament in Georgia and since 1951 a Greek parliament member.

He just exploded in his lovely Pontic accent while moving his stick up in the air.

– 'They are hiding. They are all hiding. They can't face the wrath of the nation.'

His ire could not, however, remove the polluted air of the building. Only a Clean Air Act could do it, but this was anything but forthcoming.

My job as parliamentary correspondent involved working as a rule until the early hours of the morning as the parliamentary debates would not start before 7.30 in the evening. But the stimulating sense of mission was absent. I was on a job that could not even offer me job satisfaction.

I did nevertheless enjoy it as, among other things, it enabled me to familiarise myself with the pettiness of politics and the opportunism behind several great ideas.

Even so, a few times it turned me into a nervous wreck. Those were the times when, pursued by the clock, I had to submit my report, which due to the late hour was going straight to the printers, while I still had to listen attentively to the ongoing debates.

The tenor in parliament did, however, only highlight the dismal prospect we all faced as the future's fingerprints were everywhere. We all knew what to expect: the firestorm that would burn our house down.

Indeed, we waited for it as we wait for the bus on the route to nullity.

Discussing the prospect times and again whether in a friend's house, the *Byzantium* café in Kolonaki well after midnight or during the long night walks after work was always leaving us with a sense of impotence. The bottom line was that there was nothing we could possibly do to stop or resist the coming dictatorship.

After all, you cannot stop the tanks with your bare hands.

Resigned to the inevitable, the only point of interest was where to hide when this happened, as Thales Dizelos, a colleague and also a good friend, clarified jokingly one evening to nobody's appreciation. Thales, when the dictatorship came, was arrested, taken to a concentration camp where he signed the document renouncing communism and its scions, and then returned to Athens where, sadly, he became the editor-in-chief of the official junta newspaper *Nea Politeia*.

The dictatorship could have been avoided but only if the democratic forces, Left, Centre and the moderate Right, had raised the white flag and surrendered unconditionally to the palace and its praetorian guard. If, in other words, they had agreed to sanction the role of the militarists, whether royalists or not, as the ultimate source of power and sole arbiter of political developments.

It was the same dispute that had wrecked the prospect of peaceful developments back in 1944 with the British then and the Americans now behind the king.

But this, even if some politicians were prepared to compromise, could not stop the stormy democratic river that threatened the militarist structure of Greece's post-war politics or, much less, reverse its flow.

Some centrist figures, the so-called apostates, who did so in 1965 were crushed by the force of the ponderous popular movement.

It looked as if the only option open under the circumstances was an heroic confrontation with the dark forces behind the scenes the end of which was, however, beyond the slightest of doubts.

Yet, neither me nor anyone else I knew had ever questioned the march to the bitter end, the time when all but honour would be lost.

The feared and the fearful did arrive in April 1967, just a few weeks before the scheduled elections which the democratic Centre Union was certain to win with an overwhelming majority. A military dictatorship turned Greece into a vast burnt down and silent landscape.

We were back to square one.

The military, which Churchill was so determined to protect, could not tolerate any challenge to the far right regime.

The coup d' état, colonel Papadopoulos, its charlatan leader, claimed, was just a surgical operation performed by himself, the doctor, on the patient, Greece, who had been placed for the purpose under anaesthesia in an orthopedic cast.

As Yannis Voultepsis, an *Avghi* reporter larger than life, said with his usual ferocity:

– 'What the man lacked in intelligence, he has made up for in stupidity.'

Strangely, later on Yannis joined New Democracy, the centre-right party, with his daughter Sophia becoming in 2012 its spokesperson in parliament.

Among the victims of Papadopoulos' action was king Constantine and his military. Having not received as yet Washington's green light to abolish the democratic institutions, the latter were superseded by the army's militarist element under Papadopoulos, a CIA recruit.

– 'Not the king's fault', someone known for offering his opinion on both parochial and extra-parochial affairs with considerable animation ventured to suggest.

– 'Just a traffic light problem.'

Having ostracised all other considerations, including the reasons it was sought, the West's search for security led instantly to granting the colonels all the support they needed.

The professed commitment of the Americans to the protection of the free world turned out to be as good as President Nixon's declared commitment to the rule of law. American policy looked, at least to the millions of Greeks deprived of their human dignity and freedom, like a ghastly variant of an extrahuman nightmare.

Of course, at a time that the world had revolted against the war waged by the Americans in Vietnam or against their intrigues in Allende's Chile, feelings of this kind were not the exclusive privilege of the Greeks.

5

Up The Exploration Lane

My English at the time the I arrived in London, swinging London, as my newspaper's London correspondent early in January 1967, was just good enough for Tarzan to understand.

Yet, despite my inability to reach the verbal orgasm expected in a conversation, it felt as if I had just stepped into a dream.

This was the country that six months earlier had won the World Cup, was the home of the Beatles, the Rolling Stones and host of the adrenalin driven reggae rhythms, of Julie Christie and Alan Bates, of Dr Who and The Avengers, of David Bailey, Bridget Riley and the new popular art, of Twiggy, Carnaby Street and the so economical mini skirts.

It was the country that had been taken over by a totally irresistible and also subversive youth culture.

The promised land was no longer situated in the map of the distant future. It was there.

I could touch its breasts with my fingers, relish it even though at times I should have been more discriminating. Quantitative borders were crossed only too often, but I did not mind it as, overwhelmed by the euphoria of the era and the timeless elation it generated, I had surrendered unconditionally to it.

My only complaint was that my neck was not as long as a crane's to enjoy the taste of the delicacies in my plate longer.

But life took a new twist and the 'very merry, dancing, drinking, laughing, quaffing and unthinking time' ended when in April 1967, nearly four months after my arrival in England, the tanks of the military strolled upon the streets of Athens. What a tragedy for my country, still recovering from the devastating consequences of a civil war, what a misery for me.

As it was, I did not share the fate of thousands of other Greeks – nearly ten thousands – who were sent by the junta to concentration camps. I would have certainly been one of them if my departure had been delayed. Both the police and the military police, as my father told me, had visited our home searching for me.

Being on the long list of Greece's political prisoners would have, of course, been an honour, albeit not of the kind one would actively pursue.

But I still found myself playing in injured time. The military coup in Greece had closed my newspaper down and declared me a person whose activities were 'detrimental to the country's national interests'. At a stroke, I had lost my country, job and passport.

– 'You have to go back to Athens to ask for your passport's renewal', an embassy official, who carried most of her weight at the stomach and hips, obligingly informed me when the time to renew it had arrived.

But I did not lose the almost mystical vibrations inside me that steered my optimism, energy and drive. Yet, first of all, I had to find a job.

Thankfully, a Jewish refugee from Nazi Germany, i.e. someone who had experienced similar difficulties himself in the thirties, professor at Sussex university now, arranged a job for me with the National Institute of Economic and Social Research, in London's

Smith Square. His help was a much appreciated act of solidarity. It gave me a few months of breathing space.

But a few months later I left this job, which was not for me, and looked for alternatives in the media, including that of other cities, from Zurich to Oslo. Looking back at it, it was all a crazy adventure which only my boundless optimism and thirst for new experiences could explain. In any other terms it made no sense. If it did, it would not have fixed itself so firmly in my memory.

The peripeteia started in Holland which I entered on foot. It was not, of course, what I had planned. Even in those days you did not walk from one country to another. It happened after I accepted a lift someone had kindly offered me in Antwerp, Belgium, except that he dropped me just at the frontier because he wanted to celebrate our acquaintance on the bed of a nearby hotel.

Not interested in it, I had, as a result, to walk to the passport control station on the Dutch side of the frontier, where, apart from my passport, I had also to show the officials how much money I was carrying in my pocket.

– 'Sorry, it's not enough', I was informed by one of them, someone who looked only too pleased too disoblige. 'With this amount of money you can stay in Holland for only a couple of days.'

The money was actually less than not enough after the dinner to which a well known Dutch actress had invited me at a fancy restaurant in Amsterdam. She had an amethyst hanging from her neck, important according to the Romans to maintain a husband's affections, and a watch on her wrist worth probably ten times as much as my annual budget. Still I had to pay for a meal which under different circumstances I would never have had.

On the other hand, *Trow*, a well-known Dutch newspaper, welcomed my suggestion to provide them with Greek news from London.

In Oslo, *Dagbladet*, a large national daily of Norway, interviewed me on the situation in Greece. The story appeared on its columns together with my photograph, which I sent to my mother, who responded by sending me another photograph, of herself this time looking proudly at the photo I had sent her. She also made sure that visitors did not miss the opportunity to appreciate the looks of her son, with a goatee beard like all the proud revolutionaries of the age.

– 'This is my son. Isn't he gorgeous?'

As people rightly say, a mother thinks all her geese are swans.

I left Oslo with a Norwegian girl for Stockholm where, amongst others, I met Theodoros Kalafatides, a man who within the next forty years produced 25 novels that sold over one million copies worldwide.

He was very happy living in Sweden, which, on the bus to somewhere, he described as

– 'The best place in the world to have an accident.'

For better or worse, I failed to take advantage of the opportunity.

Instead, I left for East Berlin where I contacted Marika Mineemi, a gentle lady who had ended up there as a political refugee from Greece and was *Avghi*'s contact in that city. She took an instant liking to me and kindly introduced me to the editor of *Wochenpost*, a national East German weekly paper. The latter offered me what I had asked for, i.e. being its correspondent in the UK.

But in East Berlin I also met a number of Greek students, members of the Lambrakis Youth movement who had been given scholarships to study in East Germany.

Practically, all of them were disillusioned communists.

One of them, Alexis Karageorgis, was the son of the communist leader Costas Karageorgis whom Zachariades, the party's secretary general, had denounced as a 'traitor' and murdered in Bucharest in 1954.

Alexis, a gynaecologist these days, told me something I still remember.

– 'When I came to East Germany', he said, 'I thought that, apart from a few bits, the machine was working well. It took me no longer than a year to understand that the entire machine was not working.'

The city was spiritless, the people inhibited and undemonstrative, the atmosphere depressing. Even at a party of young Germans run by some high-ranking party officials to which I was invited nobody attempted to make contact with me, the only westerner in the hall. Nobody would offer me even a courteous smile. I did not envy them.

Soon after I moved to Zurich where I met the foreign editor of a Zurich national newspaper and arrived at some sort of working arrangement with him, too. To a similar understanding I had also arrived at earlier on, before I had embarked on my continental ventures, with *The Scotsman*.

Back in London I could not, however, meet the commitments I had made. A few features appeared here and there, violently attacked occasionally, as in the case of *The Scotsman*, by the Greek junta information minister. The problems were numerous and overwhelming.

My English was totally insufficient for the purpose, and my contacts with people in Greece rather limited as people, edgy, did not want to talk over the phone. Apart from all this, I did not even have a phone because I could not afford one. I could not even afford a typewriter.

What illustrated the situation best was the time I had to walk from Shepherds Bush, where I was temporarily living, to Bayswater to borrow a typewriter from a friend, walk back home with it, type up my story, return the typewriter to the friend and walk home again. I could not use public transport for the purpose because I did not have any money.

– 'Life is hard', Costas Zouraris, an engaging and rather eccentric fellow-student and later a politician who became a celebrity in Greece, opined with a smile full of sympathy.

I nodded as though I knew this all along while at the same time looking out of the window at the Jaguar which he used to park in front of the very humble flat we temporarily shared.

At that point I gave up. My capacity for illusions was not infinite. Illusions at an unaffordable cost could just not be maintained.

I did, instead, a few odd jobs, like renovating old houses whose imperceptible melancholy pervaded my senses, or helping to stock the shelves of a Cypriot supermarket close to Goodge Street with items I could not afford to buy myself. In the process, I discovered that a shilling's worth of plain biscuits, with plenty of water, can keep the hunger away for the day. I disgraced myself in a few instances, like the time I had to pay for the coffee I thought I would be offered – and I had no money to pay for it.

–'Sorry', I explained as earnestly as I could to the Portuguese fellow I was with at the Holborn branch of a J. Lyons tea shop, 'I put money in my pocket, but then, unfortunately, I left the pocket back home.'

Occasionally I also slept rough, and then, barely eking out a living, I celebrated Jesus' birthday on my own with a couple of sausages which I ate before realising that they needed cooking.

But this was not just my own predicament. Mariza Koch, the Greek folk singer, among others told me years later she had also starved in London in those years. Yet nothing mattered as after all we were all in it together. And nothing could break my spirit.

– 'I had nothing', as Goethe's poet said, 'yet I was not poor'.

The tale was still sauntering in the field of daffodils and lilies.

Hence in the following year, 1968, I cheerfully embarked on a new venture by going to Czechoslovakia, a country undergoing a radical transformation of its communist system. We are going, Alexander Dubcek, the party's secretary general, said, to have 'socialism with a human face'.

Party members were given the right to act in line with the commands of their conscience, censorship was abolished, government incompetence and corruption were freely castigated by the media, and people, greatly relieved, were celebrating out in the streets.

I joined some of these celebrations in Prague's beautiful Wenceslas Square under the approving eyes of St Wenceslas and his horse.

With me were many other Greeks, members of the Lambrakis Youth movement, studying like those in East Germany with the help of government grants. Their views were not different to those held by the Greeks studying in East Germany. And all these were people of my age, who had, like me, grown up in Greece, shared my convictions and suffered the same treatment as me in the hands of the Greek state's security apparatus.

Members of the older generation, i.e. those who had during the civil war fought against the US-backed regime and, following their defeat, had escaped to Eastern Europe, were not just critical of the communist regime.

Embittered by their savage treatment, they were outrightly hostile.

The situation took for them a turn for the worse after February 1968, when the Greek communist party split between the Stalinist hardliners, supported by Moscow, and the euro communists. The purges of reformers in Easter Europe assumed then even more appalling dimensions. People were kicked out of their homes or even hospitals.

One of them was Yorgos Grivas, *Avghi*'s correspodent in Prague. He lost his job in the Czechoslovak media and started work, instead, as a road sweeper. Another one was P Demetriou, who used to be a member of the party's politbureau. A solemn, scrawny man who had opposed the Stalinists, had suffered a similar fate.

– 'The party', he summed up in the early hours of the morning in his humble flat in Bucharest where he received me, 'had let the people down'.

Yet I could not see eye to eye with the reformist communist party that emerged during this upheaval. Its name, incidentally, was the communist party of the interior as opposed to the communist party of the exterior, which was supported by Moscow. All my instincts, firmly anchored in my sense of fair play, were telling me to keep my distance.

And this while I was still ignorant of the arrangements made between the reformers and their new backers: Romania's Nicolae Ceau escu and North Korea's Kim Il-Sung.

The road, obviously, had no end, no relief. Hopes seemed not to have a long life-span. Like flowers, they lived for a while and died at their season's end.

In any case, the stories I had heard in East Germany, Czechoslovakia and Romania had truly horrified me. They had attacked head on the convictions I held since childhood and epitomized a world that I no longer had any desire to be a part of.

My thinking evolved further in Paris, where I spent a few months, including the legendary May 1968. Still without money, I did some work on a building site that earned me enough to ensure my survival.

'The old man', as poet Seamus Heaney would say, 'could handle a spade. Just like his old man.'

The rest of the time gave the young man, me, all I needed to plan the future of humanity at the courtyard of Sorbonne in the morning before watching a Buster Keaton film in the Odeon early in the afternoon, clashing with the CRS later in the day, and, after assessing the effectiveness of the day's tactics and the General's intentions, carry on conscientiously with my research on the original sin.

Life without French women, bon viveur Friedrich Engels thought in his time and not without good reason, 'wouldn't be worth living'. To console himself for their absence while in Manchester, he arranged a ménage à trois with his lover Mary Burns and her sister Lizzie.

Looking back in those Parisian halcyon days, I realise, of course, that in some ways we were all kids playing in a delightful playground with sex and politics, poverty and dreams, plans and ideas.

But in another, and very important sense, joy and its politics, changed radically all perceptions of reality and completely shaped the upcoming generation. The world became wide-open to experience, question and change. Thinking and feeling, intellect and passion, outer and inner walked together hand in hand up Exploration Lane.

Nothing could any longer keep shut 'the windows of the sky'.

The odoriferous flowers of fancy were presented by a dream, the vision of a better, freer world within grasp.

The dream was largely utopian, a Nephelococcygia, the town in the clouds built by the cuckoos. But this did not matter, for the '60s was, on the other hand, the sacred fountain whose crystal-clear water had the power to inspire, the signpost indicating the direction we should follow. It was also a source of tremendous strength of the kind that seems capable of moving mountains and lakes.

– 'I have a dream', I can still hear Martin Luther King, 'that my four little children will one day live in a nation where they will be judged not by the colour of their skin but by the content of their character.'

It was the power of a dream like this and its underlying spiritual message that galvanised millions into action and changed dramatically the social landscape.

The era of illusions, as I believed, was now over. The new understandings, in Nietzschean language, disturbed what was previously considered immobile, fragmented what was thought unified, showed the heterogeneity of what was imagined consistent with itself. The crystals of certitudes had crumbled. Reliance upon the transcendent had ceased.

De omnibus dubitandum, the principle that everything had be doubted, became the axiom to which every self-respecting bearded man had no choice but to subscribe. The new era, heralding the end of the prepermissive times, had just dawned.

In the Hypocrisy Park of the world all I wanted was to burst with a little sarcastic needle all its balloons just to show that inside there was nothing but hot air.

Doubting at that time had something definitely positive about it.

Unlike the nihilistic doubting inherent in the thinking of the seventies and beyond, to doubt, then, meant to challenge monolithic political structures, the domination of society by the forces of the market or the restrictive culture of the time. It represented the affirmation of faith in the power of the humans to determine their future. Rules and institutions were only a hindrance. Rather than a manifestation of impotence, it was, thus, a vote of confidence in human nature, a celebration of life.

To doubt was to hope.

Hence the annus mirabilis, 1968, was an experience that inspired and turned people into active agents of political, social and above all cultural change.

Filling its bones with wine, the world looked open, gay, beautiful and promising.

But it was not all what it looked.

Later on in the same year, the Soviets invaded Czechoslovakia. The invasion caused a tectonic shift in the thinking of the continental Left and also determined my own attitude for good. My unlicensed expectations and the 'socialist' realities, sufficiently bare to entice a Stylite off his pillar, could no longer see each other eye to eye.

What was there was not the socialism people in my country had been dying for, but national socialism they had died fighting against. We had been holding, without even knowing it, a candle to the devil.

As far as I was concerned, soviet-style socialism, to paraphrase Nazim Hikmet, the Turkish romantic-communist poet, had become the victim of the Stalinist bullets. Alternatively, it took its own life.

The Bolsheviks had 'reached out their hands in longing for the further shores', as Virgil might have said, yet, in almost no time, and under Stalin, the ruthless man whom Nikolai Bukharin, the Russian revolutionary leader, belatedly called the 'new Ghenghis Khan', they turned the socialist dream into a nightmare.

Bukharin hardly had time after that to reach his grave.

Admittedly, the Bolsheviks begun their lachrymose march in history grievously handicapped. Russia was a country which Lenin himself had described as 'one of the most benighted, medieval and shamefully backward of Asian countries'. But one could assume that as time went on the revolutionaries would justify the pride whole generations took in the first workers' state and its Stalingrad epic. They did not.

Propelled by primal instincts, fuelled by paranoia, immune from retribution and proud of their barbarism, which was heralded as 'a model of proletarian firmness', they descended, instead, into the Erebus of a purposeless, sterile madness all of their own.

Surely this was not what Marx had dreamt of when envisaging a world in which the state is withered away, the whole becomes free from coercion, and individuals contribute freely in accordance with their abilities and rewarded in accordance with their needs which, in his case, included cases of claret and Rhenish wine.

The system, caught by the long arm of its ineptitude, had certainly failed to deliver on its promises.

But, on the other hand, its appalling failure did also reflect the failure of man to overcome the dark, ugly, unsavoury side of human nature on which, it seems, we can always bank when contemplating the worst.

As the idiot in Dostoevsky's Crime and Punishment claimed anticipating Freud's theory of the death-wish, the law of self-destruction has as much force in human affairs as the law of self-preservation. Kavafy, the poet, might have had a point when he said that 'humanity has no more honourable qualities; those beyond are found among the Gods'.

Hence Orwell's bitter sense of hopelessness inherent, as he believed, in the human condition. His pigs, though superior to the other animals in terms of intelligence, were missing in moral character – it was this absence which turned them from the liberators of the farm's repressed community into the new agents of repression.

Equally well, the failed experiment had just shown, as Austrian-born philosopher Karl Popper argued, that it is not possible to 'set up' or 'direct' or 'regulate' or 'create' a whole because that whole is bound, whatever the intentions, to lead to an inhumane, repressive social order, a dystopia inimical to freedom. The twentieth century's utopias which opened the floodgates to totalitarianism, the prelude played before capacity crowd to a Last Judgment which fortunately never happened, bear evidence to it.

Less pessimistic, Jean-François Lyotard dismissed all 'metanarratives', i.e., all teleological notions used as a smokescreen to hide the will to power. Having been caught only so often in the company of undesirable characters, 'metaphysical certitudes', dismissed so disdainfully by Wittgenstein, had definitely lost their innocence.

Innocence, self-evidently, was no longer fashionable during these permissive times when the stock of virgins had so dramatically dwindled.

The West had nothing much to promise either.

– 'Both sides', Thucydides could say again, 'claimed to have the good of the community at heart, while both in fact aimed at political control, and in their struggle for ascendancy indulged in the worst excesses.'

From my perspective, Britain and from 1947 onwards the US had backed a savage regime to ensure Greece remained part of the 'free world' even if this world was anything but free. Compromises that would have averted both the civil war in the forties and the 1967 dictatorship were possible, but, blinded by their strategic and economic interests whatever the costs to human life and dignity, the West had just opted for the worst.

And the poor, as Shelley would have once again said, paid

– 'With their blood, their labour, their happiness, and their innocence for the crimes and mistakes which the hereditary monopolists of earth commit.'

Looking back in time, I still derive a personal satisfaction that in my earlier years I managed to overcome the fear the age generated and do what I saw as my duty to the world. Somehow, the memory of the pain endured along the way has been consigned to oblivion just like, I suppose, the memory of a woman's birth-giving pain.

I am also satisfied that, despite the huge obstacles, we managed to conduct effectively the offensive against the ossified and corrupt right wing regime, even if at the end we were defeated.

But, unlike the calendar, thoughts and feelings, often inchoate and half-articulated, do change before they settle like bubbles in a glass of sparkling wine. If they do, of course, because the past is not just our experiences, but also their echo and after-effect, coloured by subsequent events. Time, bent, as Euripides said, on his own business, does not care to preserve even our basic assumptions.

At some point, one may even wonder whether the past has been a reality or just a dream. When events are shaped by forces beyond our control emotions are just neutered.

Though we did not really expect a dream world, we had given everything in the fight for a better future and this without any thoughts of personal gain. This idealism was the source of our strength. But it was also our Achilles heel. It turned us, without realising it into the victims of the various power centres and of our illusions. What remained of it, in a bottle, had the taste of wine gone sour.

Even worse, self-scanning raises an unsettling and unanswered question which cultivates further one's inner confusions, often moist with emotions. We had all offered ourselves as a sacrifice to the altar of the future, to a fair and decent world, only to witness zero returns on our investment. In the new black and white minimal reality, even the colourful dreams that held us together were no longer there.

While in the Leros concentration camp, Yannis Ritsos, the man whose only sin was poetry, reflected in 1968:

– 'We went inside ... searching for some deeper correlation, some distant, general allegory, to soothe the narrowness of the personal void. We found nothing.'

Hope seemed at that point as if it had assumed an astral body.

Yet socialism, as the ultimate goal, had not disappeared from the picture like the dying flames in the iron stoves of a caravansary.

Abandoning its humanistic premises, it looked utterly inconsequential, unprincipled, unethical, immoral, tantamount to abandoning ourselves to the winds of fate.

But re-radicalised, going back to its roots to rediscover its early spiritual commitment, its soul, and recovering its humanistic ethos, it would regain the high moral ground.

If not, we would have to accept that we are all too miserably human or too humanly inhuman.

But, in the meantime, I cancelled my EDA membership, and I have never since joined any political party either in Greece or the UK. In my still unwedlocked concepts, party politics was not there to provide legitimacy to the élite that runs the show. It makes sense only if it aims at the empowerment of the community through the public's participation in planning and the decision-making process at all levels, and if it rests on full accountability.

In any case, politics, as I discovered later, has little to do with what the political parties say or do.

Politics relates to our entire culture.

As Aristotle said while walking in his 4th century BC Lyceum off Athens' Rigillis Street, politics actually begins with the family.

6

School of Danger

Early in 1969 I had become once again a student having registered for a Ph.D in History at London university. History was a subject dear to me from my school days, when, having read lots of books, I could mischievously raise questions with my teacher which he could neither answer nor was he really expected to answer.

– 'Who was responsible for the infertility of the royal couple, king Otto, the first king of Greece, or Amalia, his wife?' was one of those questions raised while my classmates were not even trying to suppress their impish smiles.

As if let down by a linguistic infirmity, his answers would come in sounds that refused stubbornly to turn into words.

In May 1969 I had also met Dina Glouberman, a student at Brunel university, who later became my wife.

Dina at the time was sharing an apartment in London's Swiss Cottage with Tonia Marketaki, a journalist and friend from Athens. Tonia, incidentally, a sparkling character, made after her return to Athens in 1974 three full-length feature films and directed a number of theatrical plays. She died suddenly in 1994.

Whom the gods love, as they say, die young.

Meeting Dina through Tonia had something which I still view as truly extraordinary. Looking for someone to share a flat in

Swiss Cottage, Tonia had placed an advert in London's *Evening Standard*, and Dina had responded. If the advert had been placed a couple of days earlier or later, if it was on the right day but Dina had missed it or had gone for something else, if Tonia had chosen someone else as her flat mate or if Dina decided, after visiting the flat, to opt for something different, I would have never met her.

This means that Skyros, as a holiday company, and all that went with it, would have never come to life. It follows that my choices, forced or otherwise, would have been radically different and my course in life would have followed an entirely different route.

What hits me here is that one can make the best long term plans and prepare the ground carefully for their realisation only to end up in a situation in which the future hangs on somebody's reading or missing a classified ad in the *Evening Standard*.

The most important things in life apparently happen by chance.

– 'Chance', Jocasta said in Sophocles' king Oedipus, 'rules our lives'.

My journey in the student politics world started in 1969, the time when in Lund, Sweden, I was elected by a number of Greek unions in Europe as the head of the Greek National Union of Students (EFEE), in exile. I had gone to Lund together with Yanis Yanoulopoulos, an ex-president of EFEE, and George Grammatikakis, later rector of the University of Crete and after 2014 a member of the European parliament.

The journey to Lund, by ferry from Copenhagen, was hilariously unforgettable.

As this was a journey I had done before, I knew that for a few krones you could help yourself freely to the delectable seafood available on board the ferry. So this time none of us had eaten anything for almost 24 hours in order to take full advantage of this supreme Scandinavian opportunity. Yanis called it:

– 'The Vietcong mentality'. Eat as much as you can now because you do not know when the next meal will be coming.

It sounded good advice except that when you have not eaten anything for some time, your stomach shrinks and you cannot have even what you would normally have. The disappointment is still with us.

Left-wing student politics at the time were rather amusingly preoccupied with ideological purity, clarity and an unambiguousness as rich in pleonastic amphibologies as the sheikhs in petrodollars.

The effort to establish the precise meaning of words which are vague by design often resembled Thomas Aquinas' attempts to work out the number of angels that could dance on the point of a pin. In the process, however, and as soon as I started my episodic journey in the world of European student politics, I familiarised myself fully with the give and take nature of politics, its rhetoric and practice and also, in the world I was moving in, its hazards.

Regarding the latter I did not have to wait for the tide to turn.

A week after the Lund conference I had to be in Frankfurt for the European conference of the United Democratic Left (EDA) as the representative of its UK members. I had, therefore, a few free days between the two events, which I chose to spend in East Berlin just in order to see some old Greek friends and also the staff of Wochenpost, the East German weekly publication.

The latter's staff was quite welcoming. They offered me coffee and cakes when we met plus smiles and even a joke.

– 'What's the shortest book ever published?', their international editor asked me with sparkling eyes. The answer, he himself laughingly offered, was

– 'One hundred years of German humour.'

His sense of humour, I freely admitted, was far superior to that of any German or a communist I knew.

Soon after I left their office for the *wursts* with that distinctive spicy sauce I had discovered in Alexanderplatz during an earlier visit. I enjoyed them again. Nevertheless, a day later, following a request by the local representatives of the Greek communist party to the East German authorities, I was arrested, detained in a police cell for a day and then expelled unceremoniously to West Berlin.

Stasi, the *Schild und Schwert der Partei* (Shield and Sword of the Communist Party), had ensured a serious threat to the communist state had been averted. I imagine, the Inca empire, which had been seriously weakened and demoralised when Columbus had unwittingly brought smallpox to the New World, would have wished to have acted with the same efficiency and speed.

The Moscow-backed Greek communist party of the exterior had declared war on us and everybody who refused to submit to its rule.

The danger this represented in Western Europe, where the party had no influence whatsoever, was nil, but in Eastern Europe, where it was backed by the communist regimes, its influence was decisive.

In the same way it forced the East Germans to expel me from East Berlin, it could also force the Moscow-backed International Union of Students (IUS), of which EFEE was a member long before the dictatorship, to twist our arm.

The Greek student movement in Europe at the time was in shambles, just like all the other Greek democratic political forces. The blow the dictatorship had administered was devastating, the omnipotence of silence deafening, and the prospect of a quick return to what would approximate normal conditions looked as unlikely as God's chance to make a four-sided triangle.

– 'God', Paracelcus said, 'can make an ass with three tails, but not a triangle with four sides.'

To be of any help to the Greek students in Greece itself, the Greek student movement abroad had to be re-energised except that this, I believed, could not be done without the help of the non-Greek National Unions of Students. In this we had the support of the British NUS under the presidency of Jack Straw, the UK's foreign secretary later on, and of the Scandinavian NUSs.

The plan was to make 1970 the year of European student solidarity with the Greek students in Greece.

Soon a campaign was initiated, information bulletins started to be sent out regularly to the European unions and to the Greek anti-dictatorship media and a list of all Greek students held in Greece in prison and concentration camps was compiled and sent to the European unions for adoption. Further a book with photographs of all events leading to the dictatorship was printed and distributed widely together with posters and other publicity material, and rallies in support of the Greek student resistance movement started to be organised in many cities.

The goal was to demonstrate that the Greek students were fighting actively against the dictatorship, get the European student movement to support equally actively their struggle and isolate further the Greek colonels' regime.

The support we received was very widespread, from the UK to Israel, from Norway to Italy and from the US to New Zealand. People were only too happy to help.

The hard work involved was also quite rewarding from a personal point of view as at the end I received a diploma in moderation.

This was during an intense practical course I had taken when dealing with some of my confederates – Palestinians of the extremist Popular Front for the Liberation of Palestine, for example, who had hijacked three aeroplanes and had brought them to a desert air strip in Jordan, threatening to blow them up with their passengers.

For some strange reason, as if this was a tourist attraction, our international student group was taken to that spot.

All of us, with the exception of some German members of the Baader–Meinhof Group, argued fiercely against killing the hostages, whose distraught faces we could see through the aeroplanes' windows.

– 'Don't do it. Whatever your argument, these people don't deserve to die.'

Their lives were eventually spared. I was lucky that my own life was, too, during the same time, the Black September of 1970, when the tanks of King Hussein began their offensive in Amman that crushed the PLO. During a lull in the battle between the two sides I approached an advanced Palestinian unit to chat with its officer.

– 'How is it going', I asked him in the same friendly, conversational manner I would have asked the tobacconist around the corner before buying my Rothmans.

Rather than answer, he asked me, instead, to hand over the notes I was keeping for an article I was planning to write later on. The argument we had ended, however, very soon, i.e. the moment Hussein's army resumed the firing and the bullets were hitting the pavement walls left and right of me.

– 'Take cover', he advised me before returning fire.

Incidentally, while in Amman I tried to renew my passport which the Greek embassy in London had refused to renew. I had thought that in the hands of an inexperienced local consular official I might get what I could not get in London. But Greece had no embassy in Amman, and the nearest one was in Damascus to which I could not go as my passport had already expired while I was in Amman.

Yet I went to Damascus, albeit smuggled by Fatah activists, where the Greek embassy refused again to renew my passport, and then smuggled back again to Amman.

Though futile, the adventure, dancing to the frenzied tunes of darabukka drums and mizmar flutes, appealed to the John Le Carré in me.

But without a passport I had to rely on the travel documents subsequently issued by the British Home Office.

In another instance, American Vietnam war ex-servicemen were determined to set their own embassy in Helsinki on fire. More arguments here with both them and also Italian leftists committed to non-violence but strictly as a last resort.

Moderation was often backed by muddled, distemperate arguments.

My time in EFEE involved in some respects taking lessons in what Thucydides would call 'the school of danger'.

I felt this way, for example in Czechoslovakia, where I was almost caught carrying letters from London to members of the clandestine opposition to the Soviet occupation given to me by Jan Kavan, a student leader of the Prague Spring of 1968 and later his country's Minister for Foreign Affairs.

– 'Be careful', he warned me in my Hampstead flat, while handing me over what could turn into a time-bomb.

It almost went off.

The security staff at the airport of Prague opened in my absence my bag except that they did not find the letters stored in its bottom. Their attention was taken by a new shirt at the very top, which was no longer there when the bag reached my hands.

I tried to hand over these letters to their recipients in Prague, but my goal remained unachieved. People either were not in or, if they were, they would shut the door in my face before I could even open my mouth.

I never regretted these occurrences – they all had the stuff that good stories, marinated in humour, are made to tell friends later around the fire on cold winter evenings.

This was exactly what an American with a wide range of conversational topics had told me when we were both stuck on the Yugoslav-Hungarian frontier. Having spent the night there, we had to return to Belgrade to get the Hungarian visas we had not thought of getting in advance.

– 'Don't worry', he said. 'What happens will make a good story to tell later'.

In Krakow, Poland, I did, however, get into trouble with the authorities. It was during an international student gathering in which I mentioned the massive spring demonstrations by Polish students demanding the freedom the regime had been denying them.

– 'You mentioned the student uprising around the globe', I said in front of a few hundred delegates, 'but you've failed to say a single word about what's going on here. Would you please enlighten us?'

They did not, but, as a result, I was placed under police surveillance, while Polish students, despite it, kept coming to me to have their views about the marvellous state of western democracy hopefully confirmed.

I did not encounter similar problems in Budapest to which I had gone to attend a Moscow-run World Federation of Democratic Youth conference. In it, I represented EFEE in exile and Theodoros Pangalos, foreign minister in the post-dictatorship Greece, the Lambrakis Youth which no longer existed. What I found most striking here was the speech Theodoros delivered to the Budapest Greeks, all refugees since the end of the civil war, in which he 'informed' them that the dictatorship was about to collapse. The year was 1970. I told him:

– 'I don't see why we should deceive these people by telling them stories we know aren't true.'

His answer, badly in need of an operation to remove its cynicism, which, incidentally, he did not seem to mind, was:

– 'That's what they wanted to hear.'

This explains fully why later on he turned into a politician and I did not.

Like Socrates, I was really too honest to follow that route. Besides, I did not know how to match the eloquence of his delivery with the strikingly woolly thinking that supported it.

Walking in Budapest, incidentally, I was surprised to see supermarkets with half-empty shelves and assistants totally impervious to the concerns of their customers.

But to be fair to them, Lenin had not mentioned anything about customer service in his Materialism and Empiriocriticism.

In another instance, in a meeting in Helsinki, where a Vietnam solidarity week had been organised by the Soviet backed International Union of Students (IUS), I held a meeting on Greece only to be reproached by the latter for doing something 'out of order'. As much out of order was our singing the Guantanamera, the Cuban song associated with Fidel Castro, with which the east Europeans could not emotionally connect.

They were just standing in the big hall exchanging long austere silences with a disconsolate expression.

The time did also have its amusing moments. In one of them, in Amsterdam, I was standing up on the platform of the theatre where the rally was being held when at the end the hosts decided to sing *L' Internationale*, the most popular song of the socialist movement since the late 19th century.

I did not know the words whether in French, Greek or any other language.

In another instance, in 1973, I was speaking at Oxford University and for some reason my sentence got incredibly long – so long that Helen Vlachos, the publisher, who was sharing the platform with me, and Chris Woodhouse, the head of the British Military Mission in Greece during the war, who was sitting in the audience, looked anxiously at me as if I might lose track of what I was saying altogether. Thankfully I did not.

But sentences, I decided, had from now on to be short as, otherwise, I might well expect the fate of the Samian opponents of Polycrates the time they appealed to the Spartans for help. The latter, Herodotus tells us, had forgotten the beginning of the Samians' speech and could not, therefore, understand the end.

The simmering conflict with the IUS manifested itself early enough, when two days before the Lund conference started, the Prague-based organisation let us know that it could not finance it as it had promised.

– 'We thought', the editor of the IUS magazine told me later in Dublin, 'that withholding aid would break you up'.

– 'It could only be expected', Pericles Nearchou, elected as my deputy in the Lund conference, said in his irritatingly even-tempered manner, which, I guess, must have helped him later on in his career as Cyprus' ambassador in various capitals of the world.

He added: 'You don't mess with them.'

Of course, we were not the only ones to receive this treatment, as 'dissident' student unions of other countries such as Spain, Venezuela, Iran and even France, could among others testify. And the IUS did not break us up.

The conflict with the IUS reached its first peak in Nicosia in the summer of 1970 during the annual conference of the Cypriot student unions. The Cypriot students in Athens were represented there by the officials the Greek junta had appointed, and the obvious choice under the circumstances was, together with the other European unions, to boycott the event.

Instead, and in consultation with the British NUS, we decided to attend it and challenge on the spot the legality of the proceedings.

The Cypriot communist unions, backed by the IUS, offered no support in this as, in their view, one had to be realistic and accept what one could not change. The same paraplegic argument had been advanced to me in Prague by some Bulgarian officials.

– 'The Greek dictatorship', they said while we were in the historic Prague Castle which housed the offices of the Czechoslovak communist party, 'is a fact of life which the socialist countries cannot ignore. If that was not to be our policy, we would end up relating to only a handful of countries.'

Nevertheless, this kind of realism could never appeal to us even if we had to pay a price for it. That was, indeed, the case when the Greek student unions in East Germany and Czechoslovakia were banned by the authorities because their policy was 'incompatible with the foreign policy' of those countries.

In any case, for us, the children of the Paris Spring of 1968, realism meant only the pursuit of the impossible.

– 'Be a realist, demand the impossible' was the motto.

In the presence of Greek army units outside and dozens of Greek security men in plain clothes inside the Cypriot hall, I challenged the presence of the 'honoured guest', the junta appointed 'president' of EFEE.

– 'You represent nothing but the colonels who appointed you', I shouted at him. 'Get out of here'.

I did not expect, as a result, the fifty Nereids to start performing a spiral dance on the white sands of Cyprus while the Cypriots opened cases of claret. But I did expect that in the ensuing battle that destroyed the theatre, I would manage not to be lynched. I did, and for this I have to thank also the communists, particularly the Andreas Fantis family, who, for personal reasons, offered me their support.

Andreas Fantis, in whose home I had stayed, was the deputy Secretary General of the Cypriot communist party and Astero, his daughter, my friend from Athens.

Yet the agents of the Greek military junta seemed determined to send me, handcuffed, back to Athens. I was told that this did not happen following the intervention of the Cypriot Republic's president Makarios himself.

The IUS representative, a Hungarian who could not for his life manage a smile, on the contrary, backed up the policy of the 'pragmatic' Cypriot communists and denounced us, the 'extremists'.

Soon after, the IUS opportunistic policy was denounced in Dubrovnic, Yugoslavia, in a conference of thirty-two western unions from all over the world. No matter how diplomatic I needed to be, there was, however, a limit as to how much I could tone down my disappointment.

– 'You've just failed to back us up against the monstrous Greek military regime', I eventually said to the displeasure of the present IUS representatives. They liked even less the sentiments behind my words.

The same Hungarian who had graced the Nicosia conference with his presence was once again present, silent again as a brick. I wondered if he was not an alien.

It was in that town, Dubrovnic, incidentally, that I discovered the irredentist claims of the 'Socialist Republic of Macedonia' that a number of years later would, like the hiss of demons, send shivers through the stars over the Athenian sky.

– 'We're Macedonians', Slavica, one of our hosts, insisted while we were dancing at a night club. Rather thoughtlessly under the circumstances I ventured to suggest that there is no such a thing as 'Macedonians'. She stopped talking to me altogether.

In 1971 a new EFEE executive was elected in Copenhagen, where the most massive and most representative conference the Greek students had ever held abroad was held. I was about to get out of the picture.

Before doing so, I had, however, to go to Prague for the bi-annual IUS conference. This was the time the IUS decided to stab us in the back again.

I was refused entry into Czechoslovakia.

In protest, and without cost-effectiveness in mind, I staged a 24-hour sit-in at Prague airport, which nevertheless had no effect whatsoever.

Though ignored by the authorities, I had, however, all the attention of the airport staff who surreptitiously supplied me with fruits and sandwiches accompanied by clandestine smiles.

This event took place a few weeks after a rally held by CND in Trafalgar Square in which Jiri Pelican, Alexander Dubcek's Information Minister, and myself had denounced both the Greek dictatorship and the Soviet occupation of Czechoslovakia.

Following my entry-ban, EFEE, appalled, withdrew from the IUS, while the latter, in Prague, accelerated its move to the periphery of the world student politics. The withdrawal from the IUS was confirmed by EFEE in Athens after the fall of the dictatorship.

And this was the end of my journey into the fascinating world of European student politics. I do not know what I achieved, if anything, but the effort to make our voice heard was worth much more than all its moments of frustration, fear and exertion.

Trying to do what you must may at the end fail to achieve the results hoped for. But I do not know what is better than trying.

7

'Facts' and 'Values'

Time, however, as Kazantzakis said, 'has cycles and fate has wheels'.

The new era of optimism generated in 1968 did not last longer than an opened bottle of Beaujolais nouveau. Crude realities led in the '70s to a reconsideration of passions, the deconstruction of the vision, the departure of the grand designs. The dream of '68 had in no time become a memory which had already taken its rightful place in the museum of the West's folkloric history.

The Left had, indeed, been left with nothing but memories of a propitious past, which now looks as remote as the fall of Syracuse to the Romans, and a teenage boy, Tony Blair, for a future.

Its vocabulary, humiliated, had the sepulchral looks of deposed nobility. Its vision the backbone of a wet sock.

In the 'gloomy' seventies, the hangover decade or the decade 'forgotten by taste', a time that the cost of living was rising fast, unemployment in the UK had hit 1.5 million and the world seemed to be coming to an end, practical concerns tended, instead, to dominate everyone's agenda. The unions, determined to stop the erosion of their living standards, and the miners, in particular, on strike in 1972, forced prime minister Edward Heath to introduce, in a bid to save energy, the three-day working week.

Power cuts and lengthy blackouts became the order of the day.

That was when Aline, in a song by the popular 1970s Lancashire folk group The Fivepenny Piece, asked the last person to leave Britain to 'turn out the lights'.

The oil shock of 1973 that resulted in an oil price bombshell, followed by the 1973 – 1974 stock market crash, the worst since the Great Depression, made the situation far worse. Britain had turned into 'the sick man of Europe'. Prime minister James Callaghan told reportedly his colleagues that if he were a young man, he would emigrate.

The thought had not crossed my mind, but if it had, I would have looked for a place that had not heard of Benny Hill, the TV comedian.

This, a friend had let me know, only confirmed that Britishness was not yet in my blood.

Disillusionment, resignation, even cynicism crept in, with nothing to look forward to. Amphion was no longer around to rebuild Thebes by the music of his flute, said to be so melodious that the stones danced their way into walls of their own accord. Philip Larkin's 'never such innocence again' became the new wisdom of the learned. Dreams, not wearable any longer, went out of fashion and so were the visions of a different world.

The fierce denunciation by Isaiah Berlin of any attempt to enforce a single order on the grounds that it was bound to turn into a totalitarian straitjacket for the human condition somehow summed up the spirit of the time.

For many Greeks detained by the Greek military junta in concentration camps, the new world could only be 'chaotic' by design. Their very early and yet fully-blown postmodernism pronounced the disintegration of purpose or the disintegration as purpose, a life, as Albert Camus would say, without appeal.

– 'All ideas are rubbish', Angelos Phocas, a respected Greek activist, tried to impress upon me in the office of the Greek

Committee Against Dictatorship. 'We've just entered the realm of real freedom.'

Our heart, as Aeschylus would say, had lost 'the precious confidence of hope'.

Ideals worth living for, let alone dying for, and strong beliefs were considered now to be the monopoly of single-issue fanatics and the self-appointed thought-police. The rest of us, if sufficiently motivated, could always write a letter to *The Guardian*.

Besides, there were more things to look forward to. After all, popularity pills were not yet available, the secret of everlasting youth had not been cracked, and a genuine cure for death had still to be found.

Grounded, intellectually mature and also immersed in triviality, we were, thus, ready to pursue only practical dreams, those whom we could see signalling their sexy presence in the corner of our eyes, things achievable by individual effort such as a job with Westminster Polytechnic, a semi in Crouch End and a woman to take care of our frustrations.

Having witnessed both the growth of conceptions of primal integration and then their later disintegration and disgrace, nauseated by vacuous, expansive words fertilised with 'purpose', overwhelmed by feelings of utter powerlessness, and unable to see even 'a fragment of tomorrow', I ended up myself, too, with nothing worth believing in apart from my own self.

Nothing seemed, likewise, worth doing apart from a Ph.D. on the necrotic fermentation of illusions or the reasons people do not like queuing. Alternatively, I could join the Nudist International.

The fish had to learn how to walk because the water was no more.

The only thing that enabled me to keep my feet on the ground was the brutal situation in Greece which was still under the 1967 military dictatorship and the plight of the Greeks, particularly those in prison or in concentration camps.

During all those ill-fated years I was happy to give my time and energy to the Greek Committee Against Dictatorship, chaired by the venerable University College professor Yannis Spraos, to help the dislodgement of the military from its position of power.

Members of the committee included Takis Lambrias, later Karamanlis' minister by the prime minister, Nicos Garganas, later governor of the Bank of Greece, George Catephores, later special economic advisor to prime minister Andreas Papandreou, and euro-MP, Spyros Yannatos, president of the Greek NUJ when the colonels took over, Yanis Yanoulopoulos, president of EFEE in its most glorious times and later history professor at Panteion university, Rigas Doganis, later CEO of Olympic Airways, George Krimpas, political economy professor at the university of Athens, and many other Greeks who distinguished themselves after the fall of the dictatorship, including Spyros Mercouris, Marcos Dragoumis, and Raphael Papadopoulos.

The Committee worked together with many other distinguished Greeks such as Helen Vlachos, the publisher, Aspasia Papathanasiou, the actress, Maria Farantouri, the singer, Yolanta Terentsio, the BBC journalist, George Plytas, later minister of culture or Amalia Fleming, the physician and wife of Alexander Fleming, known for his discovery of penicillin.

A frequent visitor to the Committee's office was also, among others, Richard Clogg, a man who later on specialised in modern Greek history and published several insightful books. At the time, he was, however, as demonstrative of his thoughts and emotions as a fish in an aquarium.

It was rather difficult to get to know him.

Hence chats with him were usually in length no longer than a centimetre.

Occasionally, I would also offer some help to the League for Democracy in Greece, an English grouping formed in 1945 and headed now by the unflagging Diane Pym, a relation of Francis Pym, foreign secretary in the Thatcher government. In her truly extraordinary work for which the Greeks can only be grateful, Diane was supported by Marion Sarafis, wife of the resistance leader Stefanos Sarafis to whom she would always refer as o στρατηγος, 'the General'.

Next to them was Betty Ambatielos, a woman of ferocious goodwill, member of the British communist party and wife of the prominent Greek communist Antonis Ambatielos, who, in his London flat, had just dismayed me with his patronising attitude. Betty Ambatielos had organised the 1963 massive demonstrations in London against queen Frederica, who was forced to seek refuge in a stranger's house, sealing as a result the Greek government's fate.

Occasionally, I would also give a bit of time to the African National Congress and particularly to Thabo Mbeki, a friendly, unpretentious young man, who later, in 1999 was elected president of South Africa.

The ANC office was practically next door to the Greek Committee Against Dictatorship.

Commitment to the freedom of Greece was for me a political but also a personal decision. Identifying with Greece, I needed to feel proud of the country, not ashamed of it. But at the same time I decided to take Sancho's advice to Don Quixote to stop rambling about 'from Ceca to Mecca' and do, instead, what I was supposed to be doing in the first place as a student, i.e. complete my doctoral dissertation at the University of London.

A grant from the Swedish government through the International University Exchange Fund and also from Birkbeck College, for both of which I am most grateful, made this possible.

The subject was history, the foreign policy of the South and Central European Powers at the time Hitler ascended to power in Germany.

Researching the Foreign Office and the State Department's unpublished records in Washington DC as well as those of other

Foreign Ministries to reconstruct the period was not, of course, as exciting as planning the 'revolution' in the Che café of Paris.

Nevertheless, this was a work which I grew to like because in terms of political insights offered, it was as edifying as that undertaken by Machiavelli when he was about to write The Prince.

Politics, as seemed from its adytum, was based on the most immaculate conception of self-interest. The politicians did, of course, have a view of the world in line with some convictions, commitments to some fundamental articles of faith and well-articulated concepts of the right and the good. But the wholesomeness of their policies was almost always compromised by calculations of self-interest.

Quoting Darius, Herodotus made this point beautifully.

– 'Men', the Persian king said, 'lie when they want to profit from deception and tell the truth for the same reason'.

This did not necessarily imply that policies pursued were faulty or morally repugnant. But politics in the last analysis was not about ideals.

History read, as a result, almost like the malefactors' bloody register.

Erasmus was said to get nauseous at the smell of fish. I felt likewise at the smell of politics.

The thirties were of course a most disturbing time that unleashed the worst in people. Fascism, in boots, loved to play in democracy's field of daffodils – this was the Churchillian depiction of the era, embellished and convenient. But the looming conflict that started taking shape in the thirties had nothing to do with ideologies and everything with redistribution of territories, wealth and influence. And the democracies, though less aggressive, were as unscrupulous in protecting what they possessed as the dictatorships who were trying to take it from them.

What upset Churchill was not the immorality, but the ineffectiveness of the Western policy, the shopkeeper's view of the world, which, in its circumscribed wisdom, almost gave Hitler a hand in hoisting the swastika in Westminster.

In the process, as I discovered rather unexpectedly, history may be about truth, but truth is, as Oscar Wilde wisely said, 'rarely pure and never simple'.

Subscribing to the rather old-fashioned latter-day positivism that had completely dominated the field until the mid-1950s, I begun at first to look for 'facts', in Leopold von Ranke's dictum, 'simply to show how it really was'.

The concept had been championed by the French sociologist Auguste Comte, who coined the term 'positivism' in the 1830s to describe what he called the scientific status of historical laws. Historians, according to positivist historians, had to begin with the documents and the facts they revealed and then develop their scientific generalisations on a scientific basis.

'Facts' were a measurable quantity, but 'values', i.e., subjective evaluative judgements based on philosophical, moral, ethical, social, political or religious considerations, man-made and illusory, were something like soft earth, excellent for flower-beds.

They were cognitively meaningless just like the subliminal or encoded references that render sub-tweeted messages meaningless to outsiders.

Jacques Derrida called this passion for 'facts' 'archive fever'.

The massive study of documents, I had, thus, been encouraged to believe, would be good enough to establish and confirm verifiable empirical realities on which I could, with the Olympian detachment of the historian, proceed to develop my own 'scientific' general interpretations and build the castle of my saga.

The idea appealed to me for the additional reason that I had never before had access to written sources. The Athenian public records of any age were as inaccessible to researchers as God's correspondence with the Virgin Mary.

I could not, thus, resist the temptation to be the willing casualty of the 'archive fever'.

Documents did, indeed, provide an astonishing amount of information.

In the process I realised, however, that separating the object of my research from my own 'truth' was an impossibility. I had to recognise that value judgements interfere not only with the assessment of the collected facts, but also with the constitution of the facts themselves, meaningful only within a structure that gives them meaning.

Interpretations, coloured by the beliefs of the historian, do not emerge after the collection of facts. They come, instead, before the facts and guide their selection because they have to fit into one's perception of the world and its implicit theoretical framework. In other words, there is no way one can be 'objective', take 'God's perspective'.

One can account only for what he or she experiences.

And that meant that my account of historical developments could not be detached from my own background which coloured it and underpinned it. One could, indeed, go as far as to say that facts are there only to support the historian's initial assumptions.

Interpretations are, therefore, bound to be mutually exclusive. Yet, different perspectives are anything but mutually exclusive. As Appleby, Hunt and Jacob argued in their excellent book Telling The Truth About History, insects living on grass eaten by sheep can be expected to look on the sheep as ferocious predators, but the wolves are bound to be seen as harmless and benevolent creatures of God. Although mutually exclusive, both views are valuable.

Different perspectives, rather than contradicting, complement each other. A slave's point of view does not obliterate the perspective of the slaveholder.

There is a diachronical dimension, too, for the view of the past is not engraved in marble like Praxiteles' aesthetic understanding. History is ceaselessly being reinterpreted, even reinvented, in line with new political and social values and the truths that come in and out of favour, which the historian reflects. Historical judgements, E.H. Carr, the British historian, said, reflect the assumptions of the periods that produce them.

Just like art or fashion.

History, like memory, is a psychological process prone to editing, interpolation as well as contamination by subsequent events. It moves as invisibly in its incessant transformations as our body cells, the building blocks of life.

To take Eric Hobsbawm's view, expressed when he 'deconstructed' the traditions of modern nationalism, 'history is the raw material for nationalist or ethnic or fundamental ideologies as poppies are the raw material for heroin addiction'.

I had, thus, to question 'truth' and 'objectivity', accept their artistic verisimilitude, and thereby acknowledge the relativism and subjectivity of all historical accounts, including my own. I was handicapped by my own limitations – my background, priorities and values, interests and skills, choices and prejudices, my own sense of right and good, even my gender and psychological make up.

My early experiences did, thus, and still do reflect the climate in which my thoughts, which, unfortunately, I never had the inclination to place within the safety of a book, had grown. Time passes but it is not separated from us. You cannot live outside time.

My views on the political developments in Greece, as discussed in this book, reflect, therefore, only what I identify with: the interests of a small country which does not wish to be invaded, coerced into compliance or exploited by a powerful 'friend', and the right of its people to express themselves freely, choose what they want to choose and enjoy all the privileges to which they feel entitled.

This is what gives me the moral high ground to argue the case against foreign intervention and domestic oppression.

But looking at the same developments from a different angle, the story is bound to be different. The Greek Liberation Front represented a potential threat to the imperial interests of Britain, and as such it had to be nullified. Making the moral case, Britain did, of course, argue that it acted in the interests of the free world and all it is supposed to stand for.

Right and wrong are in the last analysis not coloured by morality but self-interest in whose pursuit all means available can be almost effortlessly justified.

We get a taste of it in the way we run even our own personal or business affairs. Our choices are not dictated by some sort of eternal moral laws, but by our own interests. The two do not necessarily coincide.

More interestingly, whether they do or not, we are always ready to claim the high ground.

In my assessments I did also remain intellectually attached to justice, which, as Theognis of Megara, the lyric poet, and Phocylides, the poet of Miletus, said, 'sums up the whole of virtue'.

But again justice, just like history, is subject to different interpretations, too. Fire, Aristotle explained, burns both in Athens and in Persia, but justice is not subject to the same immutable laws. There is, as he said, a thing such as natural law, but, on the other hand, everything in our world is subject to change.

In any case, from the '70s onwards history was increasingly being viewed as a subjective, partial, even propagandist, indeed fictional, account of events. It was even denounced as a discipline, a fool's obsession with 'the rear-mirror view'. The nominalists reduced it into a multiplicity of disjointed episodes, and the subjectivists into myths originating in different national, class or gender groups.

What was also questioned was the universality of values when these values simply reflect our own standards.

Foucault dismissed the usefulness of general world views, the metanarratives, whether Christian, liberal or Marxist. Each society, he argued, has its own regime of truth, its general politics of truth, shaped by language and enveloped into an ideology. Together with Barthes, Derrida, Baudrillard and others, he questioned the western search for truth – the prime western illusion – and objected to immortal verities, the eternal self-deception into which we are pushed by the grand designs.

'Truth' had turned out to be something as personal as our hiccups.

Protagoras, the sophist, had said so already and so had Gorgias.

– Nothing exists, the latter maintained, and if anything exists, it is unknowable. But even if it exists and it is knowable, it cannot be communicated. That was the time, the 4th century BC, that, when talking about virtue, the Athenian's first reaction was 'what you mean by virtue' – a question nobody could answer.

Tradition had been destroyed, faith in the polis had been shaken and justice, as sophist Thrasymachus declared, served 'the interests of the stronger'. Justice had been subsumed into the callousness of reality.

Like our contemporaries, rather than citizens, the Athenians had turned into connoisseurs, content to spend their life exchanging jokes about cooks and the price of fish, shrewish wives and incompetent doctors.

The thinking of the French postmodernists exerted a profound influence all over the West though the UK intellectuals, reputedly hostile to abstract thought, especially when championed by foreigners, kept their distances from it. At a time that technology tries to eliminate space, the latter must have certainly felt honoured by the favour.

But I never really subscribed to the kind of relativism that declares universal ethical and moral values null and void.

Emancipation from every value is not the answer, but the problem.

8

The Unfinished Business

In 1974, following the ill-fated Greek military intervention in the affairs of the Republic of Cyprus, the Greek dictatorship collapsed.

I heard about it in London's Belsize Park from my friend Sofia Roumbou, a leading Greek movie actress. We hugged each other and danced ecstatically in the middle of the street. The embarrassment, which we did not feel, could only come as a poor second to the relief experienced and joy.

– 'Ignore us', I told the passers-by, who, so British, pretended not to notice us. 'We're just lunatics on vacation.'

The feeling was overwhelming. We could breathe again and look forward, after such a very long interval in the dark, to the enjoyment of democracy's sunshine. Athens, to which I went soon after, elated, full of creative energy and determined to curve a new path in history away from the disconcerting past, was able to smile self-confidently once again.

The stone had, perhaps, decided to blossom.

But something at the same time did not look right to me. In the first place, the dictatorship had given birth to a new ruling élite, composed of the most unscrupulous and greedy elements who backed the colonels for their own benefit. These people had now been removed from power, but what was still there was the legacy of an aneurysm-inducing corruption they had left behind.

I smelt the stale cabbage as soon as I set foot in Athens. One person I knew stole at that time the records of the export company she was working for and started her own export agency. Another one suggested to me the setting up of a fraudulent business, something like selling brand-new antiques. A third one, a member of the communist party who also happened to be a relation, was caught stealing.

They all had the looks of someone who had never in their life got away with anything, which was what had given them that ignominious sense of entitlement. I had never come across such incidents so untainted by rectitude before 1967 and I felt an immediate twinge of discontent.

Equally bad was my experience in Skyros island soon after, when I came face to face with a flourishing culture of corruption as epitomised by the giving and taking of bribes. It was as if it was all part of an eternal plan to which one had for his own survival to adjust and dress accordingly.

People, when I questioned this practice, looked at me as shocked as if I had proposed wife-swapping or, alternatively, as if I had just come out of the ark.

– 'You live in your dream world', I had often been nicely reminded.

If not so respectful, their language would have appeared in its Monday-to- Friday plain clothes.

Apart from all this, the road to a new world seemed to be a journey through acres of confusion and valleys of obfuscation and I just did not feel at home with it.

The country was enraged, and its anger, which could activate the smoke alarms, had to find an outlet, in the tumultuous rejection of everything that exemplified or symbolised the hypocrisy of the West. The US, in particular, professing strict adherence to democratic rule while backing up a dictatorial regime, most feared and utterly detested, was the most hated target.

A new generation of communists had, in the meantime, redefined both the communist part of Europe as the promised land and me, who had tried on several occasions to dispel their illusions, as part of the reactionary establishment.

The country, in a Third World 'revolutionary' delirium, was looking for the cathartic end of the tragedy and at the same time for the redefinition of its role in the contemporary world.

I understood the feeling behind this anger, but, as the years went on, I found its political expression frivolous, shallow, manipulative and at times outrightly vulgar. Ineffective, too, like the pill the story's grandmother was taking because she did not want any more grandchildren.

Because of it or despite it, I did nevertheless want to make my contribution to the future I felt Greece deserved.

Going for it, I should have made sure I did not wear my best trousers as Ibsen's Dr Stockman had advised those who wanted to fight for the right and the good. And I had not!

The problems begun when I re-entered journalism with the Athens daily *Avghi* which had by that time moved outside the Soviet ideological sphere of influence and aspired to become the voice of the decent Left.

Things ran smoothly for a while, i.e. when they were happy with me as, for example, when I gave them a list of Greek police officers trained in US police academies and later identified as torturers of political prisoners.

The list was confirmed by the Greek government.

As welcome was the text of the interview granted to myself and a few other Greek journalists by ex-king Constantine just a few days before the November 1974 referendum on his return to the throne which went against him.

– 'Your Majesty', I said when I met him at his home in Chogham, Surrey, 'the Athens correspondent of *The Times* has just reported that 90 per cent of the Greeks consider the US responsible for the arrival of the Greek dictatorship. Do you share this view?'

I believed he could never answer such a question in the affirmative as he would never cross swords with the Americans. The latter would certainly appreciate it, but the 90 of the Greeks would definitely not.

– 'To make such a claim, you must have the necessary evidence. Do you?', he asked me rather than answer my question.

His boyish face had suddenly become very serious.

– 'Don't you?', I retorted with gingerly concern. His eyes narrowed in apparent concentration before his head started moving upwards.

That is the way the Greeks say 'No'.

What I did not know at the time was that the word 'Americans' did not mean all that much as US policy on Greece lacked the anticipated coherence. One was the policy of the State Department and the US embassy in Greece, which backed the planned royal dictatorship, and another that of the CIA and the Pentagon, which conspired with the colonels.

The private chat after that involving his Danish wife Anne Marie, who gracefully served the coffee, and his children who were playing noisily around, was quite friendly. Constantine even asked me to convey to my mother his best wishes – that was after I told him she would vote for his return to the throne.

I did not expect to encounter any difficulties with regard to anything relating to the above or the story about the rumoured decision of Turkey to turn herself into a nuclear power.

The story that appeared in Greece for the first time when *Avghi* gave it prominence had emerged following an agreement on the subject between Turkey and India in April 1976. It was followed by speculation that Turkey was about to buy six nuclear reactors from France.

The Foreign Office I asked did not go, as one might expect, beyond a confirmation that it was against the proliferation of nuclear weapons, while Giscard D' Estaing, the president of France, a little bit more straightforward, told me in London that

– 'Nothing had for the time being been arranged.'

And Yashwantrao Chavan, the Indian foreign minister, of whom I asked the same question in Colombo, Sri Lanka, said that his country's agreement with Turkey provided for their 'technological cooperation' but nothing more than that.

Incidentally, nothing of it gave the true picture as nuclear weapons research had long been underway in Turkey since its association with NATO under conditions of extreme secrecy.

As much of a 'secret' was the storing of 90 thermonuclear B61 gravity bombs at its Incirlik nuclear air base, revealed in February 2005 by a National Resources Defence Council report. Fifty of these bombs were reportedly assigned for delivery by US pilots, and 40 were assigned for delivery by the Turkish Air Force. However, no permanent nuclear-capable US fighter wing is based at Incirlik, and the Turkish Air Force is reportedly not certified for NATO nuclear missions.

Though this was confirmed in 2010 by George Robertson, former Nato Secretary-General, Turkey remains an 'undeclared nuclear weapons state'.

Even so, as the president of the International Strategic Studies Association revealed in 2010, despite its denials, Turkey still pursues the development of its own nuclear weapons programme. The latest of these denials, in September 2014, was contradicted by the German newspaper *Die Welt*, which, citing sources from within the German Federal Intelligence Service, reported that Turkey had, indeed, been secretly developing nuclear weapons.

Avghi had no problem giving publicity to such issues or to the answers to questions I had asked Henry Kissinger, the US secretary of state, in Brussels.

But other issues were in the grey area. I did not know, for example, whether the opposition I expressed to the execution of the 1967 military coup leaders, who had been sentenced to death for high treason, would be published.

It was, and also thankfully the putschists' sentence was commuted later to life incarceration. As Aeschylus had said, retributive justice inflicted in plain revenge leads to chaos.

Pleased as rain falling in dry wine, I also saw the publication of an article on the 1936 – 1941 Metaxas dictatorship that challenged the prevailing view according to which Metaxas, the dictator, was in Hitler's pocket.

Though ideologically pro-German, partly for reasons of self preservation, partly because Greece could not side with the Powers defeated in the first world war and now demanding the re-drawing of the European map, and partly because he believed that the British would at the end emerge victorious from the war, Metaxas had aligned himself with the latter. The British were not always comfortable with him, but they never really worried as king George II, a man who told the British ambassador that he viewed himself as British rather than Greek, seemed to be in total control of the country's destiny.

Incidentally, for the right-wing press, the article signified the rehabilitation of Metaxas by the Left. This was not the case, for Metaxas himself was a miserable fascist and a tyrant. Thankfully, the reformist communist party behind *Avghi* responded to the allegation stating that my 'iconoclastic' views were 'food for thought'.

What I wanted to emphasise was that ideology does not dictate foreign policy.

In September 1975, *Avghi* dared also to publish a controversial long article that challenged the prevalent assumptions on Cyprus.

The article had been written following a long discussion with Rauf Denktas, leader of the Turkish-Cypriots, that strangely I cannot recall where it took place.

All I remember is that we were sitting in the garden of a countryside pub drinking beer.

Glafcos Clerides, later President of the Republic of Cyprus, had offered me his time, too, and so had James Callaghan, the UK foreign secretary at the time. The latter's advice, offered in Brussels, had, however, something that resembled the Delphic oracles' statements.

– 'Those who live by the sword, die by the sword', I remember him telling me, while I was trying to work out the meaning of his and Matthew's words of wisdom in our context.

My conclusion of it all was that Turkey was not going to end the occupation of the 40 per cent of Cyprus or allow the return of the 200,000 Greek refugees to their home whatever the circumstances. Greece and Cyprus had, therefore, either to prepare for war to evict the Turkish troops, if they thought that was possible, or, alternatively, look for the best possible compromise. Greece and Cyprus were doing neither.

Quite a few people said it was the best ever article written on the subject.

Another story that was again published refuted the views expressed by Tasos Vournas, a senior member of its staff on the Iranian revolution. The author had been arguing that the 1979 Iranian revolution was based on socialist ideas because the 'resurrection of dead ideas, i.e. Islamism, is unknown in history'.

My argument was that Islamism is an ideological train going in the direction determined, not by the Koran, but by those who have chartered it.

Driven by the bourgeoisie, it intends to perpetuate its dominance, driven by social discontent, it strives to bring in a regime of social equality, driven by patriots, it intends to fulfil the country's national aspirations, driven by nationalists, it serves their expansionist aims or driven by fanatics, it aspires to accelerate the march towards the end of our 'evil' world. In theory, and politically speaking, it could be a progressive or an utterly destructive force desperately happy to slaughter our fellow human beings in the name of God .

But this is, of course, in theory, for in practice I have not seen as yet a progressive Islamic state. Political movements growing on the back of a religion can never be a progressive force.

The road to renewal was, nevertheless, full of obstacles, for the old guard was still able to make its influence felt. Clashes of perceptions appeared any time I would question old-held beliefs.

Hence Costas Hatziargyris, the co-editor of *Avghi*, wanted me out of the picture.

– 'He's dangerous', he told Thanasis Tsouparopoulos, the other co-editor, as the latter did at some point inform me.

Eventually, however, it was Hatziargyris who was moved out of the picture.

In one instance, for example, I challenged the Soviet foreign policy on Cyprus as articulated in a book published by Novosti, the Soviet international news agency.

Turkish expansionism resulting in the 1974 invasion and occupation of the 40 per cent of Cyprus had been caused, as far as the Soviets were concerned, by the imperialists' attempt to overthrow president Makarios. The Turkish invasion was, therefore, none of their concerns. Of sole importance now, Andrei Gromyko, the Soviet foreign minister, quoted in the book said with an air of profound indifference for the fate of the 200,000 Greek refugees, was not to turn the island into a NATO base.

Hence the Soviet foreign minister called for the preservation of Cyprus' independence, but forgot to mention the UN decision calling for the return of the 200,000 Greek-Cypriot refugees to their homes.

The article was never published. Another article on the Soviet education system, which another contributor had praised for having removed the class barriers and I rejected as a thought-killer, had the same fate.

In another instance I questioned the credentials of the 'anti-imperialist' Libyan dictator Muammar Gadhafi. Those opposing US power were, however, at the time in Greece above criticism. Andreas Papandreou, the 'socialist' leader, shared after all, as he had said himself, Gadhafi's vision of radical social transformation and an end to dependence on US power.

It is tragic, I wrote, to view Gadhafi's fascist state as the new 'socialist' model. Regardless of his anti-imperialist tone, Gadhafi is a tyrant. But right and wrong are not always as clear and unambiguous as right and left. The article again was never published.

The problems, thus, persisted and came to a head in 1976 after my trip to Sri Lanka to attend the conference of the non-aligned nations. In its course I enjoyed meeting people like Indira Gandhi, who approached me to ask me where I come from. I told her: Greece.

– 'Oh, from a Nato country', she responded with a melodious smile, thinking perhaps of her Italian daughter in law, Sonia, whom her son, Rajiv, had met when she was a waitress at a Greek restaurant.

My discomfort with her was similar to that experienced by Miguel de Cervantes' Sancho, who could eat as well, or better, standing and alone, than if he were seated close by an emperor.

It was in Colombo that I also met Yasser Arafat, to whom I complained that, despite my efforts, I had not been able to see a few years earlier in the Middle East, Kenneth Kaunda, president of Zambia, and also ministers of foreign affairs of several countries including those of India, Vietnam and Kampuchea.

The interview with the latter turned into a very controversial affair as the only questions one could meaningfully ask at that point related to the genocide which was being carried out by his government in his country.

–'How dare you raise such issues?', my furious Cypriot TV colleague asked me afterwards with a voice intended to radiate earnestness. In his view, I just could not ask the representative of an anti-imperialist state such questions. That was the privilege of only the British and the American media.

I told him he was a drooling idiot. The Italian correspondent of *Unita*, the Italian communist daily, who had joined the two of us for the interview, chose to remain silent preferring instead to swap his whisky from right hand to left. The rumours that followed this bamboozling story, stuffed with unpleasant components, did not do me any favours.

In theory I was, of course, in sympathy with the aims of the nonaligned movement. Its divisions, however, running so deep, made its existence a mockery. Cuba had nothing in common with Saudi Arabia and North Korea nothing in common with Morocco. I wrote a number of articles highlighting the problems which made almost by definition sure that this organisation would never turn into an effective force. Some of them were published, others not.

The censorship was due to the fact that Ceausescu's Romania, one of the most prominent leaders of the non-aligned movement, did not want to hear any criticism of it, and *Avghi*, did not want to displease Romania. At that point, I submitted my resignation.

My problems with *Avghi* were, however, only a reflection of the problem the reformist wing of the communist party had to deal with. On the one hand, the party asserted its own identity, abandoned its dependence on the Soviets, and committed itself to the country's democratic institutions.

But on the other, as Leonidas Kyrkos, its leader, told me clearly and succinctly over a coffee near the Tottenham Court Road Tube station, the Soviet system and its practice were not to be questioned.

The same was more or less the attitude of Santago Carillo, secretary general of the Spanish communist party, whom I interviewed in London in July 1975 and, despite the warmth he exhumed, never felt the urge to meet again. Carillo, now a euro-communist, held that socialism and democracy were indivisible and that, as importantly, the communist parties should not interfere in each other's affairs.

But that was the theory, not the practice.

– 'Some', he said, meaning the Soviets, 'do not respect the principle of non-interference', which, however, he asked me to emphasise for the benefit of the Greeks, 'can be established except that one has to fight hard for it'.

For some reason, I did not trust the man – he reminded me of many within the Greek reformist communist movement as proud for the numbness of their mind and will as he was. The rust accumulated on his beliefs was heavily interfering with his judgement.

The Greek reformists had, meanwhile, entered into an electoral alliance with the Stalinist party only to regret it as they were swallowed by it before, in the mid-eighties, their lamp run completely out of oil. They recovered in a spectacular manner but only in 2012, when in the midst of the economic crisis an entirely new Left emerged.

Their attitude was incomprehensible to me. As I wrote to the editor of *Avghi* repeatedly before and after my resignation, the party had to reconnect with the power of its convictions and break for good with its dreadful past – a past without a future.

My views on it were, perhaps, less coloured by ideology and more by the dreadful experiences I had in Eastern Europe. I could not forgive the inhumanity of the Greek Stalinists after the Greek communist party split in two. Brutality was to them what maternity is to a woman.

Having consulted once again their encyclopaedia of evil-doing, they had discriminated against their reformist opponents, all refugees from the preceding civil war, in everything, from housing to passports and from studies to work and pensions. They even kicked them out of hospitals.

Let us not forget either, I wrote to my editor, the regime of terror and their corrupt practices through which the Greek Stalinists secured their reign, the divisions they instigated and the slanderous lies they could not do without that they threw on their opponents. I was one of them.

In a 1975 issue of the Athenian *Anti* magazine I expanded on the difficulties I had experienced as head of the Greek National Union of Students in exile (EFEE) in its relation with the Soviet dominated International Union of Students (IUS).

In the same article, I also mentioned the Trafalgar square CND rally and my expulsion from Czechoslovakia.

In response, a member of the Communist party's central committee denounced me as an 'agent of imperialism' and claimed the Trafalgar Square rally had been financed by the CIA.

If I were living in the Soviet Union a few decades earlier, I would have probably been forced to admit that I was 'an heretic, an apostate, a sorcerer, a sodomite, an invoker of evil spirits, a soothsayer, a slayer of innocents, an idolater, working evil by deviation from the faith'. But, thankfully, I was not.

Soon after, April Carter, CND's chairwoman at the time, explained patiently in the same magazine that the CND was one thing and the CIA another. CND, she added just in case someone still thought otherwise, was not financed by the CIA.

Still it was like trying to sell the bible to the devil.

The reformists, I wrote in 1982 in *Eleftherotypia*, the Athens daily I joined a few years later, had failed to realise that the Soviet model, though still alive, was as good as dead. There was no oil in its lamp. Its institutions and social fabric had disintegrated, the Warsaw Pact countries were desperately trying to end the Soviet hegemony and large sections of the European left denied the Soviet system any democratic legitimacy.

Ideologically, politically and economically, the Soviet Union was nothing but a giant with clay legs. Its collapse was only a matter of time and the only issue now on the agenda was what to do with the body, bury it forever or embalm it.

I am kicking myself I have never tried to sell my prophetic skills. If I had, my meagre salary might have been upgraded, in which case my fried eggs would have appeared on my breakfast table in the company of some bacon.

But while receptive in private, the reformists would not break, in public, with the past. This was partly due to their political calculations, i.e. the fear that if they broke with the past, they would lose the support of the Left's hardcore. But I think it was also psychological.

They could see the lunacy they had given their lives for, but they were still in denial.

Rather than look outwards, they looked impotently inwards, and rather than move ahead, they settled on the bridge of hesitation. Happy in their dogmatic certainty, and despite the tensions that lingered on for years, they just kept hoping for the best.

Hostages to their ossified mentality and encrusted habits, they could not let any measure of doubt enter their comforting certainties. The past, framed and hung up on the wall as testimony of their living was bound to remain their unfinished business.

I felt very sorry about it as these same people were still the incorruptible part of the country's political forces and this at a time that many other bright stars of the Left had already joined Andreas Papandreou, the man who had promised to take the country beyond the promises of the age.

Meanwhile, in 1974 I had my first book, *1944: Κρίσιμη Χρόνια* (1944: A Critical Year), published in Athens.

It was a selection of three hundred documents from Churchill's personal files relating to Greece in 1944. Alongside the British prime minister's correspondence with his military and diplomatic personnel, I had also presented the views on each aspect of the story offered in articles and books by other leading figures of the time.

Instantly the book became a huge success with praise coming from all sections of the media like an endless row of cranes flying on high in the sky. This was partly due to its revelations which shocked the Greeks as much as they had shocked me.

To hear Churchill ordering General Scobie, commander of the British forces in Greece, to arrest prime minister George Papandreou if the latter did not follow his commands burst what was believed to be the framework of reality. Yet, though shocked, they were not surprised. They had learnt to expect anything from the country's 'protectors'.

Churchill, as the documents showed, was prepared to go to any extremes, as he often did, to ensure the return to the throne of King George II. That, as far as he was concerned, would ensure the country remained within the British orbit.

In 1977 my second book, *Οι Ρίζες του Ελληνικού Φασισμου*, was published – it was also published in Norway by the university of Bergen as part of a larger edition under the title *Who Were the Fascists*. The title of the book – The Roots of Greek Fascism – was rather misleading as Fascism found no breeding ground in Greece and failed to turn into a movement such as in Germany, Italy, Hungary or Romania.

The establishment kept its distances from it, the few fascists could not exploit national frustrations over lost territories or unfulfilled expansionist expectations and they could not campaign against national minorities since they were insignificant. The 80,000 strong Jewish community, mostly in Thessaloniki, was too small and uninfluential to arouse the hostility it did in other countries.

And finally, fascism did not appeal to the Greek character, essentially undisciplined, individualistic and unmartial. The force to arrest the advance of the Left in Greece had, thus, always been the army, whether monarchist or republican, acting with or without the blessing of the foreign 'protectors' of the country.

These two books, which many viewed as a 'treasure', were followed in 1980 by Το Ευρωπαικο Αδιεξοδο (The European Deadlock), a book that focused on the foreign policy of the South and Central European Powers when Hitler ascended to power in Germany. This was fundamentally my doctoral dissertation re-worked.

Extracts appeared again in a number of publications.

I was told they were also enjoyed by all those normal men and women for whom book reading seems like the habit of those bored by life.

9

Days that Wouldn't Die

It seems a natural question. 'Tell us about the vision, the dream you had when you started Skyros'. Skyros is the 'magic place', a thrilling adventure into the land of hope, the reality our culture denies. Skilful in avoidances, I am happy to oblige.

Well, the leaf from my unfilled memories reads, it all begun in the languorous drowsiness of a late summer afternoon in Delphi.

At the time I was resting under an olive tree, trying, unsuccessfully, to read Eric Van Lustbader's French Kiss, this 'epic inferno of power-lust and shattering violence'. Bought at Heathrow airport, the book seemed a pretty good insurance against thought. In the rufescent light of the sunset that enshrouded Apollo's marble temple, it was, however, as tempting as the telephone directory. Reading was an impossibility.

Mesmerised by the breathing of the cypress trees that was tenderly caressing the curve of the day, bewitched by the legends of the land and in touch with my own infinite self, I had, without meaning to, let my head drop on the breast of a dream, effusive and mellifluous. In a spiritualised form, I had crossed the boundaries of the mystical. I was no longer I but its essence.

'Lo and behold', Kazantzakis's Zorba exclaims; you do not need much and 'your soul grows big, too big for the old carcass' – so big that 'it challenges God to a fight'.

But then, as I was re-appraising my own strength against that of God, something startling happened, something which even the *Evening Standard*'s horoscope had completely failed to prepare me for. A sapient voice that seemed to be coming from the far end of eternity smashed the tranquillity of the place.

– 'Man', it commanded, 'wake up'.

My self-propelled mechanism of reactions failed me for a moment. I looked around with amazement and incredulity, but I saw no man either talking, or being talked to. All that was there not previously seen was a blue pigeon standing on a nearby almond tree and looking at me sternly.

What a dream, I thought, ready to sit down once again.

But then the voice thundered again leaving me this time with a lingering look of fear in the eyes.

– 'Yes, you! I am talking to you! Listen carefully and do what I say! You will go to Skyros and set up a centre which will become the guiding spirit of humanity.'

I was acutely aware that the voice, the pigeon's human voice, was addressing me.

– 'Zeus', I cried. 'Me? Why me? I have nothing but a Ph.D – in history, if you can believe it. Of what good can I be?"'

Zeus was not, however, in an euthymic mood – Hera must have just had another of her opprobrious fits of jealousy.

He volunteered a disdainful look, invisible to the eye but chillingly discernible to the senses, and repeated what he had just said, this time with a definite finality. The ominous thunderbolt that followed his words left me in no doubt as to his decisions. I had obviously been selected for a higher purpose which I had to fulfil if I were not to share the fate of one or two of my most obstreperous friends and turn into a monkey.

Aeschylus was all of a sudden the man that came to mind and I felt the most sympathy with. Poor man. He died, it is said, when

116

a tortoise, thrown by an eagle for the purpose of breaking its shell, hit his bald head mistaken for a stone.

Being the only person I knew who had a conversation with Zeus, albeit a very brief one, I found myself in a loop of energy in the ten dimensional hyperspace. However, and although I never had a problem with abnormalities such as creativity, the weight of the mission felt very heavy on my shoulders.

Reflecting on it, I walked slowly down the hill, had a beer at the local cafe – Zeus, its prices – lit a filterless cigarette as men did before they were effeminated, and thought matters over.

Eventually, fully realising that Zeus' omnipresence, which, incidentally, looks very different from its photo, was not designed to stimulate dissent, I accepted my fate. I was damned to be famous, and cursed to lead a sinless life.

Crossing into the early evening, I had, thus, managed to distance myself sufficiently from the lower breeding of my earlier reservations, and in a more sober mood, looked for a map of Greece to find out where Skyros island is located. Then, I set out for my appointment with destiny.

Consistency, much better as a mistress, now had to be treated as the lawful wife.

Many years later, in Gothenburg, I met Sasha – Sasha White, an American real estate agent, who had also been chosen by God 'to save the planet'. It happened, she told me in the gym where she had gone to buy a sandwich, when God, rather ungentlemanly, visited her in her bathroom.

Supported by other real estate agents, executives of American corporations, diplomats and an army of mediums, native American shamans and, most importantly, public relations officers, all of them in a sprightly spiritual relation with their bank balance, she did, indeed, launch an international campaign, the Campaign for the Earth. The Campaign, at least in Gothenburg, did raise the crowds to a state of synthetic ecstasy, which, in effect, turned them into zombies.

To ensure the lasting effect of the inculcating principles established, a native American chief warned at the end everyone:

– 'Don't go away with negative thoughts. The spirits will be after you.'

Odious absurdities, I thought, when they colour a colourless existence, can sometimes be useful.

Two years later the campaign collapsed owing to internal dissensions about money, I heard. My guess is that either God had made the wrong choice or the weaknesses of his creation are stronger than his will. In either case he ought to know better.

Gary Zukav, the US spiritual teacher and author of four consecutive *New York Times* Best Sellers, a conference participant with whom I established quite a friendly connection, did not seem so enthusiastic about the proceedings, either.

No matter where you stand, it is rather difficult to endorse a simplistic approach coupled with mass manipulation techniques designed to bring people to a state of ecstasy in which human beings can happily abrogate their right to think for themselves.

I am not sure where another conference participant, the deputy CEO of Kentucky Fried Chicken, the US fast food restaurant chain, stood on the subject. But he had no problem describing the products of his company as 'this shit'.

Skyros was established by both Dina Glouberman, my wife at the time, and myself, back in 1979.

Talking about the 'vision', the 'dream' I had the time Skyros was launched, was like walking in a Hieronymus Bosch painting and its world of dreams and nightmares.

In any case, people do not want to hear boring tales and details. They want a fairy tale that will validate each individual's search for purpose and meaning in life, that will show that the power of inner conviction can triumph over the harsh realities of our world, that the mythical and the diurnal can after all blend into a happy union.

'Tell us about it' is not a question but, in effect, an invitation to affirm that the autonomous individual and the power of ideas can still make a difference in an age dominated by dystopic visions of the future.

It means 'let's believe in ourselves once again'.

I have no quarrel with this 'let's believe again' approach. But I have no fairy tale to tell. Indeed, my own involvement with Skyros started at a time that I did not actually believe in myself, when I had nothing to look forward to and little in terms of beliefs to hold on.

As it happened, this had, however, nothing to do with convictions and everything to do with my life.

Time had not been so rancid until the mid-seventies. By the mid-sixties I was near the top of my profession, journalism, and fortunate enough to be sent by *Avghi*, my Athens newspaper, to the UK as its London correspondent. Then in April 1967 the military dictatorship came, my newspaper was closed down and I lost my job.

But I somehow survived and when the turbulent years ended in 1974, the time the Greek dictatorship collapsed, I had practically finished my doctoral dissertation and published in Athens my first history book.

Nearly two years later this was followed by a second one and then by a third one. I had also re-started my work as a journalist again as London correspondent.

In the mid-seventies everything, therefore, seemed to be going my way: a decent career in journalism, good academic qualifications, three published books, and two years' experience at the very top of international student politics. Moreover, having like all primitives never made a distinction between work and leisure, I was always willing to work *de die in diem*, day and night until the light of the morning sent the stars, skullcapped, to bed.

In Shakespearean language, I had become a man 'of great admittance', or so I thought, and I only had to choose the flavour of the cream to top my cake.

Man's infinite capacity for illusion had not as yet made headlines in my thinking. I still believed in both my own serendipitous stars and the benign nature of the universe.

But the plot had taken an odd twist. For various reasons, I could not get what I wanted, i.e., a full-time job. I wrote another history book this time as its ghost-writer, which, edited, was published in Athens under the name of a well-known politician. But a steady line of work continued to be elusive.

Representing the Athens News Agency in London was not a job for me according to its ultimate boss, Takis Lambrias, the information minister.

– 'You're too good for it', resorting to a helpful lie he informed me.

The problem was my association with the Athens daily *Avghi*.

The same was the case with the Greek television despite my being backed by its CEO, Andreas Christodoulides, an old friend. Basically, I did not have the required training. Joining the London Greek embassy's press office was out of the question, too, as, unfortunately, when I applied 'all arrangements had already been made'.

A job with the Greek section of the BBC was, likewise, turned down. The problem, its director, more frank than Lambrias, told me, was again my association with *Avghi*. For different reasons, I was also unable to get a job with the International News Agency the non-aligned countries were planning to establish as, apart from anything else, this was never established, and I was turned down by other bodies such as Amnesty International, the Labour party or various universities, including Cambridge university which interviewed me for the purpose.

I had reached an age where I thought I knew all about life only to discover that I knew nothing at all. Life is not something like a walk to the nearest train station, but a maze in which you can get easily lost.

Though devastated by my failures, I still remembered, however, that Giuseppe Verdi had been rejected by the Milan conservatory and then failed to get a job as an organist.

With plenty of unused speed and no road I could race on, optimism could not, however, survive for very long. At the end, having drunk pints of refusal, I started looking for other possibilities totally alien to my interests.

The 'file of my failures', which is still in my possession as a reminder of the twists in life's tail, contains correspondence with Greek marble, wine and spirits, flokati rugs, furniture and other firms interested in exporting their products to the UK and UK firms interested in exporting to Greece their technological goods.

Nothing resulted in anything. Also fruitless were my efforts to generate some business in Saudi Arabia or Yemen. At the very end I even sought employment with an estate agency, but, no, I could not get that, either.

– 'No, I think I'll have to say No', its Golders Green manager told me after picking up from his wide range of expressions the most appropriate one. And that was as if I had appeared in front of him with ketchup stains on my suit and mustard on my tie.

'Happy the man ... whose dreams are dead or never born', Primo Levi, this so warm human being, once said. 'He fears nothing, hopes for nothing, expects nothing, but stares fixedly at the setting sun'.

If he had a point, I could not see it at the time – a time that my never conquered anxiety that one day I would be restored to the enjoyment of all my original fears and die destitute and homeless, like that old man I had met in Athens' Monastiraki square, had been re-activated. I do not know if I had picked up the right fears, but that is where I had found myself.

In the frame of mind I was, nothing actually seemed destined to work apparently in line with some silent immutable laws. I was, perhaps, too independent, moralistic, ambitious, eccentric, rebellious or just too innocent. Perhaps I had chosen the wrong illusions or, more likely, I lacked completely the marketing skills to 'sell' myself.

Alternatively, luck had just deserted me as it deserted even its own temple in Alexandria, the temple of the goddess Tyche, which the Christians turned into a tavern. Or, if you believe in this sort of thing, this was my punishment for a past life misdemeanour.

Whatever, the future seemed to have developed as great an antipathy to my aspirations as the snakes to the soil of Ireland. From the outside of the universe where I was sitting with my elbows on the waters of futility, all my efforts, to recall Kavafy, looked 'like those of the Trojans', destined to end in total, utter failure.

The great future seemed to have been left behind me, overtaken by a present lugubrious enough to grace the most depressing funeral.

The picture was actually worse as, not being a 'New Man', I could not deal with the guilt and the humiliation generated by my condition. I did not even know what to say when asked what work I do as I was after a concert in the Athens Odeon of Herodes Atticus by Eftichis Bitsakis, a theoretical physics and philosophy professor and a colleague since the student days in Athens.

I managed to gibber a few words to the effect that I write books only to hear from him, as if I did not know, that this occupation does not provide the essentials for living. Miserably, I had to hear more of the same from my father.

– 'You cannot just be supported by your wife', the latter told me more than once with a barely guarded expression of distaste while I was blushing from a piercing embarrassment.

Herodes Atticus, I thought, had thankfully no such problems. He built the theatre in 161 AD with money inherited from his very rich father.

Dina, incidentally, did at the time have a full time job as a psychology lecturer at Kingston Polytechnic.

My inability to support the family became meanwhile even more pronounced in 1977, when my son, Ari, was born. A bit of relief was, however, offered next year, when with the help of a heavy mortgage we bought a second house in London which I spent six months renovating.

Soon after, the house was rented out and I was free again to develop a hobby, perhaps put on file the best quotes on inutility. Despite my difficulties, I never, however, considered applying for a state handout and never received any. The UK owed me nothing.

During that time I also learnt to sing the Friday evening Jewish prayer:

– *Barukh atah Adonai, Eloheinu, melekh ha'olam* (Blessed are you, Lord, our God, sovereign of the universe).

Thankfully, Dina's Jewish roots did not demand anything more. And religion, whether Greek Orthodox or Jewish, unlike the oven or the vacuum cleaner was not on our home's list of requirements.

Nevertheless, my situation was not as unique as it it appeared as in 1976 the UK, the world's first industrial power, had to go to the International Monetary Fund for a loan. The country seemed to be disintegrating.

The Labour government's very rigid prices and incomes policy to cap rampant inflation had eventually forced the unions to take up arms against it. The winter of discontent, frightfully restless, had arrived – I still remember the *Evening Standard*'s headlines about the mountains of rubbish piled high in the streets, and the grave diggers' refusal to bury the dead. Even ITV was forced to suspend its programmes and Coronation Street, among others, had to go on a long vacation.

Skyros sprang up in this time of slithering despair, the time I felt as empty as a library without books. It was, indeed, the child of my despondency, my response to the emergency of my condition, a way to earn a living in circumstances that seemed to have denied me this right.

Yet, it was what helped my spirit to rise from years in the doldrums.

The idea, in the arms of the intangible, emerged as accidentally as a poppy but, as it happened, it was as original as Michelangelo's Pieta.

It popped up one evening out of a bottle of wine we shared with Brigitte Towers, a university colleague of Dina. If Dina, a lecturer and psychotherapist, could run her personal development workshops on a Greek island, I could contribute all my skills and knowledge of Greece to ensure their success. Simple.

Dina loved the idea. What I think appealed to her was, first, the expectation that the project would give me something which would take me off the streets of depression. It also appealed to her because it was coming close to a dream she had been nourishing for some time: that of an intimate community under the sun in this land of irresistible grace.

The thought that this might be the beginning of a venture to be celebrated almost a lifetime later never signalled its presence at the corner of anybody's eyes.

The central idea, coming at the time like a butterfly in the company of grey moths, as Ian Rankin, the Scottish crime writer, might say, was quite simple: transfer the education process, in this instance the personal development process, into a new environment free from the city's hustles and constraints, and, at the same time, give the holidays a new meaning which could be as rich as life itself.

The idea was innovative on either account, except that it had not really registered with us as such at the time. We went for it, my own natural daredevilling overcoming Dina's natural cautiousness, in the same way we could have booked a holiday in Tenerife.

Blessed are the innocent for they should inherit the earth.

Dina's roots were very different from mine and so were her interests.

Born and grown up within a Jewish family in this city of sundry virtue, i.e., New York, she studied psychology in Brandeis and then moved on to London where she did her thesis on Piaget's socio-psychological theories. Committed to psychotherapy, she struggled, because nothing comes easy in life, and eventually she established herself as a professional of very good standing – alert, caring, reliable, conscientious.

Our views on life were very close, but our approach to it was rather different. She was much more concerned with the visible essentials of our existence as opposed to the invisible ones, those in a gaseous state, for which I had assumed full responsibility.

In addition, she was good with people whereas I was almost hopeless. Just like Charlie Brown, I loved mankind but I was not always at ease with its constituents.

It was all, perhaps, due to the assumption that the everyday conversation is just a waste of time.

The time Skyros was launched, in 1979, was extraordinarily difficult for her. She had a full-time job as a lecturer at Kingston Polytechnic, a two-year old son, Ari, and a few-months old daughter, Chloe – our children. She was also still working as a therapist, and, even worse, she had to take care of me – a lugubrious unemployed wreck.

Yet, she was happy to go ahead with the project, confident that our boat, steered by the birds of the open sea and powered by the winds of fate, would reach its destination.

Mercifully, innocence is not always an albatross.

Dina had approached Skyros from her own perspective, the psychological. Partly because she had the initial commitment

I lacked and partly because of her different departure point her input was decisive, particularly at the beginning.

Myself, I had no interest whatsoever in inner invisibilities or intimate therapeutic communities in the sun or in the shade. Psychotherapy was as alien to me as the wedding rites of the Shamans before the industrial revolution. The voluptuous idea of coalescing with the pulchritudinous nymphs of the Aegean was, I must say, appealing.

But my involvement with the project was to be that of the mercenary.

Despite my cynicism, that was, however, the time I was able to make the first entry into my diary of the baklava-sweet thoughts, forgotten and blank for ages.

Though faithful to my prejudices, I did, thus, got fully involved with the project and in 1978 I toured the Greek islands until I found the right place: Skyros island, a land of timeless elation, neglected by time, shy of foreigners and innocent as the moonlight. I had also what was to be our Centre: the old building, at the edge of the village overlooking the valley and the *Thálassa*, the Aegean's azure-blue sea.

The building, which used to be a school at the turn of the century, was quickly renovated except that, when we arrived for the opening day it was still receiving the finishing touches – the fitting of windows and doors, for example. Somehow, however, in the end the builders managed to deliver a half usable house.

–'Thankfully', I thought later, 'the litigation culture had not taken root as yet'.

Though I helped actively in the shaping of what became known as The Skyros Centre, my initial indifference was primarily the result of my unemployment.

My pride, wounded after all the painful rejections, demanded recognition of what I considered as my birth-right, i.e., full-time employment, which to me was something like a passport to life.

I also resented being drawn into my wife's world, that of psychotherapy, that had nothing to do with my own interests, and I still had an attachment to a different set of priorities favouring the social as opposed to the personal.

Therapy sounded to me like a euphemism for licensed self-indulgence, a practice superficially as absurd as Giacometti's figures, worn thin to naked nerve patterns and racked by loneliness. Skyros rather than being the answer, seemed, thus, destined to contrive to take my identity away.

Admittedly, I was at the time unfamiliar with the shadowed side of our existence and could not grasp the amplitude of pain those given by life all the right credentials were carrying in themselves.

As a result, I found myself 'leaning', as Ritsos, stunned by all that is 'vague, perplexing, incomprehensible and directionless in life', pondered in agony, 'over the top steps of a staircase without steps, a very high staircase (I) had not climbed'.

Still looking for something else, I was left with a future always pregnant and never delivering, with the frustration of the perpetual outsider, homesick for a home that did not exist. But I could not complain. I had picked up myself, as Aragon would say, 'the bitter rose made of salt and refusal', I had made my choices and all choices have a price tag attached.

I had to accept this situation, my karma that had become so familiar I could tell the colour of her underwear from her looks.

Known in town as either the English Villa or the Madhouse, terms interchangeable as if they meant one and the same thing, the Skyros Centre instantly became a resounding success. More than that, it became the model to be copied times and again throughout the world.

The venture – powerful human bonds, fantasy parties, *dejeneur sur l' herbe* by the sea, extraordinary coincidences, apocalyptic dreams – captured the imagination and gave people an emotional home.

– In fact, as Monica from Vienna said, 'it was more like home than home'.

Monica's sentiments have been echoed ever since times and again by many others. Belief in the purpose of the Skyros Centre and trust in its methods ran so deep that once, when the administrator mistakenly accommodated the wife of one couple with the husband of the other, the two couples gamely accepted it, for it must have had a purpose.

The venture had almost in no time crossed the horizon.

Meanwhile, the same year Skyros was launched, I joined the world again as a worthy mediocrity – London correspondent of the Athens daily *Eleftherotypia*.

It was not exactly what I was looking for, and the blossom of relief, which, in earlier times would have flowered into a smile, remained faint. But under the circumstances the job was good enough – better, at any rate, than spending my life having a Ph.D.

Whatever my patternless thoughts about it all, Skyros was at any rate good enough to give me a living. Intellectually and emotionally it was, however, still a venture it took me years before I could identify with.

Although it gave me a platform to air my views, journalism, on the other hand, was largely ineffective, and writing history books could not fill the gap my ferocious energy and unflagging vitality kept wide-open.

Lacking a single and clear focus, or, perhaps, more precisely, having no active involvement with people in a stimulating political context, led, thus, inevitably to frustration.

I felt as if I had taken up residence in life's suburbs, those with fuzzy colour, outline or form. The need, picketing in front of my existence, to move from the periphery to the centre of things remained unsatisfied as the trauma of the preceding years, caused by the infinite artlessness of my condition, refused for a long time to heal.

I had, as Robert Frost would say, been acquainted with the night, but the night was still my home even after daylight had broken.

All credit for Skyros, as it initially developed, goes, therefore, to Dina. She was the visionary, the soul of the community, its guiding spirit. I do not think she knew exactly what she was doing. But she had a good understanding of people, she was bursting with positive energy, she stuck to principles, and she had the right gut feeling about the way things ought to be going.

The truth is, however, that neither she nor I had any clue as to what we were starting. The venture was a journey into the unknown, stranger than fiction because fictional events have templates and precedents.

As its website never gives you enough information, reality takes you always by surprise.

I cannot, therefore, but sort of smile when people ask me what my 'vision' of Skyros was. Soldiers of fortune have no visions. My cryptic answer at the time was out of necessity similar to that given by Gurdjieff, the mid-20th century spiritual leader:

– 'We shall see.'

It sounded, I thought, a seasoned answer of the kind given by old, wise men, its evasion and dissimulation ensuring that I was not committing myself to anything.

Yet, it was the right answer, for it subsumed the intrinsically wry unrolling of the plot, which is exactly what occurred. In a short time, Skyros, not as a therapy centre, but as a place in which one could forge a new identity, won me over completely and influenced my thinking perhaps as much as I, in time, influenced its own.

Life is so queer, P.G. Woodhouse once observed. So unlike anything else.

10

The Illusions' Corporation

Margaret Thatcher, very nice to me when I first met her in Downing Street, strove with an evangelical zeal to change fundamentally the country. Just like Tony Benn, whom I respected as much as her for the same reason, i.e. the power of convictions, she was totally committed to her goal 'to change the heart and soul' of the country, its culture and its temperament.

The Downing Street meeting, incidentally, caused me initially a huge embarrassment as, for a moment, I did not know whether to address her as prime minister or prime ministress. If we have a governor, I thought just as I was about to open my mouth, we have a governess, if we have a steward, we have a stewardess, and if we have a master, we also have a mistress.

The problem was overcome but only after a few seconds of an unforgettable silence by my not addressing her by her title.

From then on the discussion was easy. Despite her reputation, she dealt with me in an almost sisterly fashion. I even complemented her on her colourful dress – a complement she did, however, dismiss by raising her eyebrow.

It was only later that I decided that she was very definitely a prime minister. Odd, I thought, but not too odd. After all, we have Her Majesty's Army, Her Majesty's Navy and Air Force and even

Her Majesty's Prisons, but not Her Majesty's Debt. The latter is known as the National Debt.

When Margaret Thatcher won power, the system after all was not working, the Labour party was in self-immolating extinction and social democracy, with hair on its lips, had turned into a dysfunctional concept.

Following that horrific winter of discontent, nothing much could be said in defence of the old order.

Thatcher, having pushed aside her own party's old guard, those in dull stripped ties, poorly dressed trousers and a patronising superciliousness, embarked immediately on her radical neoliberal agenda which radically changed the face of Britain.

In this, she walked hand in hand with her political soul mate, the US president Ronald Reagan, 'the second most important man in her life' and the man who also changed his own country's trajectory.

Happily for her, the oil production in the North Sea offshore facilities was at the same time turning Britain into an energy powerhouse and, indeed, a net-exporter of oil. This spectacular development led to massive oil revenues and provided the crunch for the country's public finances that helped Thatcher to push through the popular capitalism she championed.

Council tenants, about one million of them, were empowered to buy their homes at a substantial discount. The money that came in was not invested, however, in new housing and millions of people were left, as a result, languishing on social housing waiting lists. Many state-owned businesses like British Gas, British Telecom, British Airways, British Aerospace, Jaguar and many others were privatised to the benefit of about four million people who had never dreamt of indulging in the stock market. Shares owned by individuals did, however, drop from 28 per cent in 1981 to 11 per cent in 2010.

Further, many factories, shipyards and coal pits that needed the taxpayers' support were forced to close down and many communities up in the north of the country that provided the manpower for the old industries were condemned to live a life of deprivation. Britain, once known globally as the 'workshop of the world' due to its strong manufacturing base, became a net importer of goods for the first time ever.

The government further cut the tax rates and deregulated the financial markets. The Big Bang led to a succession of hostile takeovers, leveraged buyouts and mega-mergers involving financial conglomerates all of which turned the City of London into the world's financial leader.

It was, however, this unregulated and unsupervised market regime that led to the 2008 crisis that was deeply felt for many years. Meanwhile, unemployment had in the early 1980's risen to levels not seen since the Great Depression. Deeply affected by it, the miners went on strike in early 1984, and which ended a year later with their defeat. Just before that, in March 1985 I shared with charismatic Arthur Scargill, the miners' leader, the fear that

– 'The battle is being lost and the labour movement won't recover from it for a decade.'

How wrong I was. It still has not recovered.

The outcome of this battle was, indeed, very conclusive. Thatcher's onslaught had left the trade unions just a pale imitation of their former selves, too weak to resist the drive to the 'flexible labour market'.

At the same time, by freeing the market from political interference and removing all barriers to business, Thatcher had also delivered the economy into the hands of the corporate élite. Choice, freedom, competition, if they were to conflict with the latter's demands, were bound to turn into words devoid of meaning, a dice without spots.

Reducing the means by which citizens could restrain the power of this élite, had, however, one more consequence: the shrinking of democracy. The banks and the corporations' empires were now beyond any public control.

Capitalism, ostentatiously virile, was since assumed to be as unsinkable as the Titanic, destined to last forever. A return to what was considered to be an antediluvian number system without even number was just unthinkable.

If the measure of a person's importance is the time taken to be forgotten, Thatcher had won her place in history.

Nothing could stop at this point the consolidation of the free market model and what was believed to be a march towards a thrilling new world of glamour and self-enrichment.

Between 1979 and 1992, the richest ten per cent of the population saw their incomes increase by 62 per cent. The great cosmic expansion following Thatcher's aggressively market-driven economy also spawned a new breed of billionaire. Yuppies, the young, upwardly mobile professionals, several of them in the City of London, enthusiastic supporters of the idea that there is 'no such thing as society', led the way in their Porsches.

This new generation of status seekers, liturgists of Mammon, armed with brick-sized mobiles and bonuses rich in zeroes, were to be found on both sides of the Atlantic.

In the US they were typified by the corrupt Wall Street financier Ivan Boesky, who re-assured everybody that 'you can be greedy and feel good about yourself'. Greed, Gordon Gekko, the fictional character in Oliver Stone's film Wall Street, said, is good. Greed, as deaf to the voice of virtue as the ass to the lyre of Apollo, is right.

Following the sale of council houses, the buying of shares in the privatised sectors and the subsequent house price boom, several other people felt wealthier, too. The 'feel good factor' was further boosted by the easy borrowing of huge sums of money in a way that had been impossible a few years earlier and the unembarrassed consumer spending frenzy on which the better off embarked.

People, Virginia Woolf might say again, joined Margaret Thatcher's revolution like 'leaping dolphins in the wake of an ice-breaking vessel'.

The political history of those years, Umberto Eco remarked, could be the story of how Red Label gave way to twelve-year-old Ballantine and then to single malt.

The new decade, the *Mail* pronounced, is one which, thanks to the creation of a new social structure based not on accident of birth but on talent, diligence and inventiveness, class barriers came crashing down. This was not true. Class deference did somehow as time went on recede, but poor children were still bound to turn into poor adults.

However, the persuasiveness of the present had made the claim look as if it were true.

The 1980s, at the end, left their mark as the decade of greed, which together with arrogance, led to the 1987 stock market crash, known as Black Monday.

The 'me, me, me' society was now in place – after all, as Thatcher herself had said with her polished vowels in a velvety burr of imperiousness, there is no such a thing as society to take care of the vulnerable. Everyone had to look after himself or alternatively everyone was out for himself. The destructive cult of the individual that nurtured the degradation of all values, their turn into mere utilities, had now won respectability. Life had to be lived in the first person singular – I, me, mine.

The main features of the new world were selfishness, superficiality and avarice. Just like poetry, ideals were all set aside as damaged goods in favour of accumulation and consumption. 'Shop Til you Drop' was the new watchword as the corporations kept leasing a larger and larger part of the consumer's uninhabited brain box.

It was all about designer labels, for labels were everything, even for the children. Even my very young daughter would not settle for anything less though at the very last moment inside one of the Oxford Street's superstores, these cathedrals of the mass production of distraction, I did manage to persuade her to take a different look at things.

Gadgets, too, in the shape of home computers, video recorders, mobile phones and microwave ovens were the items to have if you were not to be out of tune with the new age. Interestingly enough, though Thatcher talked of bringing back Victorian values, her decade in office saw an expansion of the sixties' permissiveness in terms of sex, divorce, abortion, illegitimacy and drug-taking.

Likewise, though she extolled thrift, hated profligacy and even paid for her own Downing Street ironing board, she presided over a gigantic credit boom and unleashed the power of casino capitalism.

At the same time, however, millions of people, particularly the growing army of young people, had been left with no stake in future prosperity, and income inequality grew rapidly, reaching its higher level since the Second World War. The poorest 20 to 30 per cent of the population failed to benefit from economic growth, and the poorest 10 per cent ended up worse off in actual as well as relative terms. The North-South divide widened and a growing underclass felt that violence was its only option.

The moral theory in line with Adam Smith's folk version of economics that if each person seeks to maximise his own wealth, then by an invisible hand the wealth of all will be maximised and everybody will be happy did not seem to have worked out.

Unless we were all happy and just did not know it.

The policies of social consensus had been shattered, I wrote in *Eleftherotypia*, since 'Mrs Torture', as Salman Rushdie called Margaret Thatcher in his Satanic Verses, launched her social counter-revolution. The British embassy in Athens, my editor told me, registered a protest with him about my 'outrageous' assertions.

Yet, while using a language which had won respectability in the anti- Thatcher world, I was not entirely convinced myself that her venture had no merits whatsoever.

As I told, among others, Costas Filinis, one of the leaders of the reformist communist party, the Greek Left had to re-evaluate its position.

– 'Using taxpayers money to subsidise state enterprises such as Olympic Airways in which the political parties felt free to appoint legions of their cronies was not only economically wrong. It was also morally reprehensible.'

I believe he silently agreed with me.

I had made the same point to Yannis Kefaloyannis, the conservative minister of tourism, when, in his office, I saw supporters coming in one after the other to ask him to appoint their relations to various tourist enterprises controlled by the state. Their argument was:

– 'Minister, we've always supported the party. Now it's your turn to do something for us.'

The look he gave them was similar to that a corpse would give to an undertaker, but he felt he had no choice but oblige. The price of disobliging behaviour was simply too high.

Still I urged him not to give in, albeit with the same success one expects if he tries to build a monument to failure in a day. As Günter Grass said, 'we can't just look on. Even if we can't stop anything we must say what we think'.

But the minister wanted to hear me as much as the answering machines that spend their life listening to people who really do not want to talk to them.

The triumph of the Reagan – Thatcher neo-liberal market approach and the decline of orthodox communism were, meanwhile, accompanied by the disarray of the Left.

This went hand in hand with the shrinking of the industrial working class and its increasing conservatism reflected, among other things, in the manual workers reluctance to identify themselves with the working class.

The latter, alongside the new 'non-class' or 'post-industrial proletariat', could no longer be viewed as the central agent of progressive, social, cultural and political change.

In the UK, the Labour party had entered a state of crisis, while in Greece the 'socialist' party of Andreas Papandreou had embarked upon a populist campaign to the delight of the 'under-privileged'. The intellectual vacuum of the time was filled by postmodernism – a term introduced by Jean-Francois Lyotard in 1979.

Smart as an Armani collezione, solid as New Labour's 'Third Way' and unnecessarily handsome, the concept had an instant sex-appeal. The postmodernists, as I stressed in my Trilogy, dismissed traditional historical and philosophical understandings, both enabling and disabling our interaction with both past and present. Truth, objectivity, freedom, duty, worth or merit, all these 'illusionary' ideas, went out of fashion just like Jacqueline Kennedy's signature pillbox hats.

The new thinkers, with the grace and ease of cavalry officers who did not want to dirty their shining boots, turned their back on corporate capitalism, the destruction of our environment or any kind of ethical standards. The new relativism and its solipsistic morality was highlighted by the cynical maxim 'what's good for me is good for me, and what's good for you is good for you'.

Politics, ethics, economics and history, 'the history of (our) misfortunes', as Peter Abelard, the twelfth century medieval philosopher, would have called the twentieth century's autobiography, became, just like grammar, none of the postmodernists' concerns.

Their place was taken by subjective interpretations reflecting individualism and particularity. Freedom was freedom from an objectivity sanctioned by some sort of eternal order, and from the Enlightenment's rational standards of evaluation. In no time, it did also become freedom from any sense of individual responsibility to the whole on account of its white, male and heterosexual biases.

The construction of hybrid identities, the inclusion, in Stuart Hall's terminology, of voices excluded from the narratives of western culture, became, instead, the epicentre of the new rejectionists' attention. The notion of the whole was rejected altogether with an elaborate weariness in favour of the particular, and homosexuality turned into a cause worthy of attention over and above world poverty, the nuclear arms race or environmental degradation.

Disengagement from politics as advocated by Baudrillard, micropolitics, i.e., piecemeal reforms at local level as recommended by Lyotard, Foucault and Rorty, or identity politics as pursued by ethnic, gay and feminist groups captured the new mood.

In the new populist fashion, so did pleasure and consumption. Ernesto Laclau, the Argentinian post-Marxist, happily concluded that humankind had at last arrived where it should. Humankind, therefore, was 'for the first time the creator and constructor of its own history'. Greek political theorist Nicos Poulantzas' rejection of micro-politics and his call for the construction of a broad, radical democratic, socialist alternative was a voice in the wilderness.

A brand-new, albeit dysfunctional, conscience had just been acquired in the chic postmodernist market. We were no longer meant to have faith in anything. As a Greek saying goes, after you have burnt yourself with porridge you even blow on the yogurt.

But, as I soon realised, illusions had anything but disappeared.

The old ones had, of course, gone, but their place had been taken by new ones, those which have no fear of being recognised as such – or so we liked to believe. Wearing more make-up than clothing, they embrace, as Ernst Bloch, the Marxist thinker, said, 'wishful images in the mirror', the dreams cultivated by the advertising industry, the fantasies the department stores promise to fulfil, the 'wishful world of eccentricity and precise dexterity'.

The utopia they promise was embedded in the TV monoculture that has redefined reality itself, in escapades from reality offered to us in fiction and in films, in the 'fantasy bribe' which meets in imagination what is missing in real life.

Subsumed in rampant materialism and its fantasies, it was also propelled by the emergence of celebrities unhampered by achievement, consumerist escapism and the frenzied pace for the new as dictated by technology.

Disillusioned for too long, it seemed that we had, at last, regained our illusions.

Upset by this cultural steamrolling, free spirits were only too thrilled to discover the virtues of some get rich quick schemes, the treasures of one or another unknown minority culture or, faced with a haunting loneliness, invent new concepts like independence or aloneness.

Alternatively, they found consolation in the number of goals scored by Manchester United.

Yet, the utopia the new illusions promised, a micro-utopia, remained where utopias have always been since the time we used to get wrinkles with age – out of reach. In spite of their alluring looks to which we had succumbed, they could not deliver on their promises.

The stone has once again betrayed us by postponing its blossoming. The river had once again refused to return to its bed.

We can buy cans of synthafood never seen on shelves before, stylishly furnish our silence, programme on our wrist computer the timing of our spontaneous human moments, go for some new, untried pleasures or get all the sex we want on our Master Card. At the cosmetic surgery we can even order a Brad Pitt pair of lips or a Nicole Kidman nose.

The tomato-red-haired market can meet all our needs, and the system is ready to recognise all our 'rights' as customers, employees, patients, voters, viewers or taxpayers.

It cannot, however, meet our needs, and recognise our rights, as human beings.

Capitalism has enshrined the doctrine of individual choice, often hopelessly promiscuous, but it does not know how to nurture it outside the market context and its moneyed tranquility.

The new utopia's gorgeous tits, big enough to hang on our Dolce & Gabbana jacket, offer little, if anything, to the happiness they promise.

Neither does the digital replica of the age's enchantment in time sequestered from existence offered to us as life. Reaching out in the free market's realm takes us no further than Selfridges, in Oxford Street, and to Tesco's empire.

Of course, to the lackadaisical eye my mumblings resemble those of that Persian who complained that he had no shoes until he met a man who had no legs.

Perhaps they are not even very fair, for the new utopia manufacturers, always populist and manipulative, do give their customers some breathing space. They are also certainly old-fashioned, an otiose reflection of times when, as Ritsos said, man was 'certain that the longer road is the shortest road into the heart of God'.

But even if I am the guardian of the extinct, in a holy communion with the inscrutable, the postmodernist rejection of truth has not taken us all that far.

'Purification', as Greek poet George Stoyannídes said, seems to be 'late in coming'.

Whatever its merit, the postmodernist argument failed to break with the logic of the market. And however convincing it may have been, it could not measure up against the omnipotent power of the new, corporate-managed world order.

Myself, I left the postmodernist premises a long time ago, i.e., as soon as my patience grew weary in the barren, desolate land of purposelessness.

'Truths' need to be questioned and this necessitates, first of all, a vigorous and constant questioning of all our assumptions. It calls for a brave rejection of anything which by being 'sacred' is above questioning.

Though valid, doubting cannot erase, however, every single certainty. As Descartes, the doubter, acknowledged, 'nobody can doubt of his doubt and remain uncertain whether he doubts or does not doubt'.

There is some certainty even in doubt.

Albert Camus made the same point.

– 'Man, he said, 'is told that nothing is. But this at least is a certainty'.

Truth, though invisible like the Holy Spirit, is out there, despondent and screaming, at least for those who have eyes to see. It is in the tears of Africa's children, the rage of the Palestinians, the manmade disasters – Chernobyl, Exxon Valdez, Bhopal, Fukushima Daiichi – or the appraisal of life only in terms of what money can buy. Neither of them speaks the truth. They are the truth.

Claiming the opposite is only the expression of powerlessness before the mighty, gigantic forces of capitalism, which, having marched like the Lydians against Miletus 'to the music of pipes, harps, and treble and tenor oboes', and overwhelmed its opposition, have since been celebrating the feast day of St John the drinker.

Although fearful of my disembodied thoughts, quite radical within our traditional political context and often blushing in embarrassment my wanderings in the whispering galleries of the mind caused gradually a fundamental shift in my thinking.

I decided that, in political terms, positive change can come only if rooted in the conscience of the individuals rather than the action of the politicians, and it is possible only if it is supported by the culture of the country. The ideal is unattainable if the psyche of the nation is hostage to some greedy, corrupt, and violent prince of darkness, if humans do not learn to live for, rather than against, each other, and support, rather than antagonise, the fundamental conditions of our existence.

The disagreeable status quo is, after all, perpetuated not by brutal force, but by the system of meanings and values embodied into the culture's living order.

It was at that point that the importance of politics, as I understood it until then, began to diminish as rapidly as the concept of personal responsibility was dawning on me.

My wanderings gradually alienated me from my earlier conscious existence. Politics, the 'sweet wine of youth', had lost its sweetness.

The new understanding that began to emerge rested again on a vision, but this vision did not depend on some ultimate 'truth', so often associated with arrogance, intolerance, sectarianism, violence, or even intellectual racism. It did not depend, either, on the arrival of an 'enlightened', charismatic guru.

Gurus are not part of my tradition which has taught me never to surrender the right to think for myself. It is, instead, the kind of vision that produced the cultural 'revolution' of the sixties, the feminist rebellion of the seventies and the green movement of the eighties.

Yet, although disenchanted with politics as one might be with his Brobdingnagian nose, I could not distance myself from it – or more precisely from its presumed large gestures. I could not resist the warbling persuasiveness of the present and all its conflicts that, in obscureness, had to be negotiated and sorted out for the benefit of a future that I no longer remembered.

Perhaps, I had taken too seriously Pericles' pronouncement that a man not interested in public affairs is a useless character, and I believed, rather too innocently, that involvement in public affairs is a duty a man has, not to the community, but to himself.

In moments of distress, I feel, however, that this was a commitment I needed as much as a fly needs a spider.

11

The Rise of Populism

Greece was at the time on a path of its own. Andreas Papandreou had won power in 1981, ending a seven-year transition period, when the country was neither a caterpillar nor a butterfly. He won power on an agenda that promised radical 'change' in favour of the 'non-privileged' Greeks.

This was the group that everyone identified with irrespective of possessions and wealth. After all, even if someone did better than Shakespeare, who had only three horses, someone else had certainly more.

On the back of this novel and also meaningless distinction, the 'non-privileged' Greeks, i.e. the large middle class, built a culture of entitlement that, under envy's mean gaze, went far beyond anything the previous generations had dreamt.

The same middle class, radicalised politically during the 1967 – 1974 dictatorship, also responded favourably to Papandreou's nationalist calls focusing primarily on the 'liberation' of Greece from the yoke of Nato and the EEC. An anti-imperialist foreign policy was a vote winner. It did not cost the middle class anything, it gave the Left a bone to chew, and it united the people behind the government in pride.

I had met Papandreou in the years the country was under dictatorship, and every time this happened I had felt irritated by his arrogance and controlling instincts, his refined target language and his unquestionable certainties. But his passion for something he cared for, whatever that was, looked like an irresistible flood.

Last time I met him before his electoral triumph was in November 1980, when, invited by prime minister Margaret Thatcher, he was talking to British and foreign diplomats at the London-based Royal Institute of International Relations.

That was the time that, capitalising on the country's post-dictatorship pathological condition, he had led the people to an anti-foreign paroxysm. If he were to be elected, he had promised, Greece would leave both Nato and the EEC.

But, as he told his Chatham House audience, parliamentarians, diplomats and military men, that was in reality never going to happen.

His government, he said, would propose a referendum on Greece's membership to both organisations with a view to opting out, but the holding of the referendum would have first to be approved by the president of the Republic, Konstantinos Karamanlis.

And Karamanlis would never give it his blessing. In other words,

– 'You've got nothing to worry about.'

Telling the Greeks the opposite, i.e., selling favourable winds for a sixpence, was something destined to go down the history of cruel jokes.

It was, I thought, unseemly and contemptible, something that made a mockery of democracy itself. At the end of the briefing, and in order to ensure his intentions were not made public, Papandreou phoned me and demanded that I do not report what I had heard. To be sure, he also contacted Serafeim Fyntanides, my editor.

The story, indeed, was never published, but not because I wanted to oblige.

It did also show me how wrong I was in thinking that trying to ride two horses at once was very difficult even for a conjurer of Papandreou's calibre. It was not. As others before and after him have discovered, it is, indeed, as easy as expelling intestinal gas.

The deception involved is naturally infuriating, but the breathtaking audacity of the tricksters, so beautifully portrayed in the Yes Minister series, can even make you laugh.

It was the latter aspect that Andreas Lentakis, a member of the new generation of political leaders, chose to see when I told him the story while sipping a coffee in front of the National Museum. He knew what politics is all about. If the man had not died in 1997, he might have been Greece's foreign minister from 2012 onwards.

Incidentally, the same thing happened again later with the president of the Republic of Cyprus Spyros Kyprianou. Speaking to MPs in the House of Commons, he re-assured them that he did not intend to interfere with the status of the British military bases in Cyprus. As his story in Cyprus itself was somewhat different, he phoned me home later in the same day to ask me not to report his statement.

Papandreou had no intention of either withdrawing from NATO, dismantling the US bases in Greece or taking the country out of the EEC. Indeed, one of the reasons Margaret Thatcher had invited him to London was to strengthen the ties between Greece and the UK within the EEC so as to weaken to the same degree the ties between Greece and France to which Karamanlis was committed.

I suggested this to Papandreou himself and also to Malcolm Rifkind, a member of the Thatcher cabinet and later Foreign Secretary. They both concurred, albeit vaguely, with the suggestion.

By that time Greece had already one leg inside the European club following the 1961 Association Agreement reached by prime minister Karamanlis with help from Charles De Gaulle, president of France. In 1963, while in the army, I had, incidentally, paraded In front of the General in the Sedes military airport, close to Thessaloniki. Our performance was nothing less than spectacular.

Despite Papandreou's rumblings, full membership of the European community was viewed at the time as a step towards lessening Greece's political and economic dependence on the US. The EEC, it was also believed, would further back up the newly re-established parliamentary democracy against any future threats.

Whatever the exact calculations of the impact the country's entry into the EEC might be, the overwhelming consideration behind the decision was, thus, political. The country's full and formal entry into the EEC by the time Papandreou won power in Greece, in 1981, did not, therefore, cause all that much soul-searching.

It looked as if Melisanthe had just let her hair down over the balcony for Pelleas to climb in.

The belief was that losses in one area would be counter-balanced by profits in another. Industry would be hit, but Europe's Regional Development Fund and the Common Agricultural Policy would compensate Greece for its losses.

Talking to BBC radio at the time Greece's entry was being negotiated, I did, however, point out that the unequal size of the community's member states was bound to create unequal relations between them.

Greece could possibly, as a result, turn into the community's satellite state.

Ariel, the French interviewer, did not seem surprised at the thought. He thanked me with his endearingly polished voice, folded his papers and left to meet Patricia, his girlfriend, for dinner.

The entry came at a time that expansive fiscal policies, including private sector protection and nationalisation of firms in difficulty, pursued by Karamanlis, Papandreou's conservative predecessor, had hit badly the Greek economy. Against the backdrop of global recession, stagflation in Greece was rampant. GDP growth was negative (-1.6%) and inflation had risen to 24.5%.

Given all this, Papandreou promised to turn the economy from a dependent service economy based on semi-skilled labour to an independent industrial economy based on skilled labour, improve the welfare state and modernise Greece in tune with the demands of his time – universities, hospitals, new administrative services and research centres.

He further undertook to tackle patronage, clientelism, graft, bribery and corruption, which were the legacy of the past, and put an end to the close links between government and the private sector. The latter, including the big media corporations dependent on the state for their advertising revenue and licences of various kind, had never failed to secure lucrative deals from the party in power in exchange for political favours.

The relations between the political parties and the media, too intimate for comfort, were, in fact, one of the factors that kept undermining the country's newly re-established democracy.

Papandreou's task was monumental and the opportunity the powerful support on which his power rested totally unique. Fifty years of right wing rule had just ended and the country looked willing and ready to go through its revolutionary transformation into a modern European state.

The vision looked as refreshing as the heart of a watermelon.

Papandreou's election had, indeed, changed dramatically the political landscape. Greece felt as free as never before in my memory.

No person felt any longer persecuted for his political views as all remaining discriminations against the Left were lifted. Papandreou's policy was power to the people. The trade unions were turned into power houses, local authorities were given unprecedented powers and so were the farmers' cooperatives and various other special interests bodies. Students were given the right to vote in the elections of chancellors and department heads as well as seats on administrative committees – this was repealed by law in 2011.

Further, following the removal of legal barriers, the legal status of women was enhanced and equal pay guaranteed, parental leave for both parents and maternity allowances were introduced, civil marriage was made legal, adultery was decriminalised and divorce was made easier. Artistic and cultural centres also received support.

To a large extent these measures were long overdue and welcome, but even so I could not share the euphoria they generated among the vast majority of the Greeks. Even on the day the 'socialists' triumphed, Spyros Mercouris, Melina's brother, greeted me in the London Greek embassy with the loud, triumphant roar: 'we' won.

But my instant and spontaneous reaction was to shout back at him from the top of the staircase, over the head of numerous other guests:

– 'Who's we?'

I just could not identify with the 'socialists' and the crowd of sycophants Papandreou had assembled around him or his ostentatious proclamations that had become his trademark just like the absurdities of the Monty Python team. I did not believe the 'socialists' had what it takes to deliver on their promises.

In fact, I would not believe Papandreou even if he told me that he had two ears.

Whatever he did was, I thought, not an end in itself, but a means to an end which was the full control of the country by the party apparatus and for his and their own benefit. Perhaps I was too cynical. But that was what my guiding instinct was whispering to my ear.

Months later, I accordingly turned down an invitation, handed over to me by the 'socialist' party during an official lunch in London's Mayfair, to take an 'important' position in the 'socialist' administration.

– 'Perhaps, an ambassador somewhere or general secretary in a ministry?'

The invitation surprised me as I was the only person on their list I had not heard of. Besides, only a couple of years earlier I could not get a job even as an estate agent's assistant.

Nevertheless, despite its brilliantined wording, the invitation meant association with a world tainted with deceitful promises and compromises, corruption and the ruthless pursuit of self-interest. A responsible government encourages the participation of the people in the running of the country, but it also strengthens the institutions to make sure they remain loyal to the cause of an efficient and fair state.

Papandreou, an authoritarian 'socialist', was not interested in it. Considering in particular that the system had, or so I thought, no ability to transform itself from within, the idea of joining it was, thus, outrightly unattractive.

Declining the offer at that stage of my life was, however, a turning point. In moments of uncertainty the decision looked as if it had condemned myself to live outside the world's laboratory. Yet, it was a decision I have never regretted. Considering that what we usually regret is not what we have done but what we have not done and wish we had, the absence of regrets was even more gratifying than I had originally thought.

Even if, as a result, I ended up not entitled to a chauffeur.

As it so often happens, it did not take all that long for the 'socialist' dream, abandoned in the back streets of yesterday, to degenerate into a nightmare.

Though beset by long-term structural problems, the economy was not restructured. Foreign business interests, a large and incompetent bureaucracy and a parasitic élite, the kleptocrats, never allowed the 'socialist' or any other government to plan effectively the creation of a competitive economy on which the survival of the country is dependent.

This, incidentally, is historically the ultimate cause of the Greek failure that manifested itself times and again until eventually, a quarter of a century later, Greece collapsed.

This failure was particularly painful at the time as all protection of the Greek industry in the form of subsidies and tariffs as high as 500 per cent had already been removed. The Greek industry, which could not hide its peevish displeasure, lost instantly its competitiveness – exports declined from a peak of 17 percent of GDP in 1981 to less than 10 percent in 1987 – while EEC import penetration in the traditional sectors that accounted for nearly 60 per cent of manufacturing output quadrupled.

At the same time, the anticipated investment from foreign multinationals never materialised. Greece, an unattractive market for foreign capital, lacked the infrastructure or market proximity necessary for the purpose. Domestic investment through an élite-controlled banking system did not produce any results either.

It only helped, instead, most of the Greek 'industrialists' to borrow huge sums from the state banks in order to divert most of it abroad.

Investment in manufacturing was not attractive in any case as commercial and land-speculation activities were considered to be much more profitable. The wealthy went for what was profitable and useful, Aristotle would have said again, as opposed to what is beautiful but unprofitable. The low labour productivity, far below that of the EEC countries, and the small size of the market for domestic manufactures discouraged further potential local investors.

The result was the doubling of EEC imports to Greece from 13% in 1980 to 25% in 1987. With the market flooded with foreign consumer products offered at a more competitive prices, the Greeks, as a result, had no choice but to go for them. The trade deficit widened.

Karamanlis, who, as prime minister, had negotiated Greece's entry into the EEC, expected the shrinking of the Greek industry, which, in any case, consisting mostly of small and medium business, could not compete against its international competitors. But he had also, albeit mistakenly, anticipated that an industrialised and export-led agriculture would make all the difference. Industrialisation of the agricultural sector was nevertheless not easy given again the very small size of farm holdings.

Whatever the reasons, agricultural exports decreased, agricultural imports increased and the trade balance got even worse. Even the agricultural trade balance had turned negative due to increased dependence on imported food products.

The absorption of the massive European structural funds, on the other hand, was hebetudinous and, unlike the sun which moves always west, they were not always used to boost growth. The farmers, or at least those I knew, rather than invest the subsidies to modernise production, used the funds to buy instead flats in Athens and BMW cars. Others I could see on television used the tractors, bought with subsidies, to block the highways in protest to anything that affected negatively their interests.

It was as if the bonanza was going to last for ever. Blindness is not the misfortune of the blind only.

The signs of the crisis to come were already in the horizon. Shocks, as the American economist Hyman Minsky stated, are the product of the system's own internal dynamics, when during periods of economic stability, banks, firms and other economic agents sleep happily in the shade of their complacency. They assume that the good times will keep on going and begin to take ever greater risks in pursuit of profit.

So the seeds of the next crisis are sown in the good times.

Meanwhile, the number of the public sector employees grew from an estimated 344.000 in 1974 to 467.000 in 1981 and 693.000 in 1989 – almost a fifth of the active population. Their numbers increased further in the following years until in 2009 they reached the implausible figure of 952,625. Many of them were under fixed term contracts or seasonal – a practice which enabled the government to by-pass the legal employment procedure. In just a few years public expenditure was beyond any control.

All this had nothing to do with the restructuring of the economy both needed and promised. The main intention behind Papandreou's drive was to reward the party faithful and place them in positions of influence so that the party in power would be able both to control the state and buy the votes it needed in the future. Though in line with the time-honoured practice, this went, however, far beyond anything experienced since 1935, the year the Right assumed full control of Greece for half a century.

As poet Kavafy might say again, perhaps the time had come to call in a political reformer.

12

Socialism on Credit

Papandreou had just succeeded in reinventing and re-organising the patronage system and on a scale never seen before. He could not, obviously, rely on the bureaucracy he had inherited after fifty years of right wing rule, but what he did amounted to the deconstruction of the state.

The result was a state apparatus too big, too expensive, too inefficient and also too corrupt.

The clientelistic networks the 'socialists' had inherited had become clientelism on an industrial scale involving also many special interest groups demanding as clients favours from their politicians. As Dimitris Bourantas, a professor of management at Athens University, put it:

– Rather than fostering on entrepreneurship, competition, an industrial strategy or banking on competitive advantages, the political system was focused instead on growing public administration. 'We, thus, ended up as the last Soviet country in Europe'.

This went alongside an increase in salaries above the inflation rates and without links to productivity and higher remunerations of the overabundance of overpaid liberal professions. Spending on welfare did also increase dramatically mainly due to the huge increase in pension payments and also to the lowering of the retirement age down to 55 for men and 50 for women in about 600 professions considered 'arduous'.

Included among the latter were hairdressers, radio announcers, waiters and musicians.

According to the Organisation for Economic Co-operation and Development, pensions in Greece rank among the most generous in the world. This generosity left, however, by 1989 a 9 per cent GDP deficit.

Papandreou's broad social agenda led further to an ever increasing public expenditure due also to the implementation of a range of distributive and redistributive policies in terms of health and education. He expanded health coverage, social insurance and social welfare that included even state-subsidised tourism for lower income groups.

As a result, the primary budget deficit more than trebled as a proportion of GDP from the seventies to the eighties and debt ratcheted up. His policy, which promised a Cornucopia, always filled with whatever food or drink was desired, was enthusiastically received by the people except that its costs went far beyond what the country could afford.

The galloping deficits were also helped by the high degree of tax evasion, the national sport of doctors, lawyers, economists, architects, civil engineers and other professionals and also entre- preneurs mostly in the service industry. The black economy, esti- mated to be around 30 per cent of all economic activity, was flourishing.

Tax evasion, as someone I know told me, was totally justified because you do not get anything in return for your taxes as the state fails to provide the essential services as expected. The tax on corporations remained, meanwhile, extremely low by international standards.

The collateral damage all this caused was the heavier tax burden that fell for reasons that had nothing to do with gravitation on the wage and salary earners, i.e. the low income groups, and the poor through indirect taxation. These were the groups, like Atlas who was condemned to support Heaven on his shoulders for all eternity, who traditionally carry the load.

The rampant tax evasion went hand in hand with what George Papandreou, son of Andreas and 'hereditary' prime minister from 2009 to 2011, called 'systemic corruption'. But that was much later, when Greece had collapsed.

Until then, everything was wrapped up because, as Moliere's Tartuffe said, 'evil's not evil until it's known'.

Very pervasive, corruption infected all spheres of life, from obtaining a driver's licence and passing the MOT to receiving the hospital doctor's attention, getting falsified state documents or pocketing undeserved state benefits or subsidies. On a massive scale, it involved people from all spheres of life: farmers and professionals, civil servants and business people, working people and retired people, monks, priests and petty criminals, rich and poor. They were all tainted by it and contributed generously to its unrestrained growth.

Reaching a level never seen before, it awarded most people an MA in its practice, proudly framed and exhibited.

The situation reminded me of a story recounted by Herodotus concerning the blind son of Sesostris, the Egyptian king.

He was told he would recover his eyesight, if he washed his eyes with the urine of a woman who had never slept with any man except her husband.

The poor boy never recovered his sight.

What was extraordinary here was the absence of reaction by the public itself as if all this was part of their quotidian existence. People, content to sleep in the shade of their complacency, just did not bother. Their expected disdainful looks were reserved for other occasions, when, for example, someone would prevent them

155

from jumping the bus queue. And those who did not like it had no power to stop it.

The rest did not mind it as long as they themselves could profit from both the inefficiency and the corruption of the system. But acceptance of corruption, coupled with fatalism about the chances of preventing or resisting it, is what drives wrongdoing and perpetuates the bottlenecks in institutions that hamper reform.

At the same time, the age of the traditional Greek frugality seemed to be over as several people had ended up better off than before.

Everybody's purchasing power had increased with many doing far better than others, including the recipients of both government favours and also, more importantly, the massive EEC grants and loans. The latter, given for the development of the country's infrastructure – transport, tourism and commerce, agriculture, communications, science and technology, environment, health, culture, employment, fisheries, rural development etc. – were overall either abused or just wasted.

Nevertheless, together with the extensive corruption, continuous pay rises and pension increases plus cheap credit, they fed the illusion of affluence in a country in which income inequality still remained very high.

All decent people had now to live beyond their income to enjoy 'the fatness of their pursy times'. The new spirit of consumerism was restrained only by the infertility of one's imagination.

The Greek market was saturated by cheap foreign-branded products which in the 1990s expanded rapidly to Mercedes cars, designer clothes, luxury items and anything the fashion industry produced. The import of demand by the surplus countries was nothing less than 'beggar-my neighbour' policy. Meanwhile, the money borrowed was not invested in tradable activities which could subsequently service the international debts.

People were buying all the things they thought people of a certain class wanted in order to look different, looking, as a result, just like all the other people of that class. But there was nothing new in all this except the scale of the shopping.

Even in Skyros island, when invited to the home of a shepherd who smelt the sweat of the earth, I was offered neither ouzo nor wine but whiskey in a water glass full to the very top.

– 'Are you crazy?', I asked the fellow while screwing a finger into one of my temples.

– 'Enjoy it' was the answer given to me by a face which, though not smiling, was full of amiability.

Having emerged from the hard, sober labyrinth of necessity, there was no way I could take all this. If nothing else, the image of my mother mending my socks on a wooden egg so that we would not have to buy another pair, still vivid in me, would not allow self-indulgence or anything resembling extravagant spending.

It was not that I was cherishing unwarranted prejudices against all demonstrations of newly-won wealth. I was just endowed with an insurmountable shyness in regard to luxury, even horrified of comfort.

Just like Byron, I was a man of frugal habits.

A comfortable bourgeois texture did, however, cost money, more than the Greeks could earn. But the banks, which borrowed from French and German banks, were there to lend the consumer all the money needed to buy French and German consumer goods. Nothing could interfere with this new consumption process even though the production base to sustain it had been totally missing and the euphoria's bottom rested on unsustainable debt.

But as nobody was obsessed with reality, nobody bothered. Nobody cared.

As the old Greeks used to say, 'it's all the same to Hippocleides'.

The saying sprang from a story involving Cleisthenis, the sixth century BC Athenian statesman who consolidated democracy in the city and hoped to see his daughter married to Hippocleides. The latter lost, however, the favour of his would-be father-in-law when on the crucial day he danced on a table standing on his head and beating time with his legs up in the air.

– 'You've danced away your marriage', Cleisthenis shouted to him.

– 'I could hardly care less' the drunken, would-be bridegroom retorted.

Masquerading ignominiously as 'resistance' to the incorrigible capitalism the 'socialists' were administering since 1981, the new culture obliterated, meanwhile, any sense of personal responsibility to the whole – the state, the community, the environment or the future. The self-image of the middle class as the knights of progress that had been hatched earlier, in the mid-seventies, on account of its opposition to the dictatorship, its hostility to the Americans and its nationalist stance against Turkey, meant nothing.

'Leftism' in the eighties was nothing more than a self-serving 'ideology', quite crude and rather frightful. Papandreou's policy had just cultivated this mentality but also reflected it.

Yet, this same middle class, content on account of its relative economic strength that enabled it to use private resources to meet its needs, was only too happy to preserve the terribly unequal economic and social structure of the country. Despite all the social measures, which the country could not afford, Papandreou's 'non-privileged' were only too happy to attend to their own interests and, in the process, destroy many things they valued, primarily their integrity.

The 'me' society, supported by the 'socialist' nationalisation of vice, had arrived. Inner search for the after shave that is really you replaced the search for authenticity and values.

This conclusion was being reinforced every single time I visited Athens. People seemed to act as if civility was taxed.

The change was evident in everything:

The obstreperousness of the drivers, the professionals or the law enforcers who seemed to have no terms of reference, the corruption of the civil servants, the abuse of public funds, the establishment of networks of vested interests associated with elected public servants and middle-men who earned from each public deal more than a family earns in a lifetime, the fraudulence of the trading classes, the widespread tax avoidance practised by professionals and entrepreneurs who would often pay as much tax as a cleaning lady, the deceitful claims of all kinds the state was only too eager to meet, the deeply undemocratic use of 'connections' for the acquisition of undeserved benefits, the pursuit of personal interests over and above the public interest, the judgement of all values on the strength of their monetary worth, the attachment to the superficial pleasures of life.

They all seemed as natural as sex in the spring fields.

Distorting heavily both market and moral values, the new ethos *contra bonos mores* acknowledged only one objective: to become effortlessly rich.

The young people, the *ephebe*, without faith in anything and resolutely reluctant to put their trust in the future, would rather barbecue eggs in front of St Peter' gate than aspire to eternal blissful life. And their elders, in their learned wisdom, opined supinely 'never such innocence again'. The mental constructs of the past had become now a prison more confining than the economic determinism of Marx or the psychological determinism of Freud.

The age of crude materialism and vulgar commercialism, flying on the wings of fatalism, had triumphally arrived like the plague which hit Athens in the first years of the Peloponnesian war and nearly destroyed it.

Exchanging looks consciously devoid of any meaning, we had just buried God obtusely and unceremoniously.

159

The deontological decline had affected journalism, too. Ruthless media barons, emotionally drained-out editors, and ambitious youngsters with no honest beliefs in anything turned what was once a gallant profession into a branch of the entertainment industry without, as a rule, any moral boundaries. In what looked like a post-orgasmic postmodernist euphoria, all keyhole journalism was concerned about was ratings and circulation both increasing in reverse order to the syllables of the words used.

The media, like politics, was, of course, only the mirror in which Greek society could see its reflection. To protect the innocence of its eyes it did not, however, choose to look.

True to my instincts, I fought my way – a few times I won, in most cases I lost. Unfortunately, the intellectuals of Greece, hitherto marginalised and impoverished, having been given by the 'socialists' some sort of a chair on which they could seat their mundane ambitions, chose uncharacteristically to keep their reservations to themselves. Domesticated, they turned instead into managers of Greece's new academic empire.

But this did not bother the pilgrims jostling for space in the politicians' shopping malls.

Time, as Cervantes said, is the devourer and consumer of all things, including the ideas we cherished most in our early days. They had all been swallowed up by the night and turned into their shadowy abstraction.

Apparently, when the battles and struggles of conscience have profitably ended, people can live only too easily with ideals and no principles.

The 'socialist' policy was plain populism, the barren child of a long iniquitous night. But it was also exactly what the middle class, 'socialist', 'revolutionary' and on the 'left' of everybody, including itself, wanted in order to live in peace with its conscience and, more importantly, without any cost.

I felt altogether out of place, once again a rebel. Though I continued to live in London, I could not stand the hypocrisy that had transformed democracy into an accomplice in the killing of its own essence, the aphonous default on moral obligations, the abundant lack of political integrity.

The new hard-boiled ethos was reading like a B-horror novel albeit twice as mean and half as entertaining.

Margaret Thatcher was, at least, honest – she never used the double-edged words of 'socialist' Andreas Papandreou. Moreover, the new culture she championed was being fiercely resisted by a considerable body of opinion, including the honest British Left, with which, although my ethical beliefs were rooted in a different tradition, I could easily identify.

I could not say the same about the Greek Left.

Arguments that were never to deviate into sense were waiting for me around every corner. The road to unflappability was rugged, full of disruptions. There was no way I could fit into this world. But I was not the only one feeling this way. There were, thankfully, a few others, too, including of all people George Dalaras, the celebrated Greek singer.

Betrayed by the 'socialists', he told me when in London for a concert in 1986, he was swimming in a political vacuum, which, however, he did not seem to mind.

My 'socialist' experience during the years Andreas Papandreou was in power, i.e. from 1981 to 1989, vertiginous as it was, had disillusioned me for good. Instead of appealing to the high spirits of the Greeks, the 'socialist' leader had appealed to the lowest possible common denominator and got the response he expected.

The common seems as if it is bound by the rules of nature to triumph over the exquisite.

It did not, however, take all that long for the 'socialists' to come face to face with the fruits of their policies – an explosive economy in 1985.

To restore part of the lost competitiveness, the government went, first, for a controlled but drastic depreciation of the Greek drachma which lost more than 70 per cent of its value against the dollar. The depreciation contributed to an inflation explosion without a significant effect on the balance of trade. Foreign exchange reserves fell below safety level. This was followed by an explosion of foreign debt which by the end of the decade had more than quadrupled.

It all necessitated continued heavy borrowing to meet the mounting service payments on past loans.

The loans that were granted in 1985 were given on the understanding that they would be used by the government to restructure the economy in order to increase Greece's competitiveness within the EEC. An austerity programme was also introduced in the period 1985 -1987.

Short-termism in the interests of political survival ensured, however, that the economy was not restructured while the austerity programme was abandoned altogether in 1987. Restraining measures could not be implemented against the will of vested interests affiliated with the party in government and 'socialism on credit' continued unabated to render certain the constant 'improvement' of the consumption standards.

Eventually, in 1990 the 'socialists' lost power and a new, conservative government was formed under Constantinos Mitsotakis, a Cretan politician very familiar with the shenanigans of his trade.

I knew the man from 1966, when I was covering the parliament affairs for *Avghi*, and I had met him in London in 1980 when he was the country's economic coordination minister. He had come together with his daughter, Dora Bakoyannis, 'a real woman, a veritable frigate', as novelist Kondylakis might say, who later became Greece's foreign minister.

The event, incidentally, was marked by a bitter dispute between myself and all the other journalists Mitsotakis had brought along from Athens.

Having contacted a number of Greek and British sources, I had published exclusively in *Eleftherotypia* all the protocols

Mitsotakis had signed in the UK immediately after their signature. All the other journalists waited for him to hand them over to them on a piece of paper 24 hours later so that in the time in between they could enjoy uninterrupted their Oxford Street shopping.

They were furious with me.

– 'You broke our code of practice', Nikos Nikolaou, formerly an *Avghi* and at the time a *Kathimerini* reporter, shouted at me in the bar of a Marble Arch hotel.

It was not the code of practice I had adhered to.

The new government had to apply for a new loan to cover the deficits, which was granted but on the understanding that the number of public employees would be reduced by 10 per cent, indirect taxes and the price of services provided by public corporations would go up, and the market would be deregulated.

Mitsotakis promised in this instance and did pursue a programme of fiscal order including severe cutbacks in public services and a privatisation policy which encountered the fierce opposition of the unions. But his commitment to the change required was as sinewy as our New Year resolutions. The difficulties he faced were, in any case, quite formidable as debt servicing alone in 1990 absorbed over half the total tax revenues versus 25% in 1985.

The government fell after three years due, among other reasons, to Papandreou's hard nationalist policies on 'Macedonia' pursued against the government for its political benefits. With Papandreou again in power until 1996, Greece reached the very threshold of the debt trap. Still the Greeks, in the comfortable arms of self-deception, could not see the writing on the wall.

The truth, so outrageous, could just not be accepted.

13

Stories Destined to be Forgotten

I n all my years as a journalist I tried consistently to do a decent job whatever the difficulties. It was always a matter of professional pride.

Pride, in one instance, kept me in the House of Commons finishing a report on a meeting between general Bernard Rodgers, Nato's supreme allied commander, and several Nato officers and also British MPs on the return of Greece to the integrated Nato military structure despite a sudden, prolonged and killing pain in the stomach.

While working for *Eleftherotypia*, the *Guardian* of Greece, I kept filing reports on the Thatcher revolution and its impact on the economy and the people, the Labour party crisis and the election of Michael Foot and then of Neil Kinnock as its leader, the Iranian London embassy siege, the 1981 riots and the royal wedding, the Falklands war, the Greenham Common Women's Peace Camp, the tragic developments in Northern Ireland, the miners long strike, the acrimonious talks between Margaret Thatcher and the European Union, the 1984 IRA bombing attack on the Brighton hotel, where Margaret Thatcher was staying, and so much more including the Hyde Park and two hours later the Regent's Park bombs the Provisional Irish Republican Army had detonated killing a total of four soldiers and seven bandsmen.

The latter stayed with me as it embarrassed me as a journalist.

It was in that July 1982 day, when my phone rang. The call was from my editor, Serafeim Fyntanides, an easy going, witty character, cynically attached to politics, who wanted to know about the bombs. As I had switched off for the day to focus on something else, I did not have a clue as to what he was talking about.

– 'What bombs', I asked.

– 'Those in Hyde Park!'

– Did the Provisional IRA, I wonder, have to bomb its targets that very day?

News coverage required hard work and constant awareness of what the day or the night might bring. A minor newspaper's foreign correspondent is not, of course, expected to cover everything – all big events are in any case covered by the news agencies. What that foreign correspondent can basically offer is, perhaps, a view from a different angle and/or a personal touch in the presentation of a story that, in my case, Greek readers might find interesting.

The Lancaster House negotiations regarding the future of Rhodesia makes the point. These negotiations were fully covered by the news agencies, but given the struggle of Cyprus to end the British colonial rule, still fresh in mind, I wanted the personal touch.

Lord Carrington, the British Foreign Secretary, helped a little bit, but what I wanted was an interview with Robert Mugabe, the representative of the Zimbabwe Patriotic Front and ruler of Zimbabwe for the next one hundred years. There was, however, no way I could persuade him to show his face, which incidentally never matched his glasses, and give me a bit of time. He was too busy trying to outmanoeuvre the Brits.

Others, including Lord Carrington, the Syrian ambassador in the UK, the representative of the PLO and a number of MPs, were much more easily available for comment when the EU was considering the idea of a Greek initiative in relation to the perennial Palestinian problem.

As if such an initiative could produce any results.

Also agreeable was Geoffrey Howe, the British Foreign Secretary after the 1983 national elections, who received me and a few other Greek journalists in his office for a long conversation on this and other issues.

In other similar instances, I wanted to give space to cultural phenomena such as the punks, whose subculture had a largely anarchic, anti-establishment character, almost frightening, or the fascinating job done by the BBC when it presented John Le Carré's Tinker, Tailor, Soldier, Spy in which George Smiley, his hero, hunts an upper-class traitor within the ranks of MI6, the British intelligence.

Interesting stories are not, of course, by definition interesting. The idea, for example, of interviewing, if that was possible, the teenage granddaughter of Josef Stalin, who was at the time in a boarding school somewhere in the country, as the editor of my newspaper's Sunday edition had requested, was of no interest to me whatsoever.

Impervious to his encouragement, I just refused to oblige.

– 'Private lives', I told him quite bluntly, 'are not for the readers' yellow pleasures'.

Anything that had to do with Greece had, of course to be given time and space. When the Socialist Republic of Macedonia, as it was still called before the early nineties' break-up of Yugoslavia, embarked on a huge campaign in the UK to advance the 'Macedonian' cause, I made it a point to see in London the president of their Republic. He did receive me and I was dismayed to hear him attacking both Greece and Bulgaria for the ethnic repression of their 'Macedonian' population.

– 'Bulgaria', he said, 'was dreaming the occupation of Macedonian territories, and Greece represses the Macedonian population'.

But, at the same time, he refused to accept the post-war national borders as expressing today's realities as he refused to rule out any future territorial claims his own country might make against its neighbours.

Even so, what he stated was miles behind his country's propaganda machine. The latter's material, maps and books, claimed as ethnic 'Macedonian' the greatest part of the Greek Macedonia, including Thessaloniki, its main city. Ethnic 'Macedonians', the propaganda material claimed, made up in some cases the 100% of Greece's population while in others they made up the 50% or less.

The president of the former Yugoslav Republic proceeded then to deliver a history lesson which highlighted the 'fact' that the 'Macedonians' were perhaps of pre-Adamite ancestral descent or at least existed as an ethnicity since the day Athena, the goddess, punished the crows for something they had done by turning their white feathers to black.

Incidentally at the same time Athena, shocked at the crows' behavior, accidentally dropped a huge rock she was carrying in Athens, which the Athenians later called the Lycabettus hill.

The Greeks, who were not as yet aware of the 'Macedonians' claims, including their implicit territorial ambitions, were, obviously, appalled.

Their reaction marked the beginning of a diplomatic war which still has not ended.

Meeting Turgut Özal, prime minister and later president of Turkey until his mysterious death in 1993, to ask questions about the ongoing difficulties between his country and Greece was another memorable occasion. Its importance might have escaped me if it had not been preceded by the London Turkish embassy's refusal to let me join his press conference.

I did eventually, but only after the Greek foreign ministry made representations to the Turkish embassy in Athens and the

Greek embassy in London to the Turkish embassy. Özal, in his statement, professed support for the UN efforts to terminate the Cyprus dispute, but at the same time asked for the recognition of the 'facts on the ground' as created by the Turkish invasion of the island.

I argued with him that the UN proposals were incompatible with the aims of his country, but, of course, I did not expect him to agree with me. We could not even agree on the terms of our disagreement.

Interestingly, at the end of the interview, when I walked with a Turkish journalist outside the conference hall, where Turkish demonstrators were denouncing the oppressive Turkish rule in their country, I was asked by him how Özal compared to Andreas Papandreou.

– 'Though both have wings', I answered rather wickedly, 'you can not really compare a chicken to a hawk.'

Turgut Özal, incidentally, may well be remembered by history following a statement he made later on, when he said:

– 'We do not need to make war with the Greeks. We just need to send them a few millions illegal immigrants from Turkey and finish with them.'

There were other instances, however, when my lack of tact caused some really awkward moments. That was the case when talking to George Rallis, the 1980 – 1981 conservative prime minister, at a time when Greece was ravaged by waves of forest fires.

The question to which the Greeks wanted an answer was who was responsible for those fires. The prime minister, a decent man with a gentle background, exiled and tortured during the colonels' rule, and humble enough to walk unguarded in the streets of Athens even when he was the country's prime minister, was kind enough to receive me in London's Greek embassy.

But he could not provide the answer. I am sure he did not have one in which case my aggressiveness was bound to lead to nothing.

Looking back at it, I think I ought to be more considerate or, at least, less aggressive.

– 'Sorry, Mr. Rallis, if you can forgive me from wherever you are'.

My first encounter with George Papandreou, prime minister of Greece from 2009 to 2011, was even less agreeable and blissful. Of all places, I met him in a local authorities' conference in London and invited him for a coffee.

A few days earlier he had joined a reception at the White House where he had the chance to say 'hi' to president Reagan – an event presented by my own newspaper, *Eleftherotypia*, with the words Ταπανε in letters as long as my arm. *Ταπανε* means they chatted for a long time like old friends.

I mentioned it and we both laughed at it.

– 'Newspapers!', he said, as if this explained everything, which by a strange coincidence it did.

Another issue that came up did, however, inject an edge to an otherwise friendly conversation. That was when I asked him to talk about his political plans and ambitions. Naturally, he did not want to elaborate.

– 'I hope', I said at the end, 'you will not seek to prolong the life of the Papandreou dynasty. We have just managed to get rid of the Glücksburg dynasty and we can do without another dynasty, republican this time, in its place'.

Though described as a 'friendly Labrador', George Papandreou at that moment did not look like one. He did not say a word while the silence gathered pace. But the looks he gave me before excusing himself because he had, he said, to make an urgent telephone call, implied much more than his unspoken words.

I had spoiled his morning like milk in the coffee that had passed its sell-by day.

169

What spoiled his day even more was the party the Anglo-Greek Labour party committee of the London borough of Islington had given in his honour. The speaker welcomed Papandreou, whose personality and talents he generously extolled, and then proceeded to shake hands with him.

The hand he shook was, however, that of Tasos Panagides, the Cyprus' High Commission boss.

The problem was that I could not even pretend to be respectful towards the politicians. Despite my efforts, in many instances I was actually rather impertinent.

This was the case particularly when dealing with cabinet ministers such as the oleaginous Menios Koutsogiorgas, Akis Tsochatzopoulos or George Katsifaras, a man whose pronouncements rested always on a pretentiousness claiming to be either profound or witty. What guided my negative reaction to them was an instinctive dislike generated by their pomposity or the feeling that they were after something beyond the scope of their duty.

I was as brusque when talking to Makis Arnaoutis, the ex-king Constantine's aide-de-camp, at London's iconic Claridge's hotel to which he had invited me for lunch. What I wanted to know from him, while enjoying the delectable sea bream, was the business interests of his boss about which he was, however, rather evasive.

I had clashed with him earlier, too, when discussing the purpose of the Hellenic college the ex-king had established in London in 1980 with the support of the Greek 'socialist' government. Though I had argued fiercely in my newspaper against it, Constantine, incidentally, when I subsequently met him at a reception joined by princess Margaret, the Queen's sister, was still quite gentle and friendly.

The Greek government reckoned later on that its support for the project was misguided and in 1983 severed its links with it. Following the dramatic decline of the number of its students, the college eventually closed down in 2005.

There were instances, however, when I was also quite respectful to people, as in the case of Yannis Haralampopoulos, Greece's foreign minister from 1981 to 1985. He was a decent, proud and also unassuming man who once received me in his hotel room in his pyjamas. Above his party's machinations, he carried on in his high profile job for years without, however, the power of the job which had been kept in Papandreou's own hands.

Rather bitter about it, Haralampopoulos once asked me:

– 'Please don't forget to mention my role in the making of Greece's foreign policy.'

I did have some sympathy for him.

Konstantinos Karamanlis was another politician I had respect for.

A towering political figure, he had spent, between 1956 and 1995, 14 years as prime minister and 10 years as president of the Republic. He had, indeed, as the leader of the Right, dominated the political scene of Greece in the second half of the twentieth century.

The man was self-centred, almost infuriatingly self-confident, blunt in his talk, in full control of his high-powered ministerial teams and decisive in action. According to my friend George Votsis who, as a journalist, had acquainted himself fully with the man, he was also a politician with integrity, 'standing head and shoulders above all his contemporaries'.

I met Karamanlis in London when he paid a visit to prime minister Margaret Thatcher. At first he complimented me by saying he is an avid reader of my reports, but then he refused to oblige when I asked him to talk about himself.

The questions I wanted to ask him were all about things such as the influences he received as a youngster, the things he would like to be remembered for, his views on his own strengths and weaknesses or the differences, as he saw them, between the pre and the post-dictatorship Karamanlis.

The latter question was, indeed, the most important. Before 1967 he was fully committed to upgrading the infrastructure of the country in order to turn Greece into a modern state. Yet he remained an authoritarian figure relying on the repressive state machinery to keep the opposition at bay.

The extent to which he masterminded the horrendous state violence of the late fifties and early sixties is nevertheless still an open question.

The parakratos, the 'deep state', beyond any government control and above the rule of law, commanded by the palace and the military, was in place long before he won power. The military section of the parakratos was, however, split between the royalists, i.e. those looking forward to a military dictatorship under the king, and the militarists, i.e. those looking forward to a military dictatorship without, or even against, the king. This split, which had become part of the country's political tradition since 1922, became all too evident in 1967, when the militarist wing of the army rushed to impose its own military dictatorship before the king had a chance to proceed a week later with his own.

The right wing political establishment had on the back of the militarist element in the army often challenged, albeit unsuccessfully, the royalists, who, in order to preserve the status quo, were always ready to declare a dictatorship. They did not do so but only because they were held back by the Americans.

But relations between Paul and his wife, Frederica, on the one hand, and the right-wing politicians, on the other, were very often out of control.

In 1952, having lost patience, Marshal Papagos reached the conclusion that it was time for king Paul to go.

Papagos died in 1955, and the palace, without consulting the right wing political establishment, appointed Karamanlis as prime minister. The king had assumed that Karamanlis would be in his pocket. He was wrong.

Karamanlis' controlling instincts and also his anger at the continuous interference of the royalist parakratos in the running of the country brought him, thus, inevitably in conflict, not only with the opposition, but also with the traditional power centres, i.e. the palace and the US. Eventually, in 1963, in disgust at the actions of the royal family, he left the country.

The rhetorical question he asked but never answered was:

– 'Who runs this country?'

When he returned to Greece in 1974, after the collapse of the dictatorship, he was, however, a changed man. He championed the firm establishment of the parliamentary institutions, ensuring, among other things, the failure of the monarch to return to the throne. The solid institutional framework he oversaw prepared, indeed, the ground for the uneventful rise to power of Andreas Papandreou, his rival.

To secure the smooth functioning of the country's institutions, he also lessened the US influence in Greek politics by attaching the country as firmly as he could to the EEC and particularly France. He even confronted the Americans at some point by withdrawing Greece for a number of years from NATO's military wing.

Interestingly, despite his conservatism, he encouraged state intervention in support of numerous business in financial difficulties, and nationalised several sectors of the economy, from banking to transport.

In the last few years of his presidency, he had detached himself from the political routines, and, seeing himself as the grandfather of the nation, did not hesitate to describe Greece as a 'vast madhouse'.

He gave voice this way to the feelings of every Greek.

Perhaps, if he had answered the personal questions I put to him, I might have written another book on him this time.

The story I had in those years a personal commitment to was the nuclear armaments race and the possibility of a nuclear war.

The issue had re-emerged in the 80s following the 1979 Soviet involvement in the Afghanistan war which soon became the Soviet Union's Vietnam, and the decision of both the US and the UK to embark on an anti-Soviet and anti-communist crusade.

US president Jimmy Carter, unwisely, denounced the Soviet invasion of Afghanistan as the most serious threat to peace since World War II, and president Reagan upped the fundamentalist rhetoric by calling the Soviet Union the 'evil empire'. Incidentally, he also decided to support and train Muslims from around the world in their jihad against the Soviets.

The largest peacetime defence buildup that followed saw the instalment in Western Europe of a new generation of nuclear weapons, Cruise and Pershing, and the introduction of a new ground and space-based antiballistic missiles concept, dubbed 'star wars'. The Soviet Union at the same time was deploying in Eastern Europe its new SS-20 missiles.

Suddenly the nuclear threat was back and talk of nuclear war commonplace. People in both the US and the UK were supplied with do-it-yourself instructions on how to survive a nuclear attack – taking shelter under their kitchen tables, for example. They were also urged to build underground bunkers to protect themselves against it.

Life looked once again disagreeable and tasteless.

What, in particular, intrigued me at that stage was the position of Greece in case of an all-out war between the two blocs, Nato and the Warsaw Pact.

What Greece should in this instance expect to happen on the military front, what were the military plans, what was it expected by its allies to do, what the numerous military bases in the country established following the May 1959 US – Greek agreement were designed to do, what was going to happen if the Greek government refused to endorse the proposed US action and so on.

I wrote repeatedly on the subject, listing for the first time, among other things, most of the 45 US military bases in Greece.

The research was pretty long and involved interviews with both Greek and non-Greek military men, including brigadier Michael Harbottle, chief of staff of the UN Peacekeeping Force in Cyprus in the 60s, admiral Guerridge, Head of the Royal Institute of Defence Studies, or Herbert Scoville, the former CIA Assistant Director of Scientific Intelligence. I did also interview Gene La Rocque, a member of the US Strategic Plans Directorate of the Joint Chiefs of Staff, when I met him in Groningen, Holland.

This research, never conducted before by the Greek media, presented a massive amount of facts unknown to the public. However, as far as I know, the articles made no difference whatsoever in the thinking of the country. When I asked my editor what was the reaction to my research, his 'humorous' answer was that the type-setter had liked it.

My next story, I thought, might explore politics as an asseveration of male sexual vivacity. If good enough, it could even turn into a book which could hopefully become a bestseller like E. L. James' Fifty Shades of Grey.

Interestingly enough, my report on the subject attracted the interest of the London correspondent of *Pravda*, the Soviet daily newspaper, who, having apparently been alerted by his Moscow editor, took me out a couple of times for a drink. The journalistic romance he had in mind did not, however, last.

Unceremoniously, I ended it at its outset.

14

In the High Court

Despite the occasional frustration I had inevitably experienced, my commitment to my work remained intact and I continued to report on various topics from politics and economics to history and cultural events.

One of them related to the Greek merchant marine, the world's largest, whose representatives at the time were negotiating with the Greek government the conclusion of a new agreement between the two parties.

As it happened, I had managed to get an informer from the London based Greek shipping committee, who kept me up to date for several months with the shipowners' plans and the reactions to them from the Greek government, a miserable hostage to the shipping industry. The perennial issue was the perpetuation of the tax avoidance regime if the Greek-owned vessels were to keep or raise the Greek flag instead of that of Panama, Liberia or Honduras. And then it was the labour laws which Greece had to modify to the satisfaction of the shipowners.

Sadly, as Stathis Alexandris, the Greek merchant minister and a decent chap, admitted to me,

– 'The 'socialist' government's choices on the subject are utterly restricted.'

Another minister, whom I recall with affection, was Melina Mercouri, the star of the acclaimed film Never on Sunday, an anti-dictatorship activist and at the time minister of culture. I had first come across her in a fund raising ball organised in 1967 by the Greek Committee Against Dictatorship attended by hundreds of people and I still remember both her stare of exasperating amiability and the awe of the crowd the moment she entered the ball room.

– 'Melina, darling', the Anglo-Greek lady sitting next to me cried out with unbridled excitement.

The men, more reserved, greeted her with a glowing smile providing some sort of eternal reassurance.

As a minister of culture she was in London to make the case for the return to Athens of the Parthenon marbles which she went to view again in the British Museum. The visit turned into a superb theatrical performance for the benefit of the British TV with Melina touching tenderly and almost in tears the marbles and talking to them as if she were talking to her very first love after decades of forced separation.

It made me laugh and I wrote accordingly but all in good spirit.

She was such a likeable character. Even her faults made her lovable and amusing.

I reported on many other people, including Vangelis, one of the great composers of electronic music and best known for his Academy Award winning score for the film Chariots of Fire. The man surprised me when in answer to my asking where he had studied music, he said:

– 'Nowhere.'

He is a self-taught artist who cannot, just like Paul McCartney, read or write music or like Francis Bacon, the great painter, who never went to an art college.

I interviewed many other well-known personalities, too, people like Yannis Tsarouhis, the influential painter, Theodoros

Angelopoulos, 'the masterful film-maker' who won the prestigious Palme d'Or of the Cannes Film Festival and died tragically in a road accident in 2012, Manolis Anagnostakis, the poet, or George Zambetas, one of the greatest bouzouki musicians.

The latter, whom I met at a party given in honour of Constantinos Mitsotakis, the conservative opposition leader at the time, by the London branch of his party, used the opportunity to informed me that he had 'first hand knowledge of the crimes committed by the bloody commies in 1944'.

– 'I know', he rather disconnectedly added, 'because I wasn't born yesterday. I was born in the 4th century BC.'

He did not make sense, of course, but, if he had, his comments might not have been worth reporting.

Another interesting person was Jane Gabriel, whose 1986 documentary on the Greek civil war caused the biggest uproar in the history of British television. Jane in 1990 produced another film on the Greek psychiatric asylum of Leros, Island Outcasts, which took a most disturbing look at the horrific living conditions of something like 3,000 patients. The film on what *The Observer* called the Leros psychiatric 'concentration camp' shocked Europe and also led to a rapid and substantial improvement of conditions.

In 2009 the BBC reported, however, that these improvements had not been sustained.

Now and then I also used the opportunity to offer comments on various other issues, as I did in August 1984 when I raised the issue of illegal immigration. The number of illegal immigrants in Greece, mainly Africans and Asians, had by then reached the 40,000, a number that had already alarmed the public.

I suggested in several instances that the government does its best to dismantle the gangs engaged in slave-trading activities and stop unscrupulous domestic business from using cheap immigrant labour.

Illegal immigration, incidentally, has never been handled properly, resulting in the flooding of the country by Third World immigrants – over 1,300,000 nowadays. The rising social and political tensions and the inhuman treatment of poor, dark-skinned people are both as inevitable as old age.

In other instances I highlighted the inefficiency of the Greek bureaucracy, which, in order, for example, to grant export licences required the approval of a dozen different agencies.

It was all like teaching snails how to jump.

Or when I challenged Antonis Drosoyannis, the Greek national security minister, over the classification of drugs – no distinction between soft and hard drugs.

– 'You have to draw a line somewhere', I ventured to suggest. 'You can't treat something like a parking offence the same way you treat a high street robbery.'

I do not think I impressed him.

Incidentally, the only experience of drugs I ever had myself was in Ibiza in 1969, when I tried mescaline, which Wikipedia describes as a 'psychedelic alkaloid of the phenethylamine class'. I swallowed it and then forgot about it until the moment the sky looked like a Kandinsky painting and I could not stop laughing uncontrollably for no reason whatsoever.

More unforgettable were, however, the horrible sudden full-body spasms that accompanied the experience for the next three days. Drugs, I then decided for good, were not for me.

Drosoyannis had joined an international conference held in London on terrorism.

– 'Terrorism', he explained to me in words with slow emphasis, 'has no home country'.

Lapsing momentarily into a somnambulatory abstraction, I foolishly added:

– 'Like prostitution, religion or truisms'.

His eyes lost focus for a moment, but kindly he said nothing.

In a few instances, reporting was not free of trouble. The worst came in 1983.

After very extensive research, I wrote a story about Ann Chapman, a 25-year old British reporter murdered in Athens in October 1971, the time Greece was under the colonels' rule. Mountis, the man who had been found guilty of her murder, could not under any circumstances, I argued, have killed her and his conviction was intended only to cover up something else.

The report, which was very well received, was submitted to the European parliament by a British euro-MP, Richard Cottrell, and Mountis was later freed without having been acquitted or even pardoned.

This report was followed by another one, written after I had interviewed about sixty prominent British and Greeks, on Chapman's interest in the affairs of Greece. It hit Athens like a bombshell. It became the hot topic in conversations everywhere.

The reactions, as I expected, were varied – there were people who objected vehemently to it and others who endorsed it. Among the latter was Richard Cottrell, who in June 1984 submitted another report to the European parliament and then, interviewed by BBC2, said that the editor of *The Guardian* also thought highly of my story.

What I did not expect to see was the legal action against both me and the newspaper taken by one of the people I had mentioned in the report, a person Cottrell described in his book Blood on their Hands, published in the UK in 1987 as 'a serving British naval officer based with intelligence staff in Malta'.

He sued both myself and *Eleftherotypia* for libel in the UK to force me to retract what I had 'falsely and maliciously' written.

The case was heard in the country's High Court in June 1987.

The publisher and the editor of *Eleftherotypia* refused to attend the court case on the grounds that the British courts had no jurisdiction on the subject. My newspaper did not after all sell more than 50 copies in the UK, and if action against it had to be taken, it should have be taken in Greece where the 'offence' was firstly and primarily committed.

I had no choice but to attend the proceedings and defend myself for two days without any legal help which I could not afford. Costas Douzinas, now a professor of law at Birkbeck College, London University, had kindly offered me his help both in court as an advisor and during the long hours of my case's preparation. But in the end the jurors found me guilty.

I thought that at that point I had crossed the finishing line. But there was no finishing line. Damages awarded against myself and the newspaper were fixed at £450,000 and an injunction ensured that I was restrained from publishing again the same or similar material.

The phenomenal damage award, the highest ever in the UK and very far from the usual £10,000 to £30,000, instantly hit the British TV channels.

The High Court decision was denounced by the UK's National Union of Journalists for its far reaching implications. Press freedom, Jacob Ecclestone, its deputy general secretary, said in Athens where he went to consult with the Greek media and government on the story, is in danger if foreign judges deal with foreign media. It was also denounced as 'unacceptable' by the UK union of foreign correspondents, trade unions and members of parliament, including Tony Benn, the leader of the Labour Party's Left, who said that this is 'a most unjust judgement'.

The Daily Telegraph lamented 'the grotesque nature of our libel laws', the *Financial Times* saw them as 'the instrument for permissible censorship by which an individual's dignity or pseudo-dignity is to be upheld' and *The Guardian*, equally disturbed, recommended 'a modest and even-handed reform'.

Winston Churchill, grandson of the British war leader, on the other hand, was happy because, as he said in words handed down to posterity,

– 'Fortunately we have laws in this country which prevent newspapers writing lies about people.'

But Paul Foot, the celebrity investigative journalist and a nephew of Michael Foot, the former leader of the Labour party, expressed his confidence in me,

– 'A journalist of proven ability and experience, victim now of the most extraordinary libel action of modern times.'

Though in the UK the issue of jurisdiction became a hotly debated subject, in Greece the High Court's involvement and decision caused an outcry joined by all shades of political and public opinion. The Greek government, through its spokesman Yannis Roumbatis, and also the minister of justice Leftheris Verivakis, stressed that only the Greek courts are responsible in such cases, while the leader of the opposition, C. Mitsotakis, expressed the fear that 'the decision inaugurates a new international practice which can be dangerous for the freedom of the press'.

Kostis Stefanopoulos, president of the Greek Republic from 1995 to 2005, opposed it on the grounds that it is 'contrary to the laws of this country' and the same view was expressed by Leonidas Kyrkos, secretary general of the 'Greek Left'. The decision was also opposed by the president of the law society Fotis Kouvelis, who spoke of 'political egocentricity', the Greek national union of journalists, many top lawyers, trade unions or the writers society.

A similar view was expressed even by Yannis Hatjipateras, president of the Greek shipping co-operation committee, for whom the decision was 'unacceptable' and by Helen Vlachos, the publisher of *Kathimerini*, whom I knew from London and had also interviewed on the same story in Athens.

The Greek press went naturally much further in its comments: 'A shocking sentence' (*Apogevmatini*), 'Attack on the press' (*Ethnos*), 'The sentence is a shame' (*Vradini*), 'the freedom of the press is endangered' (*Kathimerini*), 'A colonial decision' (*Avghi*). *Eleftherotypia* itself told defiantly the British that 'only the royal navy could collect (the £450.000 damages), if it can manage it of course'.

But *Eleftherotypia*, equally bravely, refused to contribute towards the small amount of damages I had at the end to pay the plaintiff. Kitsos Tegopoulos, its publisher, told me it was none of his business.

– 'If I remember', he then said frivolously with a smile on his face which belied the uncompromising tone of her words, 'I'll make a contribution later on.'

– 'Make it, even if you don't remember', I mockingly responded.

– 'I make the jokes around here', he snorted back impatiently.

His dignified exit from trouble had turned into an exit from dignity.

My time with *Eleftherotypia* ended soon after. It happened when the agricultural attaché of the Greek Embassy in London, was arrested by Scotland Yard, for using the embassy's diplomatic bags for her commercial activities, i.e. to smuggle into the country tax free luxury items. For some reason, other issues came up, too.

I went to her trial only to re-acquaint myself with the mystique of the improbable. Her defence raised with the Greek witnesses, all top officials of the export department of the Agricultural Bank of Greece, issues of slush funds cash and mega scandals embroiling Greece's banking sector, the exports agencies and officials at the very top of the 'socialist' party.

The story, truly amazing, naturally made headlines and all the Athens newspapers instantly sent reporters to London to cover it, except that I could not myself stay on. My priorities had changed. I had to be in Skyros island.

That was the end of my career in journalism.

Working for the media was, as in anything else, both fulfilling and frustrating. What I primarily enjoyed was that it enabled me to maintain contact with Greece, talk to the Greeks and have a presence in the country in a way that I would not otherwise be able to owing to distance.

This important channel of communication was not, however, unrestricted, for if and when there were larger interests at stake, the publishers had the last word. Hence the occasional frustration. A source of satisfaction was also the immediate impact of words appearing in print in the next day's copy of the newspaper.

But, on the other hand, the day's news have as a rule a 24-hour lifespan. They are, therefore, destined to be instantly forgotten just like the deadened gazes of weary commuters on the tube. This sometimes makes you feel that the reason you write is to give the fish and chips industry the wrappers they need for take-aways.

But if the stories are forgotten, the experiences of the writer can be unforgettable.

I learnt about it early enough, in December 1966, when the SS Heraklion capsized and sank in the Aegean Sea, resulting in the death of 224 people. My editor sent me to Piraeus to get more information about this tragic event except that in my overflowing eagerness to transmit a picture as red hot as possible, I joined for two days a rescue boat looking for survivors in the rough winter waters with the seagulls flying hysterically over our heads.

We did not find any. But it was quite a peripeteia. More interesting than anything experienced on Facebook.

15

Arrogance or Naivety?

I
n spite of the attractions of my high-flying job, including
the inevitable delusions of grandeur resulting from meeting
some of the 'important' people of this world, despite also the
considerable freedom I had and used to challenge the corrosion of
ethical standards, I felt I had no option but to leave journalism for
good. I could not hang my hat on it.

The stories 'by our London correspondent' had been nothing
more than studious articles engraved on water in times of lost
content. At least that was how I felt.

But what also practically ended in the late eighties was my
relation with Greece. This was after the publication in Athens
of my fourth book, this time on the country's twentieth century
political history. The book, *Η Δημοκρατια του Μεσοπολεμου*
(The Inter-War Republic), was based on a long and painful
research in the historical archives of many countries and contained
a wealth of new, unknown information. But much more than that,
it offered a new and iconoclastic interpretation of events, based
on the assumption that we, rather than uncontrollable forces, are
the ingredients of the historical process. We, therefore, get what we
deserve, earn our fate.

Its basic thesis was that the Republic between the two wars
had failed because of the corruption, disintegration and paralysis

of the parliamentary institutions rather than the intrigues of outsiders.

Aeschylus had predicted it.

– Forget the law of righteousness, he had said, and the dark Furies will launch a counter-blow to crush your strength till the dim pit of oblivion swallows you.

But forgetting, assisted by expediency, is easy.

The collapse was inevitable given the total detachment of the parliamentarians from what people think life is. At the time of the Great Depression, in 1932, for example, the time that groups of starving people were storming bakeries to take bread to feed the families, all the Greek parliamentarians could focus on was nothing but the merits of the one or other electoral law.

The mid-war period was, undoubtedly, particularly dismal. It witnessed a rough, unprincipled, tawdry war between all those involved in the political process for the conquest or the holding of power. The military appropriated the power people had entrusted them with to reach as fast as possible the level of its inefficiency, and the political parties saw the country as their private property to be milked by all means available.

Violence was also used as the under-developed capitalist class strived to arrest the development of a working class movement.

People, totally marginalised, watched this soul-destroying performance with a feeling of impotence until the 1935 military dictatorship brought back the king, who, in turn, in 1936 imposed his own brutal dictatorship with Metaxas as its figurehead. So discredited, the political establishment either watched events in a state of paralysis or tried to benefit from them.

My conclusion was that democracy cannot function in a context moulded by the brutal, cruel, primitive struggle for power to the benefit of shamelessly self-seeking interests. It collapses when the party, whichever, identifies with the state, and its leaders with unashamed clientelism and patronage.

Responsible for the failure were, in this sense, all, republicans and monarchists, liberals and conservatives, military men and civilians. They all subjugated the requirements of the country and its people to their own sordid party and personal interests, and, pursuing them ferociously, destroyed the institutions.

The book was practically a flop – it was out of kilter with the times and did not fit in with anyone's perceptions of our history.

Its voice had not joined the Blame the Others chorus, i.e. it had failed to make us look as the miserable victims of British machinations and domestic miscalculations along the lines 'if the liberals had joined the communists to resist the coming dictatorship, things would have been different'.

Blaming, often generously, seems to be a most useful survival mechanism. It is what we do when dealing with our own blunders for which we are only too happy to transfer responsibility to the neighbour, the boss, the mayor, society, the wife, the traffic lights or whoever and whatever else we can think. I am even tempted to think that we need leaders only in order to have someone to blame at the end.

More than that, the book did not chime in with the mood of a country split politically between conflicting political 'philosophies' and still in awe of Papandreou, the prime minister, and Karamanlis, the President of the Greek Republic, the country's gurus.

As in the case of the Giant Rat of Sumatra, its readership was not prepared for it.

Apart from Karamanlis, who kindly let me know that, in his view, the book was an excellent piece of work, the work with one or two exemptions was not even reviewed in the press. Worse, it did not even pay for the cigarettes I had smoked writing it.

The turn things can take, I thought, is sometimes quite amazing. You take something very seriously and spend years building your tall pyramid only to end up with something that is as flat as a pizza. I wondered at that point why one, if not named Stephen King, should bother to write anything.

My attempt to initiate the process of self-examination so desperately needed had been returned unopened. It turned out to be a gift to the country as useful as a comb to a man bald as an egg. Hence the frustration generated, as Turkish novelist Orhan Pamuk wrote, by the inability to make one's voice heard, the failure to be understood, and the feeling of impotence.

The problem was not just the reception of the book, but the discontent this failure had generated.

Like Thales of Miletus, I felt I had fallen into a well, while looking searchingly up at the stars.

Arrogantly or naively, I had embarked on a journey and expected, whatever the adventitious difficulties, to arrive one day at my chosen destination. Yet, I felt, I was still at my departure point with my weather beaten suitcase, which contained all my hopes, on the station's lost property section. I imagined myself in the same section, too. And this could not be hidden by silence or vacant, premeditated smiles.

Confronting the system was not going to be simple, but living with the censorious and very disconcerting companion of futility, was anything but easy. Stuck like a fishbone in my throat, this frustration forced me to scan myself times and again to find out why I could not just accept the world as it is.

Self-doubt began devouring me again – perhaps, after all, it was all my fault, perhaps I was not good enough to make convincingly the case or perhaps I had been entertaining highly unrealistic expectations.

Alternatively, either my boat was too small for the sea it was sailing or the sea was too large for it.

Lonely in 'the enstarred vast ocean of the night', I invoked the spirit of Marcus Aurelius, the philosopher-Emperor, which, judiciously, told me that man is like a vine which produces grapes and expects nothing in return.

It sounded like pretty good, five-star advice. Stoicism seems to have the edge over other philosophies, particularly when the grapes of the vine remain unappreciated. Karl Jaspers could justifiably tell me from his grave, 'I told you so!' The man had warned the gullible that trying to be who you really are does not make you popular with the world and is in direct conflict with your own self-preservation impulse.

Scorched by the heat of my unworthiness, I never doubted, however, the good breeding of my assessments which insisted that we cannot build a future on excuses. We are responsible for what happens to us, earn our misfortunes.

I, therefore, could not play according to the rules of a pernicious and ruthless culture. Its cynicism was emotionally too distressing, ethically too unacceptable, intellectually too demeaning and aesthetically too vulgar.

Nor could I agree with the postmodernist supercilious and scornful attitude of nubile detachment. Indifference, no matter how sensible it might look to the caffè latte dilettante, was not going to be my 'strategy' for, at least, as long as the 'salt of youth' was still in me.

Whether this path was to reward me with anything was impertinent. What mattered more than anything else was to ensure I preserved my freedom and was at peace with myself. Having said the 'Great No', and this in capital letters, I could sleep again peacefully and enjoy my spaghetti carbonara Yanis Yanoulopoulos had shown me how to make the time we were sharing a house in London's Clapham Junction back in 1967.

My victory was in the 'No' itself, in managing to conquer myself, to choose myself against overwhelming social pressures, in the precious personal autonomy, the 'uniqueness' this *Gran Rifiuto* had awarded me.

Like all God's creatures, man exempted, I did not, I felt, need to prove anything to anyone – I could be myself. This was not, and it could not be, a commitment made to others, but to myself only.

But I was utterly disappointed, overwhelmed by the same feeling towards Greece as that entertained by the Phocaeans, who, rather than live under Persian rule, emigrated to foreign lands where they founded a new city, Marseilles.

On departure they dropped a large lump of iron in their harbour and swore they would return only when the iron floated like wood.

From then on and for the next ten years I did not write anything again in Greek. The lack of response makes the effort pointless – one cannot talk in a vacuum. Silence, the Tibetan monks hold, the kind of silence in which you can hear an insect moving across the ground, is the very voice of the Great Spirit. That sounds good as long as you believe they know something about it all.

If you do not, silence is as good for the removal of unsleeping, ever pacing thoughts as a course of aspirins for flat footedness. You end up, particularly when you try to stop smoking and the brain stops working, with unscripted soliloquised conversations, the time that even Jonathan Ross' show is better company than your own thoughts.

Perhaps, I did overreact – I am aware of it. Attached during the long years in exile to an ideal image of Greece, I had let my selective memory distil the past, and I had been drinking with inebriating results its succulent, intoxicating decoction.

Our nostalgia, says Seferis, the poet who had also nourished images of Greece under foreign skies, had created a non-existent country. But the Greece I expected to see, the country where 'one can pass so easily and serenely from reality to dream', simply was not there. Accident-prone, reality was different – a text with a thousand full stops but no point.

Entrapped in the web of my illusions, I could not, therefore, speak the same language as my compatriots.

Yet, as I realised at some point, my disenchantment with Greece was nothing more than a lover's quarrel.

My path in life had been carved, not by circumstances, but by the aspirations of the previous generations and the shared experiences and collective memories that had shaped my raw self. Greece, the home where my ancestors are buried, was and still is my spiritual home.

Home, really, is not a country. It is all the events and incidents, contemporary or otherwise, which have forged the identity of the individual, the emotional connection with the world in which all these events occurred, the certainties which this connection and the resulting sense of belonging generates.

Athens of my childhood is, of course, no longer there – it vanished many a summer ago. Yesterday was another country. Re-built from the late '50s onwards on columns of steel and cement on top of which the logos of the multinationals figure prominently, the city has left for good the days people were known by their nicknames.

The only building from the early days, which I thanked for its loyalty to the past, was the Panathinaikos football stadium.

The bakery in Daphnomelis Street, run by Mr Siapikas, whose divorce and re-marrying had scandalised the local community, is now part of a bakery empire, and the grocery of Mr Handrinos in Asclepius Street, has become a computer centre.

Mr Handrinos, incidentally, had managed to engrave involuntarily in my memory the agony of crossing the boundaries of life.

Taken to his death-bed when I was only ten years old, presumably to say good bye to the old man, I still remember his fast, rattling breathing, his soft moaning with little whistling breaths and wracking gasps and his sad effort to postpone the departure of life from his decaying body that once was that of a young, vigorous man.

Nikos, the imperturbable hump-backed shoe-repairer whom I used to visit regularly, had died long ago but nobody had taken up his trade. Nobody had taken either the place of Thanasis, our door-to-door milkman, who, perhaps, believing that his words were taxed, always used as few of them as possible, or of Elias, the ice-man, whose looks enabled women to pardon what we thought was a deficit in mental efficiency.

Apokavkon Road, the road I grew up, no longer has children roaring up and down, and its residents, who in the not too distant past saw involvement with their neighbours' family affairs as part of their own business, in apartment dwellings now, do not even know who the people across the short corridor of their floor are.

Nobody in the Charilaou Trikoupi bloc of flats where my parents had moved was aware of my mother's death in 1977. Sofia Roumbou, an actress and a friend, who lived opposite them, saw us assembling for the funeral outside my parents' flat, and, unaware of what was going on, greeted me like a reveller.

Had this happened in Apokavkon Road at a different time, when the interlinkage held us together, the entire neighbourhood would have been in our house to offer the family its support.

It is what tempts me sometimes to think that the better life is just behind us, over the last hill. But the temptation is, admittedly, resistible.

Though no longer in tune with the city I was born in, Athens is, however, still my home town, the place my heart belongs. There is as much of it in my blood as salt in the Aegean. And when I am there, the old world rushes back to me with unhurried dignity, and the very moment I see on the memory's screen the old smell, the odd image or the old adventure time is pushed to the background.

This is what, I suppose, gives me roots, a home and a sense of belonging. It defines me as much as its banks define the Nile. It is me.

And if we ever reach a point that, my heritage is swamped by another culture and my birthplace turns into an item in the world's archaeological museum, that 'me' will disappear.

Even at a time that no identification with anything is possible, it could not have really been otherwise. Hence I have never applied for British citizenship. Symbolic as it was, the gesture ensured that my identity was safely at home.

But Britain had also made inroads into my heart.

The English language itself had never thrilled me. It has, as Margaret Atwood put it, 'no music, it does not sing, it is always trying to sell you something'.

But the culture of the country, defined by the instincts of its people, exerted on me an allure that I found impossible, even if I wanted, to resist. What, as a foreigner, I saw in it was a fundamental decency in the way people interact with each other, a striking tolerance of differences and an innate commitment to fair play. None of these implies that Britain does not have its fair share of scoundrels and bigots and none of these erases the deep inequalities which torment the country. But this does not change the overall picture.

What also impressed me was the people's non-judgmental attitude, the non-interference in other people's personal choices, the spirit of self-depreciation. The unobtrusiveness of each one's behaviour, this live and let live approach, provides the space and protects the dignity people are entitled to.

This culture does also place more emphasis on individual responsibility and encourages accountability to the whole rather than to some higher authority. None of these things is, of course, enshrined in any legal, enforceable text, and none is easy to nail down – trying to define it, one said, is as easy as trying to paint the wind. Though undefinable, it is, however, easily recognisable, in the air, 'a different air', as George Orwell put it, that people breath on arrival in Britain. It is conjured up by numerous small

193

and different things that one experiences when coming from a different country.

Further, the power of the bureaucracy is somehow reduced in the UK by the intermediary institutions which occupy the ground between the citizen and the state.

The British themselves, unused to bending to the ukases of a bureaucratic, Kafkaesque, suffocating state, cannot treasure their institutions as much as they should.

But they should. Their state functionaries are not above the law and do not perceive themselves as the masters of the universe. The bureaucracy is neither a sadistic beast, like Tolstoy's Ivan Ilych whose power as assistant public prosecutor to ruin anybody he wished to ruin gave him pleasure and filled his life, nor a cheat to do them out of their rights. They do not trade the power with which they have been entrusted for the personal benefit of the bureaucrats themselves.

Not, of course, that the UK is free of scandals that see pillars of the establishment crumbling one by one. The financial crimes of the banks may be the most striking, but illegal insider trading flourishes in the City of London, seats in the House of Lords are often offered in return for favours to the ruling parties, 'cash for access' scandals involving prominent politicians erupt quite often, and members of the House of Commons have been often caught with their hands in the till. A number of them have even been jailed.

Fraud and price-fixing, as for example between the wholesale electricity business and retail gas supply, often make their presence felt, the lobbying industry which swarms across the government departments on behalf of corporations to influence their decisions flourishes, abuse of power by those in positions of authority and privilege do occur quite often; tabloids, resorting to interception of voicemail accounts, have broken the law or officers of the London Metropolitan police have been found guilty of bribery and other corrupt practices.

Further top businessmen, celebrities, doctors and political party donors have resorted to some of the most aggressive, albeit technically legal, tax avoidance schemes.

Yet, my sense is that, despite the publicity such scandals attract, standards in public life have been rising as have the expectations of the public. But even if I am wrong about it, one never expects to come across corrupt practices in everything daily life involves.

All the above were good enough in themselves to compensate me for the self-inflicted separation from my natural home. But, in addition, London offered me its libraries and research facilities, a stimulating environment and the kind of contact with the rest of the world which I could not really have in Greece.

My mind, in other words, has taken residence in the UK though my heart was and still is a resident of Greece. England is something like my wife but Greece is my mother.

Seferis, the poet, did not feel, I think, any different. Despite his long absence abroad, he was as passionate about Greece and its people, and this in an open-minded, non-chauvinistic way.

But probably there is something more to it all as part of the mixture is the psychology of the self-exile which had taken me beyond all known lands and corners of my thinking.

Talking about George Orwell and a significant number of other Western men, Raymond Williams, the Welsh Marxist, dwelled upon the concept of the 'exile', the individual deprived of a settled way of living and/or a faith.

The exile, he said, finds virtue in an assertion of independence which is part of a tradition that embodies many liberal values – empiricism, integrity and frankness.

Those qualities, though salutary, are, however, largely negative. The withering criticism of hypocrisy, complacency or self-deceit is usually brittle, and at times hysterical, and the tough rejection of compromise, which gives the tradition its virtue, goes hand in hand with the felt social impotence which prevents the 'exile' from believing in any social guarantee.

Given the pattern of his own living, almost all association becomes, thus, suspect – the exile fears it because he does not want to be compromised, but also because, and this is the psychological condition of the self-exile, no settled way of living whatsoever can in his eyes confirm socially man's individuality.

To the exile, society as such is totalitarian. He cannot commit himself and he is bound to stay out. Yet Orwell, deeply moved by social injustice, was convinced that only action by association, involving personal commitment, could change things. Hence his personal deadlock and the split between his committed and uncommitted parts. Hence also his belief, evident in Nineteen Eighty-Four, that dissent can come only from a rebel intellectual – the exile against the system – and the pessimistic assessment that the exile can never win.

I have often wondered how much of this I see in myself.

Choosing to be the outsider is certainly the result of my deep-rooted mistrust of institutions, ideologies and movements. But this mistrust has equally certainly been reinforced by fear – the fear of losing, if I were to get involved, my own self, my own identity. In the paradoxical situation I had found myself, I could not reconcile my need to be involved with people with the need to keep my distances from the compromises of life – and to me the two seemed to be almost mutually exclusive.

At any rate, success, as I decided soon after, could be pursued only within some well-defined ethical parameters. It made sense but only in a context regulated by purpose. And purpose could never be success itself. Although I do not demand a certificate of innocence before dealing with anyone, I could not, therefore, join what I did not believe in to further my career, to 'succeed'.

'Success', in the way it is conventionally perceived, was, thus, completely ruled out. Hence the paradox, what Umberto Eco called the desperate loneliness of parallel lines: the line of the dream and the line of my realities. Hence also the frustration that, holding me by the hand, took me unconsciously to a withdrawal into myself, my nostalgia and my revolt.

I shrunk just like a snail shrinks into its shell.

In the meantime, Greece, 'in spite of all the – so to speak – elephantism of gout – the enlargement of extremities', as poet Engonopoulos would have exclaimed once again, had since Papandreou's death in 1996 seemed to recover a sense of measure. Populist 'socialism' had given way to modernising 'socialism', i.e., the Blairite version of socialism with an 's' as strongly pronounced as in Flu. But not for long.

The conservatives who won power soon after succeeded only in accelerating Greece's march to the bitter end that gave it the vinegar faced looks.

Despite my mind-numbingly confusing thoughts, there was something in our world, however, I was pleased about and this was the collapse of the Soviet empire.

The unravelling began with the growth of the Solidarity movement in Poland in the early 80s and the attempts by Mikhail Gorbachev, the USSR president, to restructure his country. In December 1988, Gorbachev announced that the Soviet Union's European allies could leave the Warsaw Pact if they so wished and from then on a series of political changes swept across Central and Eastern Europe. Soviet authority unravelled fast.

The *imperium sine fine* had come to its end.

Free elections in Poland the following year ensured Solidarity's overwhelming victory that was followed in the same year by the fall of the Berlin Wall and in Czechoslovakia by the Velvet revolution. On Christmas day of that extraordinary year, Ceausescu, the tyrant of Romania, and his hideous wife were executed by firing squad. The communist regimes departed from Bulgaria and Hungary, too. The Warsaw Pact disappeared, as The *New York Times* put it, with a whimper rather than a bang. It ceased formally to exist on July 1st, 1991.

The new regimes that emerged embraced democracy but the authoritarianism, bureaucracy and the rampant corruption they inherited continued unabated. Whether communist, non-communist or anticommunist, corruption was in the blood of those countries. The economic reforms introduced played instantly into the hands of a new and powerful oligarchy in an orgy of stealing, asset stripping and embezzlement during the murky privatisations of state property.

– 'The fundamental sectors of our political, economic, cultural and moral life', Alexander Solzhenitsyn, the fierce critic of the Soviet era, said in 2000, 'were destroyed or looted'.

The state had just privatised virtue and nationalised vices.

But Boris Yeltsin, the Russian president, happy, when drunk to make a fool of himself, did not seem to mind it. That was the case even when, as a former Greek prime minister confided,

– 'The US President Bill Clinton and certain other officials had decided to get Yeltsin drunk in order to have a laugh.'

Being present in one such an occasion, he added:

– 'I felt, like many other guests, so embarrassed.'

Although I had never imagined that gangster capitalists would take over control of Russia and loot its assets, I had not, on the other hand, many doubts that things would go wrong. That was because in my many trips to East European countries in the 1960s and the 1970s I had always felt dismayed at the public's absence of commitment to basic values and the people's consumerist illusions which communism could neither ground nor meet.

Even someone close to Boris Yeltsin, the first president of the Russian Federation in the 1990s, whom I met in Sweden in 1980, could not detach himself from the consumerist fantasies which he demonstrated in an undignified manner which he did not seem to mind.

If some in Eastern Europe fought for democracy because communism had destroyed civil society, many more looked forward to a change because they thought it would give them the lifestyle of the rich and famous.

This was the feeling generated in all the East European countries I had visited, including Hungary, a country I experienced both in the 1970s and also in 1989, just before communism was dispatched to history.

In the latter, I had numerous discussions with senior Hungarian journalists and members of the public only to establish the illusions they entertained about capitalism and what democracy is all about. Their lack of understanding had always been hitting me in the face, for in my experience money is not rolling out on the streets of capitalism, as they all seemed to believe.

As astonished I was to see some of them, pillars of the communist orthodoxy like Andras Sugar, a top Hungarian journalist and a friend from Athens and later London, turning overnight, when the old regime collapsed, into hardline Thatcherites.

Delighted to see the departure of the East European regimes, which died with an unobtrusiveness that was totally out of character, I could not at the same time hide the melancholy generated by the utter failure of a unique experiment to improve the conditions of mankind. You can blame the failure on this or that.

But our own faults take always priority because we love them as much as Cleopatra loved men's lusting.

And, it seems, we just have to live with it. Perhaps, after all, if we were faultless, life might well be dull and dreary.

16

In the Land of Hope

A s Marcel Proust, the French novelist, suggested, the real voyage of discovery consists in seeing with new eyes. I did so in Skyros, the island favoured by a partial nature and a discriminating sky.

The island's magic is everywhere, in the sunlight which penetrates 'directly to the soul (and) opens the doors and windows of the heart', the odour of the freshly baked bread, the fleshy figs soaking in the early morning's dew, the moist brown eyes of the Greeks. It is in the youthful energy of the unfaltering eternity, the sculptured countryside caressed by the Graces, the olive trees with the wrinkles of generations and the rocks with the wisdom of all times.

I could even see there the sea-nymphs dancing naked in the diaphanous shroud of the golden sunset, and I could not help myself squeezing their beautiful breasts with my eyes.

The Skyros Centre was in the village under the orgulous and indomitable castle of King Lykomedes. Rebuilt by the Byzantine Greeks and reinforced by the Venetians, the castle graces the village and embodies the proud spirit of the locals.

It was in this castle that young Achilles had been hidden by his mother, Thetis, to escape his fate which had decreed that he would either gain glory in the war against Troy and die young or live long but unsung.

200

Not hot on heroics, Thetis had despatched the boy to Lykomedes, in whose palace he lived disguised as a girl. This did not prevent him, however, from fathering a boy, Neoptolemos, with the propitious cooperation of Lykomedes' daughter Deidameia.

But then Odysseus arrived on the island looking for him.

– 'Where's this young man', he was heard asking feverishly the king 'He has an appointment with fate.'

The king chose to remain as silent as the Apollo statue next to him, and Odysseus, losing patience, offered him some advice of an intimate nature. He then brought loudly to his attention the warning Menelaus, the king of Sparta, had given to all the Greeks.

– 'The Trojans', he said, 'have to be punished for their audacity. If not, nobody could henceforth be sure of his wife's safety'.

But neither the king nor the chambermaids, who, as expected, pretended to be busy, would come forward with the answer he was looking forward to.

Achilles himself, apparently, just like President Clinton, not eager to register for a military expedition in foreign and far-away parts, kept silent, too. This did not surprise Odysseus as he himself, in order to avoid going to war, had, when Agamemnon tried to enlist him, pretended he was mad.

When summoned to serve his country, he was flinging salt rather than barley over his shoulder, Homer tells us.

Eventually, Odysseus trapped Achilles into revealing himself. He laid a pile of gifts for the girls on the floor – Guerlain, Chanel and other perfumes, various Bulgari, Van Cleef and Tiffany jewellery, Gucci, Prada and Dolce & Gabbana steamer trunks and handbags plus a shield and a spear, and then, when he signalled, his men outside trumpet-blasted and ran to position.

– 'We're being attacked', they yelled, as if they were freaking out. 'Trojan special forces in sight.'

They then pretended they were engaged in battle against the intruders.

Achilles could not resist the call of fate. He stripped himself to the waist, seized the shield and spear and ran to battle.

Another early resident of Skyros was Theseus, the hero who killed the dreaded Minotaur and legendary king of Athens. Theseus had decided to retire to Skyros, where he had inherited an estate. King Lykomedes welcomed him with all the splendour due to his fame and lineage, but in the time-honoured tradition surviving to our day, he questioned the titles of the estate Theseus laid claim on. He regarded it as his own.

Yet, he did not say a word about it, and, kindly, took the aged hero out to show him its boundaries except that when they reached the top of a precipitous cliff, he helped him over to his death.

Later, he claimed this most unfortunate event was due to a tragic accident.

– 'Theseus', the king tweeted, 'had a glass too many.'

Full of ancient memories, the island is also very beautiful. I was taken by its primordial nature, wild and yet curvaceous and flowing, the pastel of its landscape, the scents of its mellow summer nights, the mellifluous breathing of the Aegean Sea in whose 'lustral waters Zeus himself once delighted'.

I loved the old village, too. Curved centuries back up on the hill for fear of pirates, it has narrow cobblestone streets paved with unhurried intimacy and wholesome humanness.

Its white cubic-style houses, testament of indestructible innocence of caught time, are shaded by grapevines playing voluptuously with the nuances of the glittering sunlight. In the square, the villagers, weathered by the lingering memories of the millenniums, still watch with amusement the visitors from their future and wonder in amazement what is in store for them.

I felt I had arrived at an integrated, unflappable world, at peace with itself, serene in its wisdom, ethereal as a Turner painting and yet as solid and nurturing as Mother Earth.

On a stone, a surviving vestige of what was once a Homerian wall, I had let my imagination glide back in time and acquaint itself with the shadows of posts long lost.

There, in front of me, were children of the prehistoric era playing games, Achilles, Odysseus, Nestor and Ajax, glorious Theseus telling King Lykomedes all about the dreadful Minotaur of Crete, and Athenian Kimon arguing ferociously with the surly and fierce Skyrians.

There, too, were Byzantine priests urging their flock to repent before God lost patience with their sinful lot, Venetian sailors and Algerian pirates carrying on their back flanks of wine and young women, Ottoman officials, obese, debauched and drowsy, and coltish kids Mussolini had sent to conquer the world.

And, then, Nicos Pavlis, our Skyros Centre neighbour, passes in front of me, on his donkey, with his goats and a friendly smile on his sun-hardened, lined face. 'Good morning', he says and offers me a bunch of red grapes as delectable as Aphrodite's nipples. I recall Democritus, the father of the theory of atomism:

– 'Enough', he said, 'is as good as a feast... True riches are found only in contentment.'

And, Oh God, I had more than enough. The odoriferous grapes, the convivial smile, the sensual delights of nature's breathtaking pastiche, the simplicity of life and the ancient breath of every stone had all engulfed me in a cloud of spiritual bliss. They had penetrated my soul and tuned me into the eternal rhythms of life.

Without even knowing it, I was on a spiritual journey. I listened to the whispering of the sea and I became that whispering, I absorbed the fragrance of the jasmine and I became the fragrance itself, I watched the eagles flying over the mountains and I became a proud high-flying bird circling the sky together with them.

I had extended myself spatially and diachronically, being what my eyes could embrace and what my psyche could trace in the fragmented memories of the mythical and more recent past. I felt part of it all, humbled in reverence, ennobled by the experience, mesmerised by, and grateful for, the beauty revealing itself in all its simplicity.

In this world, all I had to do was re-build my thinking and re-position myself vis-a-vis the unresolved issues of our time.

Obviously, I still had not learnt how to control my aspirations, particularly as Skyros at the very beginning was for me neither an arrival nor a departure point. For the Skyros Centre did not exactly reflect my own interests.

It flourished as a psychotherapy centre just as much of Vienna which in Freud's time had been taken over by the power of the unconscious.

But that had nothing to do with me.

Personal growth at that time meant the unleashing of primal screams, something I was not familiar with. Unacquainted with such therapeutic techniques, the neighbours, too, alarmed, wasted no time in reaching the conclusion that what had been established on their island was either a torture chamber, a mental home or a sadomasochistic clinic. And in their kindness, they often rushed in bravely to save the 'victims'.

– 'No! Don't worry – it's all play. A kind of theatre.'

– 'Oh good. When are you going to perform?'

At the end, there had to be an impromptu, if somewhat incongruous performance, in Brooke Square, high above the village, in front of three hundred breathless villagers and Costis Ftoulis, their befuddled and mystified mayor. Surprisingly, it turned out, however, to be something of an occasion made possible thanks to my grotesque optimism and the creativity of the group.

We did not become honorary citizens of Skyros, but the locals needed some time to recover.

That was the first ever Skyros cabaret, the predecessor to those which have rounded off virtually every session ever since.

The Centre had been named by the locals 'The English Villa', a term which had an automatically sinister connotation. In an English villa mysterious forces are at work and egregious things happen as a matter of course. By implication, some Australians ventured to suggest the place had thereby acquired a distinct touch of class. The French, evidently failing to appreciate this, shrugged their shoulders.

The place was also euphemistically called The Centre, 'Of what', an obviously untrustworthy member was once overheard asking.

Yet Skyros under the direction of Dina Glouberman, who had studied in the US under Herbert Marcuse and Abraham Maslow, turned into a resounding success story from day one. The venture – powerful human bonds, fantasy parties, romantic meals by the sea, extraordinary coincidences, apocalyptic dreams – captured the imagination and gave people an emotional home.

The people the Centre attracted were people who wanted to rethink their lives, discover their own truth and determine their future. As Joan Scales put it in *The Irish Times*:

– 'Our lives are "always on", but sometimes you want to just stop, get off the super-highway and breathe. You need to say "stop, I'm getting off' and have some "me time".

Skyros, the retreat that 'promotes the ethos of personal growth, creativity and self-discovery' was the place for her to do just that and burst the framework of her day to day reality.

And so it was for numerous other people who joined Skyros, individuals who, as John Torode described in *The Guardian*, were

– '...successfully holding down "good" jobs, lots of creative folk and characters from the caring professions alongside academics and the occasional business person. They had all achieved and now shared a fashionable unease about whether the game was worth the candle.'

Among the 'achievers' were at times bishops, members of parliament or top police officers, all looking for the key to a happy life lost in the corridors of their daily routines.

Writing in *Time Out*, Olivia Maxwell was more specific.

– 'Let me introduce the members of my group', she said. 'Elsa was a committed socialist living within a politically motivated community in Denmark, Thomas an engineer from Sweden, Martine a biology teacher from France. Sid was a doctor practising both orthodox and homeopathic medicine in London, Christe a medical assistant in Innsbruck, Hannes a psychiatrist from Zurich and Rosemary a language teacher in Basel.

– 'We all shared a common need – the need to grow, to confront ourselves deeply and honestly, find our inner selves and resources, uncover the games we play with ourselves and others, the different roles, unidentified fears, anger.

– 'But it wasn't all painful encounters with long-buried feelings. In the Disco on the Rocks we grappled with Greek dancing, ordered Marguaritas, were served Tequila Sunrises, and consumed copious quantities of ouzo. Later we'd pile back to the cave on the beach, light candles, banter, laugh, and drink more wine. That's the other side of the Skyros experience – the sheer, crazy, overwhelming joy of letting go and feeling alive. It's a time of change and a time for growth. A twilight time of self-recognition, of saying goodbye to tired games one has played our for the last time. It's not a reformation, but a transformation.'

What people were experiencing was nothing less than a minor miracle I could hardly believe I had witnessed myself and impossible to describe to friends and acquaintances back home in London.

A group of people who had never met before were able in a day or two to create a real, not contrived, atmosphere that exuded warmth, friendship, camaraderie and a feeling of unbridled joy and hilarity before moving together beyond all well-established social boundaries. Amazingly, most of them were going round the Middle Age Cape.

Still the people were greatly reassuring, the atmosphere enormously supportive, and the actual holiday aspect of it most rewarding.

Ann Shearer highlighted the benefits in a feature in *The Guardian*.

– 'For me', she said, 'there was not just the delight of the island but the chance to learn from the mirror others offered me and to try out bits of myself I'd forgotten were there.'

Fergus Lalor went further in an article in *The Irish Times*.

– 'I have to say', he wrote, 'that there is no other way to describe it than to admit that it changed my life.'

Excited to hear about Skyros from someone she knew, Maeve Binchy, the Irish novelist and playwright, advised likewise people again in *The Irish Times* to have a go fearlessly. I am sorry that, despite all my efforts, I never managed to bring her to Skyros. Ill-health had made it impossible.

Similar sentiments were expressed in January 1985 in the respected Dutch daily *de Volkskrant*.

The concept behind the Skyros Centre venture was to be traced to the ideas of people such as Carl Rogers, Abraham Maslow and Erich Fromm, leaders of the humanistic psychology movement that has its roots back in the 1960s.

Looking for the good life outside the parameters of the market economy, its technocratic culture and the various social and professional functions, they all anchored their approach on the full development of each one's potential. The problem, as they saw it, is the fragmentation of personal identity, the alienation of the individuals from their own nature and their transformation into abstract and functional units.

Self-actualisation, incomprehensible within the retail price index, requires, however, guts to be 'you', the 'real you' as opposed to a self conditioned by the requirements of socially determined patterns of behaviour. But who the 'real you' is?

To 'know thyself', as the Delphic maxims inscribed in the forecourt of the temple of Apollo at Delphi urge us, requires the disarming of the inner defensive mechanisms which block unconscious contact with one's 'real' self, even if that self is fragmented, and one's 'real' needs.

Hence the conflict with the self-preservation impulse and the inhibitions activated by tiresome routines.

It also requires an understanding of our world as a network of human relations rather than structures and systems, and a sense of oneness with an environment in which people find everything of value in and through each other.

The Skyros innovation was to take this concept for the first time into a community context, and this in the serene environment of Skyros island where people could, like Odysseus, when he woke up on the Phaiacian shore, rise up, look around and see who they are. They could unwind, take a good, deep and honest look at their lives, explore pain, fears, inhibitions and habits that are getting in the way of a more fulfilling life, understand, accept and respect themselves for what they are and relate to other people more openly, deeply and effectively.

All this was for me a novel and vertiginous experience which nevertheless won gradually my full respect.

Some of the courses offered for the purpose focused on particular life themes or skills while others were open-ended and deep explorations of a variety of themes. They were all experiential and not formally taught.

The course facilitators used a variety of personal growth approaches, including psychodrama, gestalt, massage and body-work, encounter, bioenergetics, art therapy and visualisation. The labels attached to these techniques were relatively unimportant as what mattered was the effectiveness of the help people received to get in touch with their deepest selves, project their genuine feelings instead of their imitations, and bring their subliminal energy into harmony with their conscious awareness and choices.

The dominant feeling in the groups, Bernard Burgone wrote in *Self and Society*, was

– 'Trust, hard work without silly, false reassurances or cosy agreements, and a steady, firm commitment to reach the parts of the self that have for far too long been shut away.'

The result was truly miraculous.

– 'It worked on every level', Gail Tresidder, the *Fitness* magazine publisher, wrote long after the experience had left a scent that was still lingering on the fingertips of her memory.

The people who would dismiss such claims as shenanigans or give me odd, subvocalized looks were anything but missing.

– But when 'I went there', Deborah Hutton, one of them, wrote in *Vogue* magazine, 'surrounded by people I came to know better in seven days than many I had known for seven years, I was forced to swallow my cynicism. It worked. Very well. I felt great. Alive and inspired.'

To do that, several had to come face to face with their pain caused by problems that shadowed their lives: career or relationship problems, issues of health and sexuality, difficulties within the family, financial pressures or a range of bewildering choices that in today's world go far beyond those of the previous generations.

Or with problems, as Saki, the witty and mischievous Scottish writer, might say, related to men who probably knew exactly what to do if they found a rogue elephant on a lady's croquet-lawn but were just hopeless with women.

I discovered the pain behind the mask and touched its textured face in the very early stages of the Skyros Centre's life. It was when a guest, an established journalist whom I see often on television, had joined Dina's course in order to file later a story for his London daily newspaper.

– 'I am here only to observe', he said with the hapless expression of a spokesman for the emotionally deserted street of his middle age, 'as I have no problems whatsoever'.

His uncertainty seemed, however, only the cover of a deeper uncertainty which became evident two hours later. It was then when he burst into tears, which he was mopping with a handkerchief the size of a small tablecloth, and started walking around with a pair of dark glasses to hide his anguish. Dina took him off the course as, she said, he was not ready to deal with the issues that came up.

He accepted it without protest and then surrendered himself to the pleasant lassitude of the afternoon idleness.

The issues that in this context do come up are sometimes quite dramatic. A German doctor, for example, could not practice his trade because he did not want in the process to inflict pain to his patients.

–'We, Germans', he said, 'have caused so much pain in the world that I don't want to add to it, even if it's for healing purposes'.

Other people had to deal with broken marriages, family splits, low self-esteem and feelings of social inadequacy, excessive burdens of family responsibility, loneliness combined with an inability to sustain new relationships, emotional vacuums, failed plans and expectations, sexual abuse during childhood or feelings of being stuck in a world in which they did not feel they belonged.

A woman even complained, while drying her hair in the sunlight, that she felt neglected because her husband never hit her back. Another one started to talk about her sexually wretched

210

married life though, as parsimonious with clarifications as she was with cash the day before, she failed to elaborate – in public.

Others would frequently raise issues relating to a work-life balance, questioning their commitment to a career that deprived them of all else life can offer. What they all wanted was the opportunity to stand back, review their lives, seek new ideas and insights and get all the support they needed to change course.

The funny side to it all, often hilarious, was anything but missing. It highlighted the absurdity of the human condition or the peculiarity of the means used by the Skyros Centre in dealing with life's puzzles. Absurdity often is part of our reality.

The Skyros Centre was taking itself seriously, but not too seriously.

But, as importantly, people were able there to amuse themselves rather than go places to be amused. That in itself was an achievement as in our days people have lost the ability to entertain themselves without help often offered from the cyberspace.

17

Like a Sunflower

Yet, despite the phenomenal success of the new venture and my respect for its work, my connection with the Skyros Centre remained somehow peripheral. My slice of bread looked as if it was buttered the wrong way. Unfamiliar initially with its concepts, I could not get involved with the self-realisation process.

But, as time went on, new ideas emerged.

I felt that the boundaries between the personal and the impersonal had to be redrawn. Psychology had to develop its political and social side to express the rebellion against the culture that stifles the individuality it itself is trying to restore. But this is what psychology avoids like a headwaiter avoids the eyes of the customers.

Hence, as the postmodernists pointed out, the evanishment of the individual as a reflective, responsible and creative agent.

The 'all-sided' individual, whom Marx referred to as 'integral' because his or her capabilities had been fully developed, could never be anything but a fugitive, if the system did not stop producing individuals with an exchange value in the marketplace.

The unacknowledged mission of the school, André Gorz, the Austrian social philosopher and a theorist of the New Left in the

1960s and the 1970s, said later, is not to prepare all-rounded individuals, but provide industry, commerce, the established professions and the state with workers, consumers, patients and clients willing to accept the roles assigned to them.

The challenge for me was the creation of a world which would confront and defy the prevalent set of ideas and affirm the power of each human being against a hostile environment. What I needed was to turn abstractions, the infinitude of the ideas several of which had been dormant for ages, and also dreams, those woven in Skyros' exuberant light, into something I could touch with my fingers.

But there was no model on which to build upon. The dream with all the élan and elegance of large gestures, captured, had to be re-dreamt.

To this I am, somehow, indebted to Prince Charles, who in 1982, a couple of years before Atsitsa raised the flag of holism, gave a speech in which he criticised modern medicine. By concentrating on smaller and smaller fragments of the body, medicine, he said, has lost sight of the patient as a whole human being.

I can still recall vividly my instant reaction to it – fascination.

The rest of Charles' speech did not enamour me – Paracelsus, the sixteenth century alchemist whom the Prince quoted extensively in support of his point is not my cup of tea.

But Charles' lecture reminded me of Hippocrates, the father of medicine, who would not treat a symptom without a full examination of the patient's whole condition which included even the political system of the city-state. This was not, however, just Hippocrates. The entire Greek culture was based on the same holistic premises, which I proceeded to explore anew. The exercise was rewarding. It highlighted what had taken residence in obscurity's back alleys.

The holistic concept unfolded was one in which unity enhanced diversity, purpose underpinned freedom, and wholeness

213

strengthened individuality. The whole of the Greeks was more than the sum of its parts.

But conceptually speaking, we had to start from scratch as at the time, there was nothing to guide us, no precedent from which we could at least draw inspiration. The concept of holism had not moved as yet outside the premises of alternative medicine.

St Benedict's communes created in the chaos that followed the collapse of the Roman Empire were not really appropriate for our purposes, and the hippy communes seemed to offer a disincentive rather than encouragement. But, although we did not know what the structures would be, we knew that it would be a community based on principles, commitment and integrity.

Simplicity, openness and trust, honesty, acceptance and self-acceptance, non-competitiveness and mutual support, loving concern for each member of the community and respect for our differences were to be the beating heart of the new venture which was, moreover, designed to accommodate different schools of thought, ensure pluralism in action, and rely on principles rather than rules or dogmas.

The whole approach was rooted in the balanced integration of body, mind, spirit and the attainment of areté. The 'lean, boyish body' of the latter, caught by poet Odysseus Elytis' eyes of the soul, was the image of physical, moral and intellectual excellence, all considered to be indivisible.

For the Greeks, the source of our inspiration, this was not the theory, but the everyday practice. The gymnasiums, where health and fitness were cultivated, were also centres for cultural activities and mental exercises. Alongside the athletic contests, the programme of the Olympic Games included music competitions, prayers and rituals, communal singing, orations by distinguished philosophers and recitals by poets and historians.

Illness, like health, was likewise viewed holistically – Hippocrates, the father of medicine, always treated a problem within the context of the natural balance of the organism.

Balance, proportion and symmetry in all of life meant that the Greeks valued no extremes of any kind, whether in the form of food fads or of religious excesses. A pure worshipper of the virgin hunt goddess Artemis, Euripides said, is as a tragic misfit. The whole person should also honour the love goddess Aphrodite.

Holism also implied that the life of the individual was inseparable from the life of one's community, the polis. Self-rule was the norm and an Athenian citizen participated in all aspects of government activity. The polis, in return, was expected, not simply to run its business efficiently, but in doing so to stimulate the intellect and satisfy the spiritual aspirations of its citizens.

The concept, I must say, developed gradually and often at the beginning, in 1984, I felt cornered by people asking me questions I could not answer as I wished. But the basics were in place. So was the place to try these ideas: the stunningly beautiful pine-forested Atsitsa Bay, the land, as Nietzsche would say, beyond all known lands and corners of the ideal.

The location is, indeed, spectacular and the allure of the bay bewitching.

The breath of the forest cuddles the bay tenderly, the sea, though as old as time, has a face as smooth as a baby's, and peace with a book, one of those without footnotes, on her side, rests asleep on serenity's commodious bed.

The elements in the winter remain, of course, stubbornly intransigent. Though the world has moved ahead since the old times, when to dance used to take two, nature has evidently not.

Atsitsa, endearingly simple, was launched in 1984 in a way which in retrospect looks rather hilarious. Our brochure – an A3 sheet of paper – went out heavily tinted in my bizarre sense of humour. The contentious introductory paragraph read:

– 'President Reagan has let it be known that he does not intend to join Atsitsa, the holistic health and fitness centre on the lovely Greek island of Skyros. White House officials revealed last night that its summer holiday programme, which aims at revitalising the body, the mind and the spirit, is not exactly to his taste. "It does not include war games which the President loves to play", a close aide said.'

Two months later we had to reprint it without any mention of President Reagan. We were forced to do so not by fans of the Star Wars project, so dear to the heart of that engagingly inept man the Americans had put in charge of their government, but by well-meaning people annoyed at our having 'invited' the President to join us in Atsitsa.

The initial public relations fiasco did not prevent the successful launch of the operation. This despite the immense physical difficulties the venture had to deal with.

Access to the building through a treacherous roadway was a hazardous affair, and all the things taken for granted in cities, i.e., mains electricity, running water, telephones or a sewage system, were all things of the dim and distant future. Some of them still are. The outside toilets had in the first year no doors, the showers no curtains, and rumour had it that the first guests built their own huts.

Guests who came looking for tennis courts did, of course, complain. But usually, though not always, everything was taken in the best of spirits.

One of the times it was not was when a photo was published in our brochure showed a young couple kissing. The couple, two very attractive young Americans, had just been married and had come to Skyros for their honeymoon. A few women objected to it and wrote to us accordingly.

Their opposition had developed on the grounds that we promoted heterosexuality.

It was the time that, as Fay Weldon humorously put it, following another cultural innovation, women now minded being hit by men and the powerful radical feminist movement was making headlines in the UK.

Emily Hynes at the office greeted their letter of complaint with a gay tinkling laugh.

Atsitsa was the Wild West of Skyros, and the guests felt like pioneers. In addition, self-discovery, creativity, camaraderie, craziness and often an outrageous sense of humour all contributed to an unforgettable experience that hardship could only enhance.

Blending facts – naked midnight swims or summer solstice toga parties – with fantasies, in which there were beds sleeping thirty, created, meanwhile, another focus for local modern mythology.

The old Skyros village, visited once a week, provided often events that could match the best comedy scripts. Once a group with Nell Dunn, the novelist, among its members, looking for a place to have dinner, sat around a table where they were politely offered water, but no menu. Quite irritated, they started to moan but communication was impossible – the 'restauranteur' spoke no English.

The story ended when they discovered that rather than a restaurant they were sitting in the front garden of a private house.

– 'I still cannot pass that house', said one of them, Michael Eales, 'without giggling'.

The courses offered in Atsitsa covered a wide range of activities from swimming, running, windsurfing and rock climbing to art, creative writing, music, theatre and movement, dance, mime and clowning, yoga, massage and naturopathic first aid, stress management, creative visualisation, dream interpretation, life choices and much more including talks on social and cultural issues and also politics.

The sheer scale and variety of what is on offer, someone wrote later, is 'an embarrassment of riches and a wealth of talent'.

Of all these what drew me in particular was clowning. Actually, I performed as a clown a few times in front of one hundred people, but what sticks in my memory is an elaborately prepared impromptu performance during a rehearsal. I finished it, smiled proudly to the other course participants and was ready to withdraw to my corner except that the course facilitator, a young beautiful Canadian with a smile as seductive as sin's, had other ideas. She would not let me off the hook.

– 'Carry on', she urged me. 'You're doing very well.'

– 'Sorry', I said apologetically, 'but I've got to go to town to give a talk on the health benefits of humour.'

She acknowledged my facetious evasion with a smile, but she left me with no choice but improvise as I was supposed to do in the first place, this time, however, overwhelmed by panic. Still, I survived it all having also learnt something about controlling the fear unexpectedness breeds when on show.

What I never tried was the various massages on offer. In one instance, in particular, more vivid than anything else, I was invited to be massaged by a young, beautiful French lady in whose presence even the cicadas, breathless, would often stop singing. Still I refused. I did not want to deliver myself to the arms of pleasure if somebody else had to pay the price for it in terms of the work necessary for the purpose. I did not want any favours. I would not want it even if I paid for it either.

When pleasure is associated with such body intimacy, it ceases to be something I would want to buy.

I am aware, of course, that normal people are expected to react differently.

Building dry stone walls in Atsitsa, which I loved and in which I became an expert, was by comparison an undiluted pleasure. What I had learnt I took with me to the Isle of Wight where, years later, I built a 25 metres -long garden staircase which I still eye with pride.

The Skyros approach was for the holiday world quite revolutionary.

Atsitsa, as the Skyros Centre earlier, had for the first time placed the holidays concept within a lively community context, they had and again for the first time introduced courses as part of the holiday experience, and they had again for the first time grounded the holistic approach to life down to earth as opposed to the metaphysical, New Age clouds. In many ways all this was ahead of its times.

– 'The fly and flop holiday is so passé', Kate Birch wrote in *Aquarius*, a UAE magazine in 2012. 'These days smart women are taking eduvacations, where learning, not lounging, is the name of the game'.

She mentioned, of course, Skyros as the epitome of this approach, as Skyros had been already in this 'game' since 1979.

The reception of the concept was stunning. *Elle* magazine described Atsitsa as 'magically successful thanks to its unique alchemy of people, settings and ideals', Matthew Collins in the BBC Travel Show portrayed it as an 'amazing place' and the Athens News Agency extolled its human values, 'the values our society should consider all-important but seldom does'.

Comments from participants, Hetty Einzig wrote in *Time Out*, 'run into superlatives – liberation, rejuvenation, bliss in massive doses. The memory of that fortnight', she said, 'sends ripples through our notions of real life'.

– 'Civilisation', Anne-Marie Conway said similarly in *The Times Educational Supplement*, 'will never look quite the same'.

Tony Crisp in *Yoga Today* was grateful for his Atsitsa experience that took him and others 'beyond boundaries' and similar comments appeared in features in many other publications including *The Observer*, the Spanish daily *El Pais*, the Swedish daily *Aftonbladet* or the German *Süddeutsche Zeitung*.

Thrilled with the experience, Jane Salvage, editor-in-chief of *Nursing Times* and advisor to the prime minister on the future of nursing in England, went years later, in 2011, as far as to write a book called Skyros, Island of Dreams. Skyros, she said in it,

– 'Has given me many gifts: opportunities to try out new things or things I have previously found difficult, and to face challenges or follow submerged desires. I have found powerful tools for my inner journey, new friendships and a renewed awareness of all life's dimensions, with a commitment to live it to the full.'

As time progressed, I was, meanwhile, able to develop further my understanding of holism as understood by the Greeks. It rested fundamentally on a sense of fairness in the way we deal with everything including our own selves, i.e. honouring all our constituent parts – mind, body and spirit. The 'just man' who has bound these elements into a disciplined and harmonious whole, Plato said, will be ready to lead an emotionally, intellectually, physically, aesthetically and morally rewarding life. For the Greeks, this meant excellence in all fields.

Hence in their vocabulary physical, moral and intellectual excellence were all described by the single word areté. The goal was balance, proportion and symmetry, a life 'beautiful and honourable'. The concept is aesthetic, yet it required not only the beauty of the form, but also the beauty of the noble soul.

Holism in this sense has, however, disappeared into the mists of history with lingering regret. Christianity abandoned life on earth, and together with it the Greek holistic thinking for the pleasures of the afterlife guaranteed by the purity of the soul.

The mind was dismissed, Reason was rejected, the body was denied and morality was identified with the denial of the flesh.

Capitalism, a system which has never fought, and never will fight, for heaven, subsequently rediscovered 'Reason' but as a weapon in its battle to turn everything into a means to an end which has always been associated with profit. In its Cartesian world, the only important part of ourselves is the mind – the rest, i.e. the body and the soul, are burdens we have no choice but to carry.

The concept of holism re-surfaced later on but without the moral and ethical values with which the Greeks had underpinned it. The Romantics attached it to a totalitarian philosophy at the service of what Jean-Jacques Rousseau called the 'general will', and the New Age, like the Gnostics in the past, aloof to the traffic of this world, saw it again in metaphysical terms.

Distorted, misinterpreted or abused, holism has been deprived of its essence, detached from its ethical basis and rendered as meaningless as the remarks uttered by the spirits of the dead when we summon them to our presence. This is so even when lip service is paid to holism, when for example the fight against terrorism is linked to a new and fair world which looks only like the negative of a dream.

Indeed, holism means nothing to the free market which is not interested in Justice but in wealth, has not set as its aim the happiness of the individual, for what matters is only his or her efficiency as a worker, and cares not about the well-being of the community, but its spending power.

The Greek holistic thought welded together Reason and morality, intellect and feeling, body and spirit, inner and outer, culture and nature, science and intuition, individuality and public realm. As parts of the whole, whether the whole was the planet, civilisation or the individual, they all had an intrinsic value, a purpose determined by their existence, and an inalienable right to be.

What, as a result of all this, was becoming clear in my thinking was that, whatever the political institutions and economic structures, what matters in our world is justice because in justice is summed up the whole of virtue, the image of everything of value.

I got attached to this ethical understanding of holism, which shaped my political convictions, like a sunflower to the sun.

18

Turbo-capitalist Times

The new era Margaret Thatcher and Ronald Reagan had launched was now in full swing and finance-driven globalisation had turned into a celebrity.

Market optimism reached its heyday later under the guidance of the two knights of progress, Bill Clinton, the US president, and Tony Blair, the British prime minister. Both had fully endorsed the reforms pushed through by their predecessors.

Almost all high-income countries and many emerging economies abandoned exchange controls, mass consumer markets appeared all over the globe and the selling of national assets, deliberately undervalued to give shareholders a first day profit, continued unabated. Technology and capital were expected to turn the earth into one giant marketplace, something like an airport, which, the neoliberals held, would dispatch earthbound governments and states to history for good.

As much as our personal lives, distinctly in favour of the 'improved' as opposed to the original, the world seemed to be rapidly improving with age.

As confident as Francis Fukuyama, the American political scientist, who proclaimed the end of history, communitarian Geoff Mulgan, director of the think-tank Demos, assured us, too, that we were 'on the brink of a real society'. The free market theorists assumed permanent economic prosperity.

Likewise, the New Age champions, those who, responding to adverts from beyond the grave, had already taken a reincarnation insurance policy, predicted the dawning of 'a millennium of love and light'. The new world order could, obviously, defy gravity and logic.

Still whatever happened afterwards, the Thatcher reforms were never reversed.

– 'You can't reverse the flow of the river', someone with switched-on looks told me before giving me a meaningful wink.

I did not know he could wink. The subsequent long silence during which you could have comfortably counted up to ten allowed him to carry on enjoying his steak-and-kidney pie uninterruptedly and peacefully. Talking after that about Octopussy, the John Glenn film with Roger Moore, was greeted like an omen of deliverance.

The big time for the corporations as the world's dominant power had arrived as had the Latin America drug cartels, the Sicilian and American Mafias, the Russian Mafiyas, the Chinese Triads, the Japanese Yakuzas, the Turkish/Albanian heroin cartels, the Nigerian crime lords and a myriad of local gangs which have penetrated the political institutions and the business world in so many countries.

Whatever went wrong with the 'New Economy' was due only to 'excesses', which, given time, the regulators would curb.

Apparently, a financial system that was flawed from top to bottom, the reckless management of its business or the 'gangster capitalism' introduced by the oligarchs of the former Soviet Union were not even worth mentioning. As unimportant seemed, too, the tax havens, this 'cancer' on the global financial system, that enabled multinationals such as Apple, Google, Amazon, IKEA or Starbucks to embark, supported by the governments, on trillions of dollars worth of tax evasion schemes.

The system was, however, anything but stable.

It was hit by the Black Monday crash of 1987 that led to massive stock market losses and in some instances the loss of hair. And it was re-hit by instability and turbulence at the beginning of the 1990s which this time led to a grinding recession. The financial markets, at the mercy of George Soros and his fellow speculators, were both savage and unpredictable. Britain discovered this in 1992, when the government was forced to withdraw the pound sterling from the European Exchange Rate Mechanism and devalue it at a great loss.

The crisis and the following 1994 sharp and unexpected rise in interest rates that wrecked the value of bond portfolios were politically a turning point. They ensured the massive defeat of the conservatives and the meteoric rise to power of Tony Blair, the Labour leader whose crisply-articulated sentences had convinced the electorate to give him a stagey chance to put his talents on full display.

This was followed by a long period of strong growth on the back of a surge of investment in the Dot-Com bubble. Inflation and unemployment went down to their lowest level for almost twenty years and ordinary investors benefited from the booming stock markets.

Still it was all an illusion.

The 'value' the corporations created was basically the product of downsizing, outsourcing, restructuring, financial engineering involving share-buybacks and mergers and excesses and abuses particularly of the internet start-ups. This, someone said, was not capitalism, but 'turbo-capitalism' that politicians from both parties in the UK and the US did not want to touch as they were in hock to corporate funding.

I wrote repeatedly about it all in *i-to-i*, the magazine I launched in London in 1989. My articles turned me into a household name in Prince of Wales Road where the magazine was based, but my words, 'oracular words, arched and summital words', as poet Andreas Empiricos might have said, were lost in the city's heavy words-traffic.

The euphoria of the moment had sent the brain on a long holiday in places inaccessible by reason. Whatever the setbacks, the markets had the power to make people believe in a future holding promises of lifetime benefits – sweet contracts, soft loans, early pensions and all the rest that appear in the book of capital accumulation. Many who believed that the welfare state, pensions and the National Health Service were bound one day to collapse, invested their hopes in private pensions, endowment policies and private health cover.

All this created for the moment the comfortable feeling of wealth which stimulated both rising consumer demand and also the pursuit of higher wages.

Anxieties were pushed aside. The market, its gurus almost religiously believed and explained with the help of flip charts, would take care of everything. Herein lies the ideological impetus for the third way advanced by Tony Blair.

Ideologically cajoled and politically coerced to gamble in capitalism's largest casino, people started following the stock market's movements as they did the sport results. Talking about the Dow and Nasdaq at barbecues and dinner parties turned, culturally, into a de rigeur activity.

In this they were inspired by the new technologies which enabled their hungry eyes to feast on flashing numbers flickering across their computer or mobile phone.

Pure greed, 'the seed of apocalypse', had taken over.

Nothing new about it, of course as we had seen the greed's hideous face earlier, in the Thatcher years. But my distaste for it, expressed in *i-to-i* with a youthful passion I had thought had taken early retirement, remained undiminished.

What in particular annoyed me was the absence of responsibility towards our community, the environment, the

225

future, even our own selves. People would not do anything before working out 'what's in it for me'. The concept of obligations in a moral and ethical sense, a dusky obscurity, seemed to have sunk to depths from which it could not be recovered.

'Our culture', I wrote in April 1995 in *i-to-i* magazine is built on 'individualism, our impacable, deadly enemy'. The principles were there, but expediency had taken the upper hand.

– 'Yes', I wrote, 'we want pollution-free cities, but we will not give up our car. Yes, we want better public services, but we will not pay more taxes. Yes, we want a caring society, but we will not give an hour of our time for the purpose. We will not even make a personal contribution to what we are ostensibly committed'.

– 'We may join a pressure group', I carried on, 'and we are happy to offer advice liberally but without any cost to ourselves. We campaign for the Mediterranean dolphins or the African elephants and let the Mediterranean fishermen or the African farmers bear the cost of our convictions. We campaign for the whales or the Brazilian rainforests and hope someone else will pay the bill of our environmental awareness. We crusade to prevent cruelty to animals. But, again, preventing cruelty to animals does not cost us anything.'

And, of course, we are all hooked to rights – the right to education, leisure, health care, rights at work, consumer rights, women's rights etc.:

– 'In the age of rights, anything we want is translated into a "right" which the institutions or society has a moral obligation to meet. Relations are no longer founded on reciprocity and voluntarism, but on law and judicial obligations. Even the care of our elderly parents, which was an honourable obligation a little while ago, has now become an individual "right" to be satisfied by the State.'

The only obligation we are willing to discharge is the obligation to pay for what we get.

– 'All this provides for a sad reflection on the decline of the civil society as we now behave primarily as a consumer, a customer, a client who is legally entitled to a series of services, facilities and forms of assistance.'

This was also a point made by Robert Reich, the former US secretary of labour under Bill Clinton, too, in January 2012. The crisis, he said, marks at a deeper level the triumph of consumers and investors over workers and citizens. As consumers and investors we have never been so empowered, but as workers and citizens we have seen our power to be heard declining.

Individualism, I persisted, is also the curse of democracy – socialism, as a matter of fact, emerged as a movement against individualism, not capitalism. Democracy cannot remain a democracy if what we value is power, possessions and the freedom to be as greedy as we like. It will not make it, and perhaps it has already had its day.

The world is now run by multinational corporations and transnational institutions and by technological, bureaucratic, financial and military élites. Well-paid fleets of lobbyists employed by large companies and generous electoral campaign contributions make sure that political parties, just like some wives, who, I heard, are paid by their husbands to adopt unusual sexual positions, are happy to play the game they do not control.

Like Frankestein, the system we, the humans, created tells us now:

– 'You are my creator, but I am your master. Obey!'

The new chichi culture that emerged was epitomised by the labour-intensive café lattes and caramel frappuccino, sleek cellphones, Feng Shui energy maps, wine climate cabinets, an abundance of fashionable peasant embroidery that a real peasant would never be expected to wear, and rejuvenation at prohibitively expensive day-spas.

Total dedication to one's own needs and self-absorption often went hand-in-hand with an 'enlightened' attitude involving an interest in Tibet, rainforests, endangered species or anything else as remote as possible from our daily realities. The Age of Aquarius which, as Marilyn Ferguson, author of the influential The Aquarian Conspiracy, stated, would bring 'a millennium of love and light' had just arrived – and as it happened, at the very moment the free market economy had triumphed.

But this, I was assured by an Arimathean priestess on the north side of fifty, was just a coincidence.

Fashionable since the mid-eighties, the New Age's 'positive' thinking, designed to 'accentuate the positive' in life, involved affirmations of the kind 'I am absolutely my own favourite person'. This became the distilled wisdom in the 'dying Age of Pisces', the time humanity was moving into the 'enlightened Age of Aquarius'.

All anxiety was from now on to be abolished.

Spiritual managers had managed in no time to turn spirituality into a capitalist commodity, expensively purchased by, and for the use of the well-off children of the money-spinning 'New Economy' and Tony Blair's 'Third Way'.

Alternative Eddie, the fictional character of Gerry Thompson, the *i-to-i* humorist, was one of them.

– 'I returned home', Gerry wrote on his behalf, 'to find a message from my ethical investment broker in New York. He had switched my assets to a really hot new item – a new product called the "Urban Shaman Kit". He reckons it's set to take the USA market by storm. The key element is a spiritually-oriented piece of electronic wizardry called the Zion organiser. It's pre-programmed with all major moon phases, earth festivals and planetary alignments. I hope this investment works out better than the others. Otherwise I might even have to get a job.'

I hope he never did, if jobs are not for the 'enlightened' minority.

They could damage fingers velvety smooth with doing nothing and doing it very well.

Others, obviously less sophisticated members of the new cultural and corporate hegemony of the new cosmopolitan, computer-savvy society, went for different fads, symbols of the new age: the Wonderbra or Jennifer Aniston's hairstyle.

Capitalism, globalised, had standardised everything, including our taste.

What we are witnessing, I wrote again in *i-to-i* magazine, is submission to the commands of the image makers, replacement of our real needs by those dictated by the market, a soul-disfiguring consumerism and the commodification of our existence. All this while we are faced with the compartmentalisation and sullen loneliness of a hectic life, the total alienation from our community, the powerlessnes which has transformed us all into pathetic spectators of life as shown on TV.

Deprived of oxygen, the spaciousness we live in is suffocating.

The new era had also signalled the end of politics. Many people, I wrote in the January 1993 issue of *i-to-i* magazine, felt a pervasive disillusionment with the political system, seen as largely corrupt and self-serving. Damaged goods.

– 'In spite of the last decade's rhetoric about rolling back the frontiers of the state, governing has become more centralised and power is rapidly concentrating into fewer hands. The institutions able to counterbalance the power of the state have lost their influence, the importance of parliament has decreased, and authority is less accountable.

Conviction, guts and vision are conspicuously absent.

– 'Today's politicians, leaders with the air of people about to be forgotten, seem to be made of standardised bureaucratic and managerial material, primarily motivated by self-interest. They reflect the dispirited world we live in, and do nothing except help to perpetuate it.'

The birds, apparently, had forgotten how to fly.

The end of politics in these rudderless and rather mean times was accompanied by the very erosion of the whole political process' dignity.

As I wrote again in January 1995:

– 'We have perhaps reached, as the postmodernists claim, the end of history, the end of politics, even the end of the individual as an autonomous, self-conscious agent.'

Still the emerging new culture had a feature that neither Thatcher nor Reagan had either anticipated, wished or just remembered to put on its website. In its ruthlessness, capitalism had also given birth to another major freedom: to be free from rigid past controls.

The West's post-1960s sexual culture, in particular, was, like so many other things, internationalised.

My elderly historian friend, Tasos Vournas, kept, however, moaning.

– 'The sea's turned into yogurt', he kept saying, 'just when we've lost our spoons'.

'There are', I wrote, 'no more dogmas, centres or rules, no leaders to lead us to new illusions and no "truths" to which everyone would be expected to abide. Our world has become less judgmental and moralistic and therefore less repressive. It has fewer external controls, less pressure to conform, more tolerance and flexibility.'

Yet nothing seems to be an unmixed blessing like the smile on the face of a child.

This newly-acquired freedom, on the one hand, failed to establish the basis for the self-realisation of the individual, and, on the other, it took away the sense of identity people used to enjoy within their tribe, neighbourhood, culture and their world.

Rather than a leaf on a tree, the individual is now a leaf detached from it, blown in the direction of the wind. Meanwhile, traditional structures are being destroyed, cultures that have existed for centuries are being eroded, and the diversity that gives our world its richness is disappearing. American values, as transmitted by Hollywood, are, presumably, good enough for everybody.

New issues – green, gender, race, ethnic, cultural and ethical or issues relating to technology, globalisation or the family – were, meanwhile, emerging cutting across traditional ideological lines and blurring the traditional distinctions between Left and Right.

Globalisation, 'turbo-charged', was questioned on account of the uncontrollable power accumulated by multinational companies following the rapid economic and technological integration.

Immigrant communities at the same time rejected integration and demanded what was called 'differentiated citizenship' that involved state recognition of their religious holidays, exemption from laws that interfere with their religious affairs, protection of their conventions, customs and family practices or state funding for the teaching of mother-tongue languages. As Joseph Raz put it, the ability of ethnic minorities to choose is intimately tied up with both access to their culture and the respect which the majority accorded it.

But, as time progressed, the ground on which financial capitalism rested was shaken.

A number of states began to run sizeable fiscal deficits – Italy as early as in the mid-eighties and France in the early 1990s. Mexico was hit by a devastating financial crisis in 1995 before the guns turned against the tiger economies of Asia. Thailand, forced to devalue its currency, was followed in 1977 by Indonesia, South Korea and to a lesser extent Malaysia, Laos and the Philippines. Russia defaulted and devalued the rouble in 1998 and so did Argentina in 1999.

Currencies collapsed, stock markets and assets devalued, private debt rose to unsustainable levels and people joined involuntarily the package tours to disappointment and resentment.

– The global capitalist system, financier George Soros said in 1998, is falling apart at the seams.

Embarrassed, the God of the markets went into hiding for an indefinite period of time.

Crony capitalism, fenced in a cloud which it believed no beneficial influence could penetrate, was, as a result, questioned. So were its main apostles, saints by trade, and globalisation itself. Political institutions and regulatory frameworks had lost trust in it and human loyalties deserted it. Many also feared that globalisation was bound to lead, as it did, to greater tax evasion by the global corporations.

The market all the sudden lost its lustre and the unfettered power of the big business was challenged as bigness can harm both consumers individually and the system as a whole. People discovered that there was something inherently insane in the way billions of dollars were churning endlessly through the global markets. Churchmen were heard talking about capitalism, which, though the 'best' system, had drifted too far from its moral moorings.

People did also start taking into account the deep scars the era had left behind – pockets of extreme poverty, high levels of ine- quality, public squalor and the split of our world between winners and losers. Fittingly the decade, a decade of increasing globalisa- tion, greed, economic insecurity and pervasive disillusionment with the political system, ended with the massive protests and riots in the streets of Seattle.

Still, at first glance, I wrote in *i-to-i* magazine, our world still holds together. The trains still run, albeit with delays, the National Health Service continues to provide some services, the institutions of learning still issue certificates of knowledge. We switch the television on and we listen to the Nine O'clock news, we go to the supermarket and we find on the shelves anything money can buy.

To all appearances this is an orderly and well-run world – never mind homelessness, unemployment, inner city decay, racism or rising crime.

Never mind plastic trees and plastic values, either.

Yet the same world is collapsing, fast. It is not just the financial markets. The glue – shared beliefs and morally and socially validated goals – has lost its strength. Christianity, the Empire, freedom, socialism or communism no longer provide inspiration. The Trade Union movement, bedazzled like a rabbit in front of the headlamps, has lost its credibility as has the Church and the political parties – even the monarchy. Society has lost its collective will, its vision and to some extent its balance.

All we see is the consumer multiple orgasm in the high street.

But we cannot survive with this 'fortress me mentality', I wrote in another instance. 'We need to belong, to be able to identify with something larger than ourselves, to share in joy and in sorrow. We need the stimulus of communication with the members of our 'tribe' and with a responsive society, interaction with others in a way that recognises and confirms our individuality, connection with the source of our social power.'

Obviously, we cannot bring back the old community. It doesn't fit into our TV rooms. And we certainly do not miss the times that women did not know how to add or multiply. But at the same time 'we don't have to endorse the computerisation of our existence. We don't have to accept being managed by a bureaucratised democracy, and we don't have to consume ourselves in the pursuit of consumption'.

And again later, in October 1994:

Content with the little we have – an income that helps to make ends meet, a job that fills the time with something 'useful' to do, and the 'freedom' to choose between hundreds of different TV channels – we do not want to think. Near-sighted, we avoid the wide horizons and let our one-dimensional, commodity-dominated, sociocultural system think for us instead.

And the system, happy as the bed in our lover's room, is ready to oblige.

It makes available at schools the skills that enable us to work for it later in life, it meets efficiently the individuals' standardised needs it creates, it gives the images of ourselves we should subscribe to if we do not want to fall behind our times, and it tells us all the wonderful things we can do in our 'free' time.

But the truth is that the system has no interest whatsoever in meeting our needs. It encourages us to buy CDs rather than sing, watch a love story on TV rather than fall in love or use cars rather than enjoy a pollution free city. It has become the Big Brother who takes care of us. So why bother to think? And we do not.

Even our interior monologues are not our own.

Hence the stress and mental disorders which have risen in the UK more than any other causes of long-term sickness absence on account of which even employers are now freaking out.

But to get real satisfaction we need to go far beyond the premises of the soul-free free market economy and its values and relations.

Looking for it means above anything else we deny the absolute power of the market, refuse to obey its rules and reject its priorities and values. All this does anything but imply a romantic rejection of modernity in favour of a return to an imaginary idyllic past, the time we commuted on steam-powered buses. It is, instead, a plea to empower ourselves, humanise our world and take good care of it to the benefit of everyone and everything.

This calls for a 'cultural liberation that can thrive on the liberation of the imagination'.

Bringing these issues to the forefront of our awareness could, I believed, affect individual consciousness, lead gradually to changes in the collective consciousness, and eventually bring about 'a cultural revolution to regenerate our society.'

Naively, just like Friedrich Hölderlin, the great German lyric poet, I was still looking forward to the 'forthcoming revolution of attitudes and conceptions which will make everything that has gone before turn red with shame', as he wrote to a friend in Paris in 1797.

But apart from Skyros that functioned as a community committed to the right principles, all I could do about it was write with a glass of what looked like wisdom within reach. And so I did.

Wisdom was not sufficient, however, to get me through the diabolical complexities of my newly acquired computer.

19

The Soul of Spring

As many as twenty thousand people have joined Skyros over the years, many of them numerous times, and relished its unbridled spirit of adventure, creativity and joy. Many explored new possibilities, tried new things and unearthed amazing layers of themselves they did not even suspect existed.

In a world far removed from daily salaried routines, others took the opportunity to reassess their life, redefine their needs and re-set their priorities.

The unexamined life, as Socrates said, is not worth living.

Yet, the walk into the garden of our existence to reconnect with life's fragrance lost in the alienated world we inhabit is not something most people would go for. Burdened by the lumpy, enervating mundane, sunk into the dailiness of life or trapped, as one woman wrote, in 'the treadmill of 50 to 60-hour working weeks in a back-stabbing academic environment', most do not even think about what they really need in life.

And this is what they do in Skyros. Not that Skyros tells any-one what to do. But it does encourage people to get in touch with their gut feeling, question and challenge our culture's assumptions and dauntlessly do what they need to do to lead a more fulfilling life.

The process is underpinned by an ethos that emphasises being rather than having, doing rather than consuming and belonging

236

rather than withdrawing into the garden of your private world. Rather than resign, accept and conform, people are encouraged to question, challenge and create.

Fulfilling our potential affirms what is best in ourselves. It also asserts man's power over his creations – the market, machines, technology, systems, fashion, ideologies or fundamentalist beliefs.

This philosophical underpinning of the Skyros culture is developed and fine-tuned through an experiential practice that makes it work. As a result, people often return home with modified, and sometimes radicalised perceptions of both themselves and the world we live in.

Life as it is lived is no longer viewed as destiny.

And this is what brings together the personal and the political, which are the two sides of the same coin. This is also what challenges the structures of our materialistic, consumerist and technocratic culture.

The context in which all this takes place is the community, the strongly beating heart of Skyros. It is the equivalent of the society we all live in at home, run, however, with different values: trust, honesty, openness and mutual support. The principles it rests on include cooperation rather than competition, participation rather than non-engagement, responsibility rather than indifference, respect for individuality rather than conformity and support for the individual's drive to unearth his or her dormant potential.

All this represents a different culture, very important in a wider context, for culture is central to the development of new, human-friendly social and political structures.

In a way, this is the working class culture re-visited – a culture, as expressed in Chartism, based on mutual aid and cooperation and a friendly expression on its face. Opposed to it stand both the middle-class culture based on rewards for individual success and the aristocratic ideal of hierarchy grounded in birth and privilege.

People in the Skyros community are first and foremost asked to be themselves. This is the key to an authentic life lost in the intricate, confusing social network of interconnecting pathways that often seem to require the placing of genuine feelings in the safe and the display of their imitations.

– 'Which of us', Elisabeth in a JM Coetzee story, asks rhetorically, 'is what he seems to be?'

To be themselves, people would have to cast aside habitual roles as a married partner, parent, boss, employee, official, client, club or union member or socialite, leave behind all features that make up their identity and re-connect with their essence.

In other words, own themselves because, if they do not, others will do it for them.

And this is not easy.

– 'To be nobody but yourself in a world which is trying day and night to make you everybody else', E. E. Cummings, the American poet and playwright, once said, 'is the hardest battle you will ever fight'.

Hence, when I am there, I ask people to leave behind the trappings of the 'real' world, a world where, as Rachel says in a Virginia Woolf story, 'nobody ever said a thing they meant, or even talked of a feeling they felt'.

– 'Do not sail under false colours', I emphasise, 'and do not pretend to be what you're not, for in this place it will not take you anywhere. Take a risk and show, instead, your real self in the certainty that you will be liked for what you really are. After all, we all have sides that we do not feel comfortable with and we are often uncharitable towards our own selves. Go for a full-blooded life, open up to the world and the world will also open up to you.'

Honesty demands, of course, courage.

Overcoming my own fears of being overwhelming, I also ask them to give generously to others as much as they can without expectations of getting something in return.

– 'Give lovingly for the pleasure of giving in terms of concern, time and attention, being also, incidentally, sure that having given your best, the best will come back to you'.

As Democritus said, he who loves no one is loved by no one.

'But be also able to accept what is offered to you with appreciation and grace, for, sometimes, accepting is more difficult than giving.'

Be also a doer rather than a spectator and give an outlet to your creativity.

– 'Try things you fancy, things you have never tried before, from singing to abseiling, from comedy improvisation to painting, from windsurfing to writing, even if you do not feel comfortable or confident about it – everybody's on the same boat. Play and be silly if the mood takes you there.

Having consulted my memory's notes, I lastly advise them to reconnect with the child within, 'the soul I had of old, when I was a child', as Lorca would say, and the child's curiosity, innocence, spontaneity, lack of fear and uncritical joy.

– 'See everything as a world waiting to be discovered, a game to be enjoyed, an opportunity for a good laugh. Focus, like a child, only on the present and experience the child's happiness at the simplest of things.

Whatever your age, playing is the salt of life.

– 'And do not worry about anything or, as the Skyrians say, do not worry about at least two things in life: those that can be fixed and those that cannot.'

As it happens, in this honest and supporting environment, people who, if they had gone somewhere else, would have made certain that they had travelled as far as possible away from themselves, do listen and, as a rule, end up as happy as swallows in the spring.

– 'Every day', David Tillett, a member of the Skyros community, wrote, 'there is a fabulous journey, a possibility of magic, an opportunity to apprehend the glory of living'.

The democratic structures of the Skyros community give people a voice, enable them to influence the day's schedule, contribute to everybody's welfare and, in doing so, interact with each other as if they were a family, albeit without the usual family hindrances.

This is done through demos, the daily early morning meeting of the entire community for the exchange of news and views, the ongoing œkos groups in which its members voice honestly their thoughts and feelings, the co-listening which involves the same process but between two people only, and the work groups which help with what is required for the smooth running of the community.

Work is occasionally controversial as people object to spending something like half an hour a day doing what people do not do on holiday.

But we have persisted because work abolishes all social, age or gender differences, underpins the individual's sense of responsibility towards the entire community, our polis, and strengthens everybody's connections with everybody else.

Freely chosen, it can also be as pleasant as the fondling by the spirit of the sun.

It all appears quite simple, yet to make it work it does take skilled leadership provided, amongst others, by the teaching staff, whose quality, as Leslie Kenton stated in June 1984 in the *Harpers & Queen* magazine, is 'very high'.

The concept of leadership in the Skyros world has, of course, a different colour. The aim is to create a community of leaders rather than followers of the enlightened one.

Leadership in any case, as Tony Benn put it when interviewed by Dina Glouberman, has various shades. Best leaders for him, as for us, are those whose presence is not noticed by the people so that when their work is done, the people say 'we did it ourselves'.

This broad and rather discernible intellectual construct places Skyros beyond the reach of any definition. It is also what puzzles me when I am asked to explain what it is all about.

How can you describe the soul of spring?

– 'Well', I have said in a few such instances, 'it's all about living fully in the moment – and making the most of it. It's about the joy of living, if joy stands for something beyond the 'fun' offered to us by the entertainment industry. It's the pleasure of going for the spectacular which transcends every preceding fear, and the delight experienced by the appreciation of things for what they are – 'a river for its riverness', as Plato said – as opposed to their benefits in this life or the next. It's also a total living experience.'

First Tuesday, the ITV hour-long programme on Skyros that was aired on prime time on the 7th of September 1993, made this point crystal clear: two weeks in Skyros, it said, is 'almost like living your life in a fortnight'.

Such a total living experience, I like to believe, could transform consciousness and hopefully lead to changes beneficial both to the individual and the world.

Cynics in the UK did, of course, dismiss it all as a hub of a Hampstead mixture of media types, people in search of sun, sea and self-importance, *The Guardian* readers' Butlin's, the Club Veg or the lentils and beards élite.

Author Nigel Gearing, author and playwright, was one of them.

As he wrote himself, he was afraid that Skyros would be a post-hippy, happy-clappy 'sharing' community, something between an encounter group and a Boy Scout camp. But, as he discovered:

– The place is run 'on undogmatic principles which embraced the profane as well as the lofty. Instead of po-faced gurus,

I found', he wrote, 'ironic, engaging teachers who could tell the difference between the edifying and the merely earnest; instead of sad, lonely participants I found mild-mannered think-alikes whose collective idea of a holiday amounted to something more than a beach towel, a bottle of sun cream and the latest Jilly Cooper.'

Like so many others who had mocked Skyros only to return home, as Maeve Binchy put it in the *Irish Times* in August 1986, 'sheepishly praising it to the skies', his spell on the island produced the perfect story.

Skyros is the moment but it is also the future.

– 'Think', I also invite people when I am there, 'what would really, really make you happy?'

The question is very simple and yet one which, if one tries to answer honestly, turns into a hand grenade exploding at the foundations of each one's existence.

People do naturally want to be physically attractive, intellectually stimulating, professionally successful and also to lead a comfortable life in line with current expectations. Their middle class background somehow ensures that they do get a reasonable deal in life, but to be happy they do not want more of the same.

Hence the answer is not a Lamborghini, but a safe space in which they can feel accepted, needed, valued and respected for what and who they are, a meaningful job that is socially validated, a sense of purpose that is larger than one's own self, and a world, their world, in which they feel they belong and to which they can relate. What most people want is a simpler and more fulfilling life, their recognition as human beings rather than functionaries or consumers, and good, decent, loving relationships.

In short, a life that makes sense.

Or, as Aristotle said, a life in tune with one's spirit and nature, community and sense of purpose – a life harmonised with everything visible and invisible.

In this context, 'more' seems to mean something different from that which our materialistic, technocratic, consumer culture provides.

Living such a life requires action in the pursuit of the right and the good, a way of life that expands the mind, nourishes the body, uplifts the spirit and helps the heart grow big. It demands an unappeasable love of beauty, from the beauty of the heart to the beauty of the institutions of a just society.

Love is the informing God of all things.

This, as articulated by the ancient Greeks, requires perfection through the development of personal human qualities embracing the whole of a man's existence and not tradable against other goods such as wealth. It involves commitment to the community and to ethical living – 'honourable living' as the Greeks would say – both of which are indispensable to the happiness of the individual and the re-establishment of a high trust society.

This is not freedom from, but freedom for one's self-realisation, the satisfaction of an entire and inter-connected range of needs: spiritual, physical, social, creative, material and intellectual. They are all part of an organic whole.

Happiness then comes, to recall Aristotle again, 'like the bloom on the cheeks of youth'.

This is what Skyros is trying to achieve in the spirit of creativity, camaraderie, risk-taking, self-discovery, tears, laughter, craziness and a scintillating sense of humour. This is also what has turned Skyros, as Gemma Bowes wrote in October 2005 in *The Observer*, into 'the doyenne of alternative holidays'.

– 'The whole set up', an Oxford university scientist wrote some time ago, 'is unconventional, almost crazy. But that was a strength as far as I was concerned or I would have gone to Margate'.

– 'Its replenishing madness', author Steve Attridge wrote likewise, is something 'I have savoured long afterwards'.

243

So have I, particularly when thinking of the frequent nine miles journey from Atsitsa Bay to the village on the Land Rover I was driving with twenty people on it, several of them on the roof. Totally stupid and very dangerous, those trips left everybody with some of the most exhilarating memories of the kind that make one feel a bit more fulfilled at the moment of death.

It would really be crazy not to enjoy such madness.

That was the view of Woolfy, too, the Alsatian dog we brought to Atsitsa, which, having been brought up by the British Atsitsa community, kept barking in Greek but with a foreign accent.

Relaxed, valued and special, people were taken completely by such thrilling experiences. Hence, as the BBC Radio Four broadcasted in September 1991, they were 'stretching beyond what they thought they could do and were popping open like flowers'.

The famous cabarets at the end of every session in which nearly everybody performed like an accomplished entertainer highlighted the incredibly high spirit in which people operated and added a special and unforgettable chapter in each one's personal history.

Such events occurred quite often. Alison Goldie, a TV presenter, gave her own stories in Jane Savage's book *Skyros, Island of Dreams*, published in 2011.

She recalled the cramming of fifty people into the handyman's kiosk for a rave with all ages and sizes waving their arms about to ultra-modern dance music or the dressing up with participants plundering each other's suitcases and swapping clothes, cross-dressing and looking more interesting than a truckload of supermodels.

She also mentioned the bar where people would sing rather than listen to songs, the sea where Susie Self, an opera composer and singer, salted with sea-spray, performed in the water for both the moonlight and an ecstatic audience of one hundred, and the women's group on the far-flung beach in the middle of the night, who kept laughing uproariously at shared stories.

Several similar stories people keep telling me all the time, stories I cannot even recall. The fingertips of my memory cannot reach the shelf they are kept on. Thankfully, however, this madness was not a conditional term in the world's judgment of us.

The impact of such a multi-faceted experience was for many people like the Oxford scientist quite 'seismic'. Jimmy Carr, the English stand-up comedian, whose Skyros experience changed radically his life, was one of them. As he told *The Sunday Times* in January 2008:

– 'I've had one life-changing holiday – on the Greek island of Skyros. I had just given up my job with Shell. I wasn't quite sure what to do with my life, so I enrolled on a creative-writing course in the hope that something would occur to me. People kept saying that I was really funny, and ought to be a comedian, so I thought I'd give it a go.'

And so he did and never looked back again.

Jennie Dempster, interviewed by *Red* magazine in its August 2008 issue, had a similar story.

– 'I had been a TV producer for seven years', she said, 'working on chat shows like Richard & Judy and Paul O'Grady. It was fun at first but, as I approached 30, I was getting increasingly disillusioned. That summer I went on a Skyros holiday in Greece. At Skyros, there's a you can-do-anything atmosphere. I realised psychology was what I wanted to do. Within six months of the holiday, I'd quit my job and was starting clinical psychology training. I now realise that helping people is what I always wanted to do. I didn't really know who I was until I went on that holiday. If I hadn't gone I'd still be a TV producer.'

As interesting is author Crysse Morrison's story as published in *The Times* in October 2011.

– 'What impressed me most ', she said, 'was something more subtle, profound, and long-lasting – the ethos of valuing both community and individuality, a way of being together that was inclusive, supportive and creative. I realised that my life was still wide open, crammed with as many opportunities as I wanted to envisage. That is why I say, without a trace of irony and with huge gratitude, that my holiday on Skyros changed my life.'

What Skyros offers is not something standardised like a toothpaste. It offers, instead, what is missing in the life of the individuals, what they want to see, experience and take away with them. Hence the totally different memories and feelings generated by events shared by everybody.

Skyros, Janet Barcroft wrote accordingly in May 1994 in the *Here's Health* magazine, is 'a magical, healing place that brings out the best in people'. But what won over Angela Neustatter, as she wrote in *The Times* in April 1994, was its 'intellectual rigour, spiritual encounters and good old-fashioned rioting in the evening'.

Some looked still unsure as to whether Skyros had its feet on the ground.

I wondered, Sarah Kent wrote in *Time Out* in March 1999, whether Skyros had entered into the 'New Age fog of earnest escapism'. But no, 'a healthy realism', she said after she visited the centre, had left no room for it. As Paul Mansfield also noted in February 1996 in the *Sunday Telegraph*, the Skyros world is, indeed, 'very real'. 'In fact', he added.

'Skyros is a hell of a lot more real than most people are used to'.

Even poet Hugo Williams, the 'licensed sceptic', described the holiday in *The Times Literary Supplement* of October 1993, as 'a lesson in uncynicism'.

Similar views were express in the *Sueddeutsche Zeitung* in March 1993, Sydney's *The Age* in December 1996 or the *Financial*

Times of May 1998 – 'some magic at work inspires people', wrote in the latter Angela Wigglesworth. Writing in the June 2003 issue of *Top Santé* magazine, Leah Hellen, likewise, said:

– 'I felt inspired and optimistic about the future and what I could make of it. I'd relaxed, had fun and learnt new skills. Best of all was the simple realisation that I had it in me to feel good about myself.'

Skyros, after all, as Deb Hunt put it in a March 2004 issue of Sydney's *Sunday Telegraph*, is 'all about conquering your fears, freeing your spirit and having the sort of fun you probably haven't since you were a small kid'.

Sue Townsend, the novelist who had been in Skyros as a creative writing facilitator for several years in a row, was even more enthusiastic.

Writing in *The Guardian* of September 1998, she said:

– 'I immediately fell in love with the place as everybody does. I kept thinking, "I am an actor in A Midsummer Night's Dream; this is Arcadia", I want to live like this forever.'

Once, while on the island, she was, I heard, in need of medical attention. Shocked as if I had just heard that Julius Caesar had been stabbed, I rushed to make all the appropriate arrangements with the local clinic. A day later, when we could all smile again, she told me she had heard from the Skyrian doctors who treated her that I had threatened to kill them if something went wrong with her treatment.

I am happy to clarify here that I had never done such a thing.

What people got out of Skyros depended largely on what they needed at that stage of their lives.

Of importance to Anne Roper, as she wrote in Dublin's *Sunday Independent* in January 1999, was the fact that she 'made bonds that will last a lifetime because the friendships were based on getting to know the real me and vice versa'. The same feelings were expressed by John Hargreaves in the March 2002 issue of *Here's Health*. In Skyros, he wrote, 'you make friends for life'.

Hence Skyros has become for so many people their second home, a real home or a home from home. Re-visiting it, as so many often do, is homecoming or, as some put it, coming home to myself.

For others 'home' meant something more. In two instances I am aware of, former Skyros participants who died and were cremated in the UK had their ashes taken to Skyros and offered to the wind, which scattered them over the island's field of memories. That was their wish.

The same happened as I am writing these lines. Eilean MacGibbon, a woman who, Ruari, her daughter, wrote to us, had 'at least two inspirational trips to Atsitsa', had requested in her will that her ashes are scattered in the Atsitsa bay.

'Thank you', Ruari added, 'for creating such a special place where our mum found love, laughter and fun'.

Debbra Mikaelsen, writing for the 2003 *Travel Insights*, emphasised another aspect of the holiday. 'As long as Skyros holidays exist', she wrote, 'none of us need ever again feel terror at the prospect of a solo vacation'. That is very true as Skyros is the perfect place to go on your own because you will never be on your own. Besides, many arrive in Skyros on their own only to depart from it with a life-long partner.

Romances are anything but uncommon. But not as frequent as one might expect because for various reasons, the majority of the Skyros guests tend to be women.

Is this, Jane Salvage wondered, because men are less in touch with their feelings or because they think that expressing them is unmanly? Is it because they do not like walking outside their comfort zone? Or is self-development outside men's cultural perimeters?

Once, in a newsletter we sent out, I suggested that men are always ready to climb to the top of the most inaccessible

– 'To read Skyros press coverage', Kate Rew wrote, 'is to choke on cliched words like "life changing", "transforming". Yet at the end of two weeks, Skyros has been all of these'.

But there were also other stories and events which, even if I wanted, I could not air-brush from my memory.

In one instance, a woman who had started seeing ghosts at night and was happy enough to share a few glasses of wine with them, was sent back to Athens for medical attention. But the problem did not disappear. A very short message on the answering machine left by Johny T, a larger than life Greek-American member of staff, who was accompanying her on her return trip to Athens, soon after informed us:

– 'She jumped off.'

That was all. He meant off the ferry.

Shocked as if I had just heard that Babylon had fallen, I rushed with Pete Webb, the Atsitsa manager at the time, to Linaria, the harbour, to see what on earth was going on. Thankfully, the only thing on the pavement was Johny T's sense of humour, in tatters, begging for our forgiveness.

What a story, we thought when we had recovered from the blow, the *Sun*, the *Daily Express* or the *News of World* had just missed.

Almost as troublesome were many technical problems behind the rough Atsitsa structures as nothing on the site was safe against the elements. Extremely vulnerable to them in the winter, it has to be completely re-vamped before the beginning of each season.

Trouble, I often thought, is welcome but only in response to invitation.

If not, it is as bad as kidney pain and often as expensive as a privately performed brain surgery.

mountain, but they would steer clear of anything that r
spontaneity, improvisation and playfulness. Being mer
just expect to perform and cannot take failure in the sar
women can.

– 'Men', I wrote facetiously, 'react to self-developm
same way, as, the story goes, Goebbels reacted to the
"culture", by drawing his gun'.

What I never expected to receive in response were the
letters sent to me by a few Jewish women, who took offence
mentioning Goebbels' name.

I left the story out to dry in the sun as it was too '
handle, and then I forgot about it.

For others, like Tracey Pocock, who wrote for the a
2002 issue of *Woman* magazine, 'the most wonderful legacy
memory of having laughed more in two weeks that I can rem
since childhood'. Vanessa Nicolson, writing in *House & G*
of July 2000, expressed similar feelings. 'I danced and hugge
sobbed and laughed', she said, 'like a schoolgirl'.

Skyros, after all, Jane Cornwell stated in *The Weekend Aust*
of September 2002, offers an environment that is 'supportive,
and, most important, a bloody good laugh'.

Hence Mariella Frostrup, the British journalist and TV pres
advise her readers in *The Independent*:

– 'Let your hair down, take risks, expand horizons, go
Skyros holistic holiday'.

This sort of superlatives', commented Carmel Thomaso
January 2009 in the *Manchester Evening News*, are writte
journalists, 'possibly far more cynical than me', for you cann
a journalist without questioning everything.

But Skyros is 'a wonderfully relaxed holiday and some o
people I met there have already found a place in my heart'.
same feelings were summed up by *The Observer* of June 200

20

Audaciously Sincere

Having distanced myself from Greece, in 1989, the year the new recession begun, I launched in London as both publisher and editor the *i-to-i* magazine.

The publication intended 'to question and challenge the dominant way of thinking and help the shaping of the concepts of the future'.

Consulting editors were Dina Glouberman, who conducted most of the interviews with celebrities later on, and Silke Ziehl, a woman with a gentle, spirited presence and an unabated interest in the affairs of this world.

– 'It's a wonderful idea', enthused by the sound of it, the latter affirmed at her place, in Richmond.

While staring at the photo of the superbly naked and charmingly immature figure of the young David of Donatello, she even recalled Friedrich Hölderlin, the great German poet.

– 'Well, well! We'll visit the spring or the rocks where the roses bloom.'

The first issue was out in December 1989. The first step in crossing 'the abyss without fear', as Hölderlin might say again, had been taken.

Tragically, my brilliant assistant Anne Frankel, a woman who could audit my unvoiced soliloquy and read my thoughts, died suddenly with only forty-three years to her credit. It happened just a couple of days before this very first issue was out. The pressure was too high for her heart. She was one of the most thoughtfully caring and emotionally intelligent persons I knew.

The idea behind the magazine was, as my first editorial explained, rather simple but also vaguely discernible.

Structures are the creation of individual perceptions as much as the latter are the creation of the former. To bring change, we need, thus, to pursue both inner and outer change and work at both the political and the individual level – politicise our individual concerns and humanise politics.

To attain this, we would have to abandon the conventional compartmentalised thinking and think, instead, holistically, i.e., taking into account the needs of the whole person – material, emotional, spiritual, physical, social, political and environmental.

This implied that the traditional borderlines between psychology, on the one hand, and political and social philosophy, on the other, had to be eliminated. Psychological notions had to develop a political and social dimension, and politics had to take also care of the individuals' concerns.

As far as I could tell, the journey was destined to take us, if I could quote Dylan Thomas, to a new land 'east of the sun, west of the moon, where each tomorrow dawns', a stirring life in a thrilling new world.

The concept made full sense to me, but not to the distributors, who, used to selling fashion or stamp magazines, were never taken by my charmless vagueness and never stopped asking me 'what sort of a magazine' *i-to-i* is.

– 'Hm... On what shelf shall we place it? With what group of magazines?'

They were entitled, of course, to their uncertainties, on which they sat stubbornly, except that I never managed to dispel them to my satisfaction.

One has, of course, to take into account that, after all, it was not easy to explain without exhausting the quota of words provided for the occasion what the magazine was about.

Yet it was a magazine with the strength and the commitment to a more honest, caring and also free world, and also the guts to pursue this commitment without compromising its integrity. It was also a magazine that had both the intellectual power to challenge convincingly the accepted wisdom and the moral courage to do so.

As I wrote in April 1993, 'the intention is not to reach a cosy relationship with our tired selves, but to push forward the frontiers of current thinking'.

The power of convictions was there, but, on the other hand, the magazine never claimed, like some men of taste, that it possessed the 'truth'. 'The "truth", whatever it is, is not something we arrive at, but what we are always looking for'.

Luis Bunuel, the Spanish film maker, had made the same point but more eloquently than myself.

– 'I would be prepared', he said, 'to die defending anyone looking for the truth, but I would send to the firing squad anyone who thought he had found it'.

The publication was not commercial in the sense that it was not launched to make me rich and famous. The celebrities' culture and its air-conditioned aspirations were totally alien to me. What motivated me was the burning desire to contribute to a better world and also the irresistible urge to do so in a creative way.

It was the urge that begged the creation of something new out of nothing, the utilisation of all powers hidden in the unreachable parts of myself and the crossing of boundaries set by self-limiting thoughts. I was in the pursuit of a wonder against a reality inert and insensitive to its thrills.

It was exactly the same motivation that had made me at about the same time, despite my total lack of familiarity with music, to write a few songs. Socrates, after all, I thought, had learnt to play the lyre in his old age.

The time to learn new things apparently never ends as Michelangelo had confirmed, too, when he said he was still learning at the age of seventy.

One of these songs was briefly performed in a concert by clarinetist Damaris Woolen at St Martin's in the Field, in London's Trafalgar Square, between pieces of Mozart and Vivaldi. Another, orchestrated by Jenni Roditi, was the original score written for the Skyros film made by SatTV.

Like Rilke, who, according to the story, heard in the wind the first lines of his elegies, I heard the music and the lyrics of this song in the humming of the Sea Nymphs while walking over the pink rocks of the Atsitsa Bay.

Financially speaking, the picture was not promising. You cannot compete against the media empires and hope to conquer the world. All I aspired with the launch of the magazine was just to break even. This despite the astrologist's assurances following the reading of celestial autocues that the publication was going to be a towering success.

– 'You'll be on top of a tower', she informed me on a day she happened to have an unpredicted bad headache, 'and the adoring crowds will be cheering you under it.'

That woman, an attractive lady aged something between twenty-five and fifty, was to be the magazine's astrologist. I informed her there was also another job available: straightening the photos on our office's walls.

Her place was taken by Paul Wright, who early in 1990 made an interesting presentation of Neil Kinnock, leader of the opposition at the time, on the strength of his astrological characteristics.

'He tends', he wrote, 'to take things very personally and his pride is easily wounded. But equally well, the applause of the crowd is nectar to him. His judgment may be sound, but it is rooted in intuition rather than logic or common sense. For him it is important to have a partner who is not only his wife and mother but also friend.'

I do not know how accurate was the description, but the astrologer's prediction that Kinnock should look forward to 'a period of good fortune, success and expansiveness' was definitely wrong. Having carelessly misplaced the manual containing the instructions to success, Kinnock released the leadership of the Labour party in 1992 following his electoral defeat.

Myself, I thought I might have a chance as, I reckoned, there was a gap in the market. But I still remember the twinge of uneasiness I felt when Anne-Marie Conway, the deputy editor of *The Times ES*, warned me in a café in Covent Garden:

– 'A gap, did you say? Be careful not to fall into it.'

Well, it was not easy, but if it were easy, it would not be worth doing.

Impervious to discouragement, I, thus, put in it all my money and so did a few others, including after a while a Palestinian, who saw a copy of the magazine in Katmandu, was taken by it and forwarded to its bank account £20K. Another donor, who still wants to remain anonymous, contributed even more.

The magazine hosted interviews with many challenging thinkers including Tony Benn, the veteran Labour leader, Tariq Ali, the prominent '60s anti-war activist, writer and filmmaker, Paco Rabanne, the Spanish fashion designer, or Michael York, the actor.

Robert Bly, the celebrated American author whose 1990 book Iron John: A Book About Men influenced the thinking of a generation, was there, too, as was Rev Chad Varah, founder of the Samaritans, Margaret Drabble and D M Thomas, the novelists, Lynne Franks, the public relations guru, Gabrielle Roth, the American dancer who created the 5Rhythms approach to movement, Denise Linn, the American soul coach or Louise Hay, the American motivational author of several New Thought self-help books.

Contributors included Kirkpatrick Sale, the legendary American environmentalist, Gary Zukav, the American best-selling author, Henryk Skolimowski, the Polish philosopher, or Rudolf Bahro, the East German dissident and later leader of the West German Green party whose 1978 book The Alternative in Eastern Europe had influenced me decisively.

Bahro, incidentally, was on the Skyros programme but had to cancel when in 1994 was diagnosed with a rare form of cancer. In his two-part article, he criticised the western state of self-absorbance and all forms of fixation on the drama of individual existence.

Tony Benn described his ambition in life, which, he said, had been to help people understand what is happening, develop themselves and use their influence more effectively. He also gave an interesting description of leadership by quoting the ancient Chinese philosopher Lao Tzu:

– 'A leader is best when people barely know he exists. When his work is done and his aim fulfilled, they will say: we did it ourselves.'

Tariq Ali, the writer and journalist, interviewed in the *i-to-i*'s July 1993 issue, called those who grew up in the sixties the 'arrogant' generation because they believed they could change the world.

Yes, I wrote in response, in this revolution against the cultural sterility of the time, or, alternatively, in this attempt to live out a dream, these kids challenged institutional power, which was despised, and dismissed expert opinion and all the over-30s, responsible for the mess.

James Joyce had somehow already made the same point as them when, at the end of his celebrated visit to W. B. Yeats, said that Yeats, still in his thirties, was too old to be helped.

Having both feet in reality, I argued, is vital and necessary. That is the lesson of the sixties. But reality includes our dreams, which shape it and is shaped by them, and dreams represent hope without which we will perish. Whatever, I concluded, I do occasionally miss that crazy, exhilarating, empowering springtime of '68.

It was not exactly nostalgia, the feeling that the better life is just behind us, but another way of looking forward into the future.

Among the contributors were numerous people whose names had figured on book jackets or the daily newspapers. All of them without resorting to glim nonsenses and airy platitudes did one way or another challenge current values, beliefs and practices.

Lisette Thooft, a Dutch journalist, did some thinking on how much money one really needs – "from birth onwards', she said, 'we have all been thoroughly trained to look outside for fulfilment'. But there is 'a fulfilment curve. It curves sharply upwards as the bare necessities of life are being met: food, warmth and shelter. It continues to climb through comforts and luxuries. After that point it begins to level out and even starts to head down again. Spending money ceases to bring fulfilment and only brings clutter'.

Like Democritus', her core message was 'enough is as good as a feast'.

This was a theme I pursued later on by asking a number of individuals for their thoughts on the subject. Many people responded including Madsen Pirie, president of the Adam Smith Institute, Bill Morris, general secretary of the Transport and General Workers Union, Alex Salmond, the first minister of Scotland from 2007 to 2014, the Rev Ian Kenway of the Church of England, Mandla Langa of the African National Congress, Jimmy Knapp, general secretary of the Rail, Maritime and Transport Workers and the authors D M Thomas and Maeve Binchy.

Apart from D M Thomas, who reminded us of Plato's view that no one should have more than four times the wealth of anyone else, and of Maeve Binchy, all the others' responses were a fountain of worn-out platitudes.

I did not want to hear that 'wealth enables us to advance charitable causes' or 'until the Third World has enough, we shall not know how much is enough for ourselves'. They did not answer the question. It was Maeve Binchy, instead, the one who put her finger on the pulse.

– 'A great many people who have enough', she said, 'will never admit it. We don't have the vocabulary to say "that's fine now". Instead, our instinct tells us that if we got this far we should go further. This is the way people identify themselves, prove they exist'.

Incidentally, when John D Rockfeller was asked the same question, his response was:

– 'Just a little more.'

His money made up for his lack of discernment.

The issue of unnecessary consumption was taken up by other journalists including Ken Worpole or Ella Young and Robert Weston, a former advertising executive. Jane Erlich, a freelance journalist, focused in particular on the 'Diet Trap' set by 'the media/fashion mafia', which, she said, entraps women through books, tapes, pills, spas, shots, food and clubs into the belief that they must have a certain kind of body.

Uselessness never seems to come in short supply.

Looking at the same topic from a different angle but as angry, Margo Maine, a clinical psychologist, said that dieting, fitness and cosmetic industries give back to women only eating disorders – anorexia nervosa, bulimia, and related problems.

At about that time satellite television had made inroads into our lives. The difference between it and ordinary TV, Jad Adams, a freelance journalist, wrote, is that every nation gets now the same transmissions, all 'homogenised as milk'. He reminded me of Milan Kundera. 'I'm so glad', he said, 'we have so many radio stations in France that at precisely the same time they all say the same thing about the same things'.

At the same time, the satellite companies are not subject to any democratic control.

– 'Satellite allows a hundred million people to be sold the same crummy tat. But we can't talk back.'

That was also the time the internet had started to have an impact on our lives. Visionaries, David Pitchford, a journalist, said, 'could turn it into a working, interactive tool of democracy. But if the commercial world or government gains supremacy, we could all be subsumed by a world of censored, monitored, pay-by-the-minute connections in which Big Brother could even steal information off your computer'.

It was a very good guess.

Interviews similar to 'How much is enough' were conducted on other issues such as Britain's responsibility to the world. If accepted, would the use of force, which would give it substance, also be acceptable? The question was raised the time the Bosnian war was raging. People asked for their views represented various shades of the human potential movement. Despite it, their answers were, however, anything but identical.

The answer to the question is, in theory, relatively uncomplicated.

Faced, for example, with the 1994 Rwandan genocide, during which an estimated 500,000–1,000,000 Tutsi and moderate Hutu were slaughtered by members of the Hutu majority, one can hardly turn his back in order to watch the 'Britain has talent' next episode or finish his online betting.

But, in practice, matters become pretty complicated as self-interest rather than principles dominates the decision-making process.

In another instance people were asked 'What is God?' For Sinéad O'Connor, the Irish singer-songwriter who in 1990 had achieved worldwide fame, 'God is truth', and for poet Ivor Cutler 'God is something you turn to as a mummy and daddy substitute, a superior type of thumb-sucking'. For Barry Long, the spiritual master, 'God is my life, my everyday unfolding life' and for Dannie Abse, the Welsh-Jewish poet honoured for services to poetry and literature, God is no mystery.

Mysteries for him existed 'in things seen momentarily in the corner of the eye, in voices just out of earshot, in odours one can't quite identify'.

My own understanding of mystery at that point was rather trifling and definitely unrefined. I could not work out why, having no car at the time, I had received a parking fine.

People, likewise, were asked whether 'marriage as we know has had its day?' The question was raised as marriages had started to collapse before the sellotape on the wedding presents has lost its adhesiveness.

Jenny Seagrove, the actress who rose to fame in 1983, thought marriage was here to stay – 'at least if there are children around', but at the same time she saw it as 'an ideological dream impossible to achieve'.

Novelist DM Thomas thought, too, that 'children should be brought up within a stable marriage'. But he did not believe in monogamy.

– The day will come, he said, that bishops and cardinals will urge us: 'Stay married, but go and have an affair.'

Otherwise, my French friend Claude remarked, it would be like having chicken for dinner every day.

Monogamy, Anne Karpf, a *Guardian* journalist, stated too, is for many people 'the apotheosis of dullness'. 'Changing sexual partners can be fulfilling and, let's not pretend otherwise, fun.'

Yet sex, Clare Jenkins wrote, 'though natural and instinctive as speech, has been denaturalised by experts. Rarely, if ever, are "deviants" advised to have the courage of their convictions when these convictions conflict with society's'. 'When thinking or talking about sexuality and sexual behaviour', Anne Karpf also wrote, 'we need to acknowledge that there is no single, acceptable form of sexual activity that holds good for all people all of the time. What is needed is a new sexual ideology which respects sexual diversity'.

Suzanne Moore, one of the big stars of the British media, focused on the floating world of modern romance fiction, peopled, as she said, by men who are as hard as steel and women who are soft and yielding and radiantly beautiful. It is a world, to put it differently, in which you

– 'Start off sinking into his arms and end up with your arms in the sink.'

Though dismissed by male critics as superficial and over-emotional trash, this popular culture, she argued, cannot be denied by anyone interested in changing the reality of many women's lives.

The way women present themselves to the world, Brenda Polan, fashion writer for *Tatler* and *The Guardian*, is another part of our realities.

Fashion, she held, gives women a simple sensuous pleasure and enables them to explore their psyches and their own bodies in a way men cannot. Feminists are not an exception to this rule.

The way women, or some women, choose to present themselves has, however, another side. Looking in the photo library for the photo of a woman radiating sincerity, serenity, care and beauty, all I could find were women with glamorous breasts, legs and bottoms. I picked one up, but then I had to face the wrath of a number of feminists. It made me think.

As I wrote in February 1991, for the women in the photos this was apparently the way forward to earn a good living and a passport to fame, or, perhaps, just the next meal. Responding to what the market demanded, those women were happy to present themselves as objects of desire. The feminists say this is the sad result of female conditioning in what is still a man's world. This may well be so.

Yet, I wonder, is selling looks really different from selling, say, skills?

Do not we all bank on what we think is our best asset to get the highest return?

It follows we cannot deplore the objectification of the female body without taking issue with our market-dominated culture.

But, perhaps, my thesis rests just in prejudice.

21

Incomprehensible but Fashionable

The magazine took an alternative and rather controversial view on many other issues such as what manhood is all about. Tony Crisp, an author of several books, argued that rather than feeling that we live in a male dominated world, many men feel dominated by their need to work, by their role and by those in power. It follows that manhood can be reached in interaction with this world and achieved when a sense of positive identity has taken roots.

But the different new heroes that emerge, David Cohen, author like Tony Crisp of a number of books, wrote, do not offer a clear vision of what it is like to be an ideal man. 'You are meant to be tough and sensitive, to express your feelings and still succeed in a competitive world'.

Men's feelings need, obviously, to be taken into protective custody.

This was the topic Robert Bly, the celebrated American leader of the new men's movement, also expanded on in an interview with Dina Glouberman.

Men are urged, he said, to develop their feminine side. But when a man does it, 'he becomes nicer, but not necessarily a stronger person. Developing this side too much means that, when the burglar comes in, the man is not going to protect you. You cannot go to a young man in a gang in the United States either and say to him "I want you to develop your feminine side". It will not work at all'.

Bly's ideal man is the Wild Man, the hunter in touch with nature, Mother Nature. Connecting with Mother Nature again, is more like connecting with women too. He emphasised, however, that we need 'to make a distinction between the inner warrior who protects the ground and the outer warrior who goes and kills'.

Interestingly, Lisette Thooft, the Dutch journalist, offered here a different view as to what a 'real' man looks like, i.e. what makes women melt. It is, she said, 'the total lack of doubt or hesitation that lures' as is the case with Arnold Schwarzenegger, 'the man without moods, the man who pursues his goal without being deflected from his course by wavering, unregulated feelings.'

Men can no longer claim ignorance.

As Green issues had from 1989 onwards moved away from the fringe image of brown bread and sandals to more mainstream perceptions of concerned professionals, I asked a number of people why we cannot manage the protection of the earth. Margaret Drabble, the author, summed up their reactions.

– 'Basically', she said, 'we all want to see improvements in our lifetime, but we don't want to have less fun in order that our children can have more'. It was and still is an attitude that I had named the 'credit card mentality' – live now and pay later.

The Green movement was at the time struggling to keep its head above water. That was perhaps partly, as Martin Charter, a man involved with projects with a Green tinge, wrote, because this Green consciousness was 'nothing more than a short lived middle class fad, a superficial guilt reaction to the decade of greed'.

But its decline was also due to reasons beyond the Greens' control.

'Exposing the threat to the environment', I wrote in April 1995, 'threatened the interests of corporations but also property, jobs and trade union power. And then the Green concerns, deprived of their substance, were appropriated by the establishment. Even prime minister Thatcher and president Bush tried to pass as Greens. Industry does also its best to appear as a force greening the planet.'

Hence the split of the Greens between the realists who knew what is achievable within the existing political context and the fundamentalists who had no faith whatsoever in institutions and called for radical action outside them.

The fundamental issue behind this kind of differences is also what our contemporary activists still need to resolve.

Poverty and violent reactions to the decade of greed like the Los Angeles riots was the focus of Ian Gregory, a freelance journalist contributing to the *Financial Times*. He warned that with long-term poverty increasing and the democratic process seemingly incapable of responding, even full-blown riots might become a recurring part of Britain's inner-city culture.

Society, however, did not seem to respond. "Politically, at least', Alex Howard noted, 'it looks like decay. There is a sense of rootlessness and uncertainty because the ideas and institutions that previously provided secure roles and routes to meaning and commitment are in decay'. In our postmodernist culture, Jim McGuigan also wrote, 'all is deconstructible. Nothing is sacred' .

What we are witnessing, Guy Claxton wrote in another instance, is 'moral despair'.

It is what we all seem to experience today, too, in a world increasingly depopulated of euphuistic ideas.

In a controversial feature, Jane Matthews, a feature writer, criticised the lifestyle of international and government agency workers and top charity personnel working in Africa. 'When you get into the bigger aid side', she wrote, 'you are looking at a person who is attracted by a sort of diplomatic life, status and the very, very large salaries you can pick up working for the UN'. Agency workers, she wrote, live in bigger houses and have servants. They like having someone to dust their shelves and mow the lawn. Many of them are there to milk the country. What might be there for the aid workers, the folk heroes of the guilt-ridden '80s, is, instead of wage packets, power, influence, a way of life that has vanished everywhere else.'

Having spent years in Africa as an aid worker, she quoted other aid workers saying that if Africans kicked out every Western expert, life would in fact for the vast majority of the population not be much worse. 'In fact, it may be a lot less disruptive.'

At the Prince of Wales Road office I offered her my compliments for her investigative skills. Raphael, a visitor, was, however, critical of me.

– 'You should have also said something about her visible assets', he said after she had gone.

The man had just failed to notice the sign at the office door saying entry not allowed to drooling idiots.

Critical of charities was also David Reed, editor of *Orbit*, the magazine of Voluntary Service Overseas. 'They have grown into sophisticated marketing organisations', he wrote, 'and public uneasiness over their role and effectiveness is increasing'. But if we question and criticise them, he added, 'we should also be aware that we are in a way criticising ourselves'.

The Third World problems were further highlighted by Kathleen Corrigan, a freelance journalist, who argued in favour of the principle 'the polluter pays' to end the destruction of the developing world's forests and wildlife. Since the developed countries created the greenhouse effect, she said, the responsibility for reversing this destructive trend is theirs.

Other large issues also came into the picture as when Naseem Khan, a freelance journalist, raised the issue of immigration and the resulting rapid changes in the composition of the population. Do immigrant communities have to endorse English values, and, if yes, what is Englishness?

Her answer was: 'Who can say?'

'Englishness', she argued, 'has always changed, and it is going on doing so. Multiculturalism, truly speaking, should be regarded as a dynamic assistant for change rather than the dreary, worthy acceptance of difference it has tended to be.'

British prime minister David Cameron did, however, warn against 'state multiculturalism' and many insist that there has to be a liberal minimum. UKIP, whose appeal rests partly on white English prejudices, is, of course, totally opposed to multiculturalism.

Yet in Britain's post-faith, post-ideology and post-everything world the uncertainty persists. Questioned during the Scotland referendum, 'Britishness', too, emerged as a concept next to impossible to define. If one is to go by what various commentators have stated, the concept is in a long term decline.

Nevertheless, even if this is the case, I find the determination of ethnic and religious minorities to treat the host country, whether this is Greece or the UK, as if a province of their own country rather disagreeable. In the long term, their refusal to integrate can change radically the identity of the host country, which, incidentally, is what an Islamist cab driver in London once told me is the ultimate aim of his associates.

Psychology, 'a religion for the well to do', and issues that came under its heading were dealt with by Petrushka Clarkson, a clinical psychologist, Corinne Sweet, author of Off the Hook, John Rowan, a leading psychologist and author of many books, Dina Glouberman and others.

Novelist and ex-therapist Rosemary Jackson took a critical view of psychotherapy, which is 'becoming an end in itself'. 'The psychotherapist's couch', she wrote, 'has replaced the church as a place of confession and renewal and the therapist as guru helps us find meaning. Fluid ideas turn into dogmas and become instruments of social power.' Preoccupation with personal growth and health, Alex Howard stated likewise, 'could itself become unhealthy, indulgent and escapist'. In its 'most decadent form', psychotherapy, he said, can become 'a comfortable pastime for the upmarket consumer and the sophisticated cultural cognoscenti'.

A similar view was taken by Will Parfitt, a psychotherapist, who deplored the fact that psychosynthesis, developed by Italian psychiatrist Roberto Assagioli, had been appropriated by spiritual psychologists and turned into a pseudo-mystical system. When the mystic takes over, he said, 'we become astral junkies, spiritual side-steppers or new age trippers.'

The New Age, a spiritual movement drawing inspiration from both Eastern and Western metaphysical traditions and also medieval astrology and alchemy, was at the time sitting comfortably among the burghers of suburbia.

Everything Oriental in particular, especially if it was incomprehensible, was now in its eyes desirable and fashionable.

Several of the *i-to-i* contributors viewed it critically. One of them, Gaie Houston, one of the founders of the Humanistic Psychology movement in the UK, was in fact furious at the New Agers. That was when she heard a lecturer at St James, Piccadilly, assuring his audience that 'higher beings' would intervene in case of a nuclear war to disarm the nuclear warheads.

– 'Only I and my companion', she wrote in *i-to-i*, 'appeared appalled at his assertion – the archangels, perhaps under the direction of an etherealised Ronald Reagan, will provide sci-fi instant protection'.

As irritated at the refusal of the New Age to entertain 'negative' thoughts, on the assumption that thought guides energy, and negative energy harms both yourself and others, was John Rowan, another established psychotherapist. He took exception of what he took as an expression of voluptuous languor when the organisers of a New Age conference refused to endorse a notion opposing racism in any form. It expressed 'negative' thoughts, they said.

But as the other side persisted, their group sat in the middle of the floor, joined hands, and hummed and moved rhythmically to dispel the 'bad' energy the notion about racism had raised. Disgusted at the spectacle, John Rowan exploded.

– 'Sometimes', he lambasted them, 'a Hitler has to be fought'.

I became aware of the absurdity of it all early enough in Skyros island, when the water pump broke down due to a mechanical problem.

The New Agers formed a circle around it, put some lit candles in the middle, and then joined hands and started humming to tune in with the spirit of the water pump to re-assure it of our unconditional love. Their positive energy, apparently in contact with some odylic force, and their messages of love, they were certain, would convince the water pump to do things it had no intention of doing.

For a moment, and as the sea was holding its breath, I thought that time had stopped several centuries ago. Or, alternatively, that someone had gained access to the daynight lamp, which, at one flick of the switch, could turn day, however bright, into the blackest night.

It was also the time I discovered the new boundaries of both communicability and absurdity, which, I thought, I had discovered a few years earlier. Someone, apparently knowing more than the rest of us, had insisted then that Plato did not like Beethoven's Ninth Symphony.

The multitude of practices that came under the New Age roof was mind-boggling. It included native American shamanism, Tibetan chanting, crystal healing, channelling, astral projections, psychic energies and out of body experiences, devas, elementals, angels, spirit guides, therapeutic touch, Bach Flower rescue remedies, reincarnation, Feng Shui and much more including many alternative medicine practices.

What connected them all was the belief of its well-intentioned practitioners in a radical shift in human consciousness which would 'change the world'. Yet, this movement, virtuous as cold porridge oats, remained disengaged from the world. Living in the present moment while attaining total detachment from the so-called 'reality', in a private vacuum, it sought only harmony with the One.

Change could then, perhaps, come on its own, like the foliage in the woods.

Spirituality to me meant something different: merging with concepts such as beauty, time, love, simplicity, rhythm, creativity, perfection, silence or energy and living their essence. Matter and spirit, all in one, create then new realities and a sense of wholeness that brings us in touch with the totality of our existence. In a neo-religious, mystical context, spirituality is, however, totally strange to me in everything, 'its curves and its volumes, its colours and adornments and its shadows'.

The flocculent nature of its belief system made, of course, the New Age far less objectionable than the strict religious orthodoxies. But the absurdity of these beliefs, which turned out to be its main asset, demanded the abdication of Reason, i.e. uninhabited brains.

As objectionable to me were its gurus. 'Gurus have no place in my tradition that teaches us never to surrender our right to think for ourselves', I wrote in *i-to-i* magazine, 'and they have no place in a world in which the people, self-realised, constitute a community of leaders – not of followers of the "enlightened" one. Visions founded on "truth" embodied in their teachings or communicated through manipulative techniques are only an invitation to move forward to the past.'

The dismissal of Reason in favour of intuition is even more dangerous.

As I often wrote, whatever comes from the deeper, mystical self is, naturally, more powerful and potentially, because of it, more effective. But our deeper self alone is not necessarily, in itself, a good guide for action.

Prone to a total, uncritical commitment, it can well respond to primitive fears and forces in us as we have witnessed so many times in history with heinous results.

Other people were as critical. Guy Claxton, author of many books on psychology and education, observed that 'in a state of spiritual "grace", psychological problems and considerations of social adjustment are not so much resolved as sidelined', and Dan Miller, a New York psychologist, focused on 'the mass manipulation techniques used on a commercial level that abuse the sincere intentions of people who follow this road'.

While in London for the Healing Arts Festival', he carried on, 'I observed many hawkers abusing the gullibility of people who didn't know what it's about'.

Jeff Harrison, a freelance journalist, focusing on shamanism, described a shaman as 'one who can perceive, communicate with and act as intermediary between the "normal" world and the realm of souls, spirits and gods'.

But he wondered:

– 'Is the adoption of shamanism in the West a legitimate instance of cultural cross-fertilisation or a form of plunder, ideal for contemporary culture-vultures?'

Having taken a long course with Avatar, a spiritual growth organisation, another journalist, Niket van Zuydam, also wrote: 'When terms such "enlightenment", "divine realisation" and even "avatar" (which is a Hindu term for the incarnation of a Hindu deity in human or animal form) are bandied about and when the founder claims to have discovered a secret technique which reduced the enlightened mystic to a redundant fossil, then I start getting goose bumps'.

From another angle but equally dismissive, Andrew Cohen, a spiritual teacher himself, talked about 'the extraordinary corruption that exists in the modern spiritual world.

– 'Most spiritual teachers', he said, 'have been found to be prey to all the usual human weaknesses like lust and greed. They feel that an "enlightened" person has transcended ordinary morality and start sleeping with the daughters of their closest disciples or telling other people to live frugally and yet they themselves live very extravagantly.'

Questioning the New Age's approach did, of course, cause negative reactions. A taste of them was offered to me by Tony Ward who, writing on behalf of the Monkton Wyld community, said that we needed to understand that 'accentuating the positive' is Alternative Realism, the answer to a world of depressive cynicism.

That was a good point, but my answer was that we cannot go blindly down an alley without asking ourselves where this alley leads. The New Age, this ill-defined movement, needed to start the process of self examination.

But this was beyond the limits of sober probability. Though happy to renew their beliefs in a sweat lodge, the New Agers did not want them questioned.

Thinking was not highly rated.

Another New Age apostle, Louise Hay, interviewed by Lisette Thooft, expanded on her personal beliefs. 'I believe', she said, 'that everything I need comes to me, everything I need to know is revealed to me, that all is well in my life, that I go from one wonderful experience to another, and that I am comfortable and prosperous and loved wherever I go'.

The new religion had been built on love – of your own self.

Thooft reminded Hay that several people thought of her as a 'phony marshmallow' and disapproved of her 'soul contract' with health, prosperity and love, which, though 'it looks sweet, is as empty inside as a soap bubble'. Still Intoxicated by the sound of her own voice, Hay answered: 'I feel very peaceful'.

Her book You Can Heal Your Life had sold 500,000 copies worldwide.

The Hay interview upset the aura of a number of New Agers for its 'judgemental' tone. It seemed that, though they had a degree in imperturbability, they did not seem to have enough practice.

The magazine hosted also features on several other topics, from how to invest your money ethically and ways to build your own house to alternative medicine and the treatment of the old, those who no longer had enough bodily substance to gratify the soul of their ladies.

Jad Adams, an author and freelance journalist, wondered why we love conspiracy theories of the kind who 'betrayed' Lord Kitchener, who 'killed' Marilyn Monroe or who was 'behind' the Aids epidemic. Conspiracy theories, he said, are fascinating, irresistible, and pure fantasy, but we never seem to tire of a good plot.

His theory was contradicted, among others, by investigative journalists Jay Margolis and Richard Buskin, who in their 2014 sensational book argued that Monroe's death was a murder ordered by Bobby Kennedy to prevent her from revealing her torrid affairs with himself and his brother, president Kennedy.

Perhaps, one day somebody will also offer the solution to the mystery surrounding the missing skull of Francisco Goya. Following his death in 1828, his corpse was interred at the cemetery of Bordeaux, but when in 1901 his remains were moved at the request of the Spanish government to Madrid the skull was found missing. It has not been located since.

Space was also consistently given to the arts: Russian constructivist art, Georgia O'Keeffe, African art, Lucian Freud,

Czech artists, the human form in art, Willem de Kooning, eco-technological art or Robert Venosa, the great American artist who graced Skyros with his presence as a teacher.

But *i-to-i* could not easily make it in a publishing world dominated by conglomerates. My enthusiasm for it, while it was running, was flying high, but, on the other hand, it was totally disproportionate to its returns.

After my negotiations to sell it to *The Guardian* failed to produce any results, I had, thus, no option but close it down.

I just could not walk on water. When autumn comes, the Tao literature tells us, 'no leaf is spared because of its beauty, no flower because of its fragrance'.

For a while I then played with the idea of launching a new website dedicated to the madness of our civilisation and the madness of our opposition to it. Irrational absurdity versus rational absurdity.

This new website could have themes such as

The thought of the day: 'Let's be twice as ordinary as everybody else.'

A New Age section: 'Aromatic oils for the afterlife.'

A courses section: 'How to identify aliens.'

A relationships section: 'Let the fingers do the work.'

A religion section: 'It gives goodness a bad name.'

A competitions section: 'The fastest watch in town.'

Its fans could also organise get-togethers to paint their fantasies, murder Deepak Chopra, have aural sex, annoy their Blairite neighbours, pee in public to raise money for a good cause or campaign to legalise grammar.

In support of the project I quoted Dostoevsky's Notes from the Underground.

'Hadn't we better kick over all that rationalism at one blow, scatter it to the winds... and live once more according to our foolish will? After all, this very stupid thing, this caprice of ours, may really be more advantageous for us, gentlemen, than anything else on earth... It preserves for us what is most precious and most important – that is, our personality, our individuality.'

It was all, of course, a fantasy to help me escape the lumpy, enervating burden of the mundane, the sort of thing that gives sanity a bad name.

But thankfully, Skyros was still there.

And I could still order the sun to rise every day.

22

'The First and Still the Best...'

Meanwhile, and as time went on, Skyros island developed a taste for tourism and the money it brings. Roads were sealed, hotels built, nightclubs and restaurants mushroomed and East European immigrants arrived. The Internet Café now electronically signposts the new era for the island.

The locals changed, too, as trends, like gravity, can be resisted only for so long. The young men frequent clubs rather than tavernas and drink whiskey rather than local wine. Young women, all graduates of the Ecole des Femmes, are as fashion-conscious as their counterparts in London's Knightsbridge.

The old days when you would not dare even to enquire about the health of another man's wife were now the stuff of sitcom script writers.

Nicos Margetis, the village taverna owner, is still there. He is still as shy as he used to be except that when in these days I take a seat at his place he comes now to ask me what I would like to order. The very first time I took a seat in his taverna, in a very hot afternoon of 1978, he ignored me completely. Years later, when I asked him why he did that, he said:

– 'I thought you were tired and had come to have a rest. I just didn't want to bother you.'

Others, like Yannis Karabinis, the town-crier, Costas Bibis, a man who, as if he were in parliament, kept talking in order to say nothing, or Stamatis Frangoulis, the old man in the traditional Skyrian outfit who was always seated cross-legged outside his village shop, have all gone for good.

Yet the magic of the island has not dissipated into the thin air of globalism. A prejudiced pride in its past and a stubborn commitment to its Greekness would not make room for it.

At any rate, even if desired, an up-to-date unconscious cannot be acquired.

The Centres also changed. The level of organisation and comforts simply had to rise from the laid-backness of the sixties. But the guests changed, too, though I still remember from 1984 that lady with an accent which made even the Queen's accent sound rather plebeian.

Rather than representing the fringe of society, the guests are now mainstream people, many of them, indeed, leaders in their fields. One of them was that fireman who had won the Skyros holiday in the BBC TV programme Tomorrow's World.

He had never thought, he wrote afterwards, that he would ever go on such a holiday, yet his experience of it was 'uplifting'.

The 'alternative' had won respectability.

Skyros, Tom Fordyce wrote in *The Times* in March 2010, is 'the sophisticated urbanite's retreat of choice'. Yet for Anne, a 1979 Skyros Centre participant who returned after 24 years, the spirit of the place had not changed a bit. Thanks to its values, upheld since the ball started rolling, Skyros' soul had successfully resisted the market's designer spirituality.

Atsitsa, true to itself, remains, however, untameable, and this, together with its countless imperfections, ensures its overriding allure. Indeed, anything different would have impoverished the richness of its stories and robbed many people of their most treasured, fragrant memories.

Yet the spirit of innovation is ever-present. Though everything may appear settled, nothing is – the creation of Skyros is taking place daily. New ideas, whether spectacularly successful or dismally ill-conceived, flow in constantly and turn the place into the imagination's workshop. What keeps the Skyros balance in place is its ethos and also its community structures.

Workgroups, for example, are still encouraged because work, as the poet said, is 'love made visible'. Work creates community. Demos, the daily gathering of the whole group, is still a cornerstone of community life, as is co-listening and œkos, both essential components of the Skyros tradition.

Of importance are also the links the Centres have developed with the local community. If it is not to be a force of destruction that allows nothing on its path to grow again, tourism has to act as a bridge between the locals and the visitors. This bridge would be left disappointed if not used in a way that is beneficial to both sides.

Respect for the local culture is in this sense important not as a matter of courtesy, but because of its intrinsic value.

After all, although wealth is not, the gift of wisdom, just like light, is equally distributed amongst all peoples of the world, and the visitors can learn something from the sagacity of the locals.

Special care is taken in this respect to honour the local traditions, and, very importantly in this sense, not to expect the locals to adjust their way of living to that of their visitors. The latter have also to understand that money cannot buy everything, including the respect and the friendship of the locals.

Leftheris Trakos, the island's travel agent, has been very appreciative of the way our Skyros guests interact with the locals.

– 'They've set an example', he has told me time and again.

Help is also being offered regularly either to re-equip the local hospital, protect the island's forest, provide computers for the local school, refurbish its theatre, support the welfare of the Skyrian horses, dogs and cats and also the work of the island's folk dance society and the local children's Tae- Kwon-Do group.

More recently, in 2013, Skyros Holidays raised €27.000 with the generous help of its holiday participants. The aim was to help with the heating of the island's schools, its health centre and its old people's home in the winter, and with the provision of facilities for its clinic. Government funds for the purpose had dried out due to the financial crisis. Another large sum towards the same purpose was also raised for the following year.

As important is its contribution to the cultural life of the island through concerts in the village plateia, exhibitions, street theatre events, yoga for the local children and also through the half-marathon Peter Webb and Kevin Whelan, members of the Atsitsa staff, organised each year with the participation of visitors and locals.

I never joined them but I most definitely would have if it had not involved running.

Skyros could now proudly claim, as *The Guardian* pointed out in March 2008, that it was 'the first and still the best' alternative holiday.

In 1992 another major step for the development of Skyros was taken, when the Writers' Lab was established. It was once again a very innovative step: holiday writing courses within the Skyros community for people who were looking for inspiration and help to start, shape, develop and turn their ideas into a book.

Writers who run these courses included celebrities such as Steve Attridge, Steven Berkoff, Rachel Billington, Clare Boylan, Lindsay Clarke, Wendy Cope, Andrew Davies, MIchael Dibdin, Margaret Drabble, Nell Dunn, Elaine Feinstein, Romesh Gunesekera, Sophie Hannah, Hanif Kureishi, Alison Lurie, Hilary Mantel, Michelle Roberts, Monique Roffey, Bernice Rubens, Kirkpatrick Sale, D M Thomas, Sue Townsend, Marina Warner, Shelley Weiner, Hugo Williams and many others.

One of those I failed to persuade to join Skyros was the Nobel prize winner Doris Lessing with whom I occasionally shared a coffee in West Hampstead where we both lived. She felt too old for the adventure – and, having been born in 1919, she probably was.

John Mortimer declined the invitation, too. Creative writing, he argued, could not be taught. My arguments to the contrary failed miserably to move him. I wonder, if he were still around, what would he have made of the creative writing courses run nowadays in almost every university.

The Writers' Lab, an overnight success story, was almost inevitably named by *The Guardian* in June 2008, as the No 1 of 'the World's Five Best Writing Holidays'. It was featured in several publications and many of its students did successfully over the years see their own work published. Others, like Roisin, are, perhaps, still trying.

As she wrote in *The Irish Times* in June 2007, she still had not written her novel, but 'after a week on Skyros I may be inching ever closer to making a start.'

Skyros, incidentally, did also welcome other celebrities such as the American actor Bob Wisdom, the singer-songwriters Tom Robinson and Dean Friedman, the singer and actress Toyah Willcox, the guitarist John Etheridge, the actress Polly James, the health and beauty specialist Leslie Kenton, the sculptor Glyn Williams, the comedians Arthur Smith, John Cremer, Andy Ford and many others.

Meanwhile, and in the midst of all this, life had in personal terms taken a disagreeable turn. At the end of 1993, I split with Dina, my wife and partner since 1969. The decision was hers rather than a joint one, but in all this I had to accept my own responsibilities. In any case, in a long relationship people's expectations change, interests diversify and outlooks are affected either by new insights or circumstances.

The divorce had a traumatic effect on me, but looking back I can only be grateful to her for the gift she gave me by her presence in my life. Despite the break-up, the friendship was maintained as did our Skyros partnership.

Soon after, I entered into a new relationship with Christine Schulz, the woman I had met in Skyros back in 1991, when she was working there as a work-scholar. Christine, partly of continental origins through her Finnish mother, is now the general manager of Skyros. My relationship with her has given me all I need to keep my certainties intact and the smile on my face.

Living with a partner you love, trust and can rely on is a blessing, one of the great gifts of life.

Relationships on life support can never do you any good.

Personal issues did not affect my commitment to Skyros and its values. Next year, in 1994, I worked, thus, with another fifty Skyros people and launched in the UK a movement embodying those values. It was in the form of the œkos movement, which soon spread to several other countries from the US to Russia. Fifty or so œkos groups sprang in no time all along the UK. Several of them are still in existence.

One such group, in Bristol, has been meeting for ten years.

– 'We've survived weddings, divorces and even death, and we're still going on', they said.

They did so because, as others said, whatever you gained in Skyros, whether it is hope, confidence, renewed faith, camaraderie, new interests, ideas or skills, needs to be nurtured. So do friendships and the spirit of the Skyros community.

Œkos in Greek stands for home/family. In our context it means a home base of like-minded people providing simple, open and honest lines of communication between them, supporting their drive towards the unlocking of their potential and helping to bring back our sense of common purpose.

As such, œkos is not an organisation but a philosophical approach in the heart of which is what E.P. Thompson, the leading marxist thinker whom I was happy to meet in Holland in the early 1980s, called 'the education of desire'. The aim, ultimately, is to bridge the gap between the personal and the social and, in the broadest sense, political, and speed up the pace towards a new society that values itself, its members and the natural world.

– 'Capitalism', I wrote in *i-to-i* magazine in July 1994, 'devalues what is outside the flow of money and has no time for it. Institutional power, threatened by grass-roots solidarity, invests no energy in it. Technology, in spite of its sophisticated "communications" systems, has given communication all the rope it needs to hang itself. And individualism, so much part of our current culture, is signing over the demise of our community. Power has turned in effect into a community vandal causing disintegration – even the family, the last bastion of communal living, is falling, fast. It's only "me, me, me", the seed of apocalypse.'

The œkos concept is rooted in Atsitsa, Skyros island, where it grew and developed.

Originally known as the UFO group, it was the forum to which people brought anything they could not raise anywhere else: a memory, a discovery, a difficulty, an idea. Though loosely defined, œkos soon became an oasis of intimacy. People could share in it feelings and thoughts in a way many had never done before. They were enabled to establish the kind of effective communication that transcended age, class, sex, race, professional or cultural biases.

Relatively free from the distorting effects of other people's projections, its individual members opened up and flourished beyond even their own comprehension. Its 'magic', Bobbie Stuart wrote from Boulder, Colorado, USA, engulfed everyone.

As the declaration adopted by the initiators stated, the idea was to bring the Skyros values into everyday life by bridging the gap between the ideal and the practical and the temporary nature of the island experience with the more permanent demands of our living realities. It was all about inner and outer change, for the discomforts of our time are as much ill-effects of our social values as the latter are ill-effects of our individual perceptions.

The aim was to foster an individual sense of identity, place and belonging and empower individuals so that they could take charge of their own destiny, free, like seagulls over the sea, from oppressive and authoritarian structures. The holistic approach of the group aimed at acknowledging all our needs – intellectual, social, emotional, spiritual and physical – in a world that needs to become more free, just and safe.

More friendly, too, as the world of strangers we all live in results in the alienation from our fellow human beings. The point was vividly illustrated to me in New York by Liu, a Chinese-American, when he advised me:

– 'Don't smile here. They'll arrest you.'

Œkos, in this sense, could be seen as a force of cultural change or, as someone wrote, 'a challenge to the status quo'. It is, Alana Woods wrote from New Mexico, USA, a 'R.Evolution', a great movement, as Satsimran Kaur added from Califonia, USA, particularly as 'it originates with the grass roots'.

The movement emerged at the right moment, Marcia Plevin wrote from Frascati, Italy, a time the 'atmosphere is ripe with a past of distrust and a "who knows what will happen" future'.

Fully autonomous, the groups determine their own flavour, range of interests, and scope of activities and are open to everyone who shares their values and objectives. An oekos group can do very well in Atsitsa's Apricot circle, but an œkos network can also be established in the neighbourhood, the college or the workplace as, for example, a group of journalists did in London.

The idea is simple. A group of six to twelve people get together with a commitment to communicate with each other openly, honestly and also confidentially. The meetings begin with a 'round' in which members take 3-5 minutes each to speak from their heart about where they are at this moment in their life.

The space is then open for feedback, discussion, exchange of ideas and planning of activities on whatever level the group feels committed to.

This is possible only in an atmosphere where people do not need to present and prove themselves. All they have to do is be themselves, acknowledge their personal needs, listen, show empathy, give and be ready to accept support. Personal issues may well have to do with 'my relationships' or 'my obligations to this world', 'my low self-esteem' or 'the authoritarian structures I find myself in'. While explored, such issues can easily generate an exchange of views on wider moral, ethical, social and other issues or focus the attention of the group to issues such as parenthood, fashion, sexuality, religion or politics.

Trust in the other members' integrity and commitment to truth is a condition for the groups' existence. Cynicism may be the dress contemporary sophistication puts on to impress, but it is hardly the material with which to build a new world. It has no place in an œkos group.

The overall positive assessment of œkos as a vehicle of change was summed up by the representative of the Hampstead group. 'The closeness, sharing, healing and joy we experience', she wrote, 'is amazing'. This was shared by the Croydon group representative for whom his œkos goes to 'amazing depths of sharing, or by the Oxford group representative, who was very pleased about the new social network œkos had created for many of its members.

Serge Beddington hailed it, likewise, as a 'most important cultural strategy', Ari Badaines from Sydney, Australia, saw in it the spirit of the human potential movement rekindled, Mario-Paul Cassar expressed the hope that it would act as 'a catalyst in re-creating community which has long disappeared'.

The œkos movement was an answer to the problem posed by our 'post-everything' world albeit in the form of a small private dream, peopled by all those who shared it. One cannot really expect much more. The time people were born into a personal community has gone for good and only its images engraved in memory, like a woman's body on the bed, are the witnesses of times bygone. All we can do now is improvise.

Yet the œkos movement was not launched in isolation from the wider movement of the social ecologists.

People like Murray Bookchin, the American political theorist, were already advocating the reinvigoration and the greening of our cities and the development of an urban 'life place' consciousness. The emphasis was on the organic, the holistic and the developmental.

And it was political. Neither in the context of party politics nor in the framework formed by special interests as represented by campaigns, societies, Rights' associations, Trade Unions or NGOs either. The latter deal only with a small portion of quantifiable concerns that make sense in the context of the institutions. They are useful insofar as they try, sometimes with some success, to correct imbalances in a disequilibrated world. But they cannot express the needs of the individual.

Politics has to embrace these concerns, too, connect to the fundamental condition of individual existence and engage into our times' cultural battles.

It is in this sense that the personal becomes political and the political personal. As I wrote in *i-to-i* magazine, inner and outer walk together hand in hand. People certainly create structures which can be good or bad, but being conditioned by them, they are also their creation.

In 1996 Skyros begun also to run holidays in the Caribbean island of Tobago and then in Thailand, Cuba, Cambodia and later Venice, Morocco and Trinidad.

Unsurprisingly, as *The Times* pointed out in June 2007, Skyros had turned into 'the most talked about holistic holiday destination in Europe'. Skyros-in-Cambodia, the same newspaper said a month later, is 'one of the top five adventure retreats'.

I would have never imagined in my early years that my activities would become the subject of stories in several of the world's leading newspapers. But anything is possible, if the impossible is true.

One day, who knows, even an egg may manage to stand on its legs rather than its belly.

In the meantime, my children had grown up. Chloe, my daughter, in 2001 was awarded an MA in English from Cambridge University and next year Ari, my son, received a Ph.D in mathematical economics from Manchester University. Ari soon after entered successfully the financial world, but Chloe first tried her luck with some acting.

It all started for her in the early nineties, when she appeared in a ten minutes TV Labour party political broadcast on education. Next day she was a celebrity and at the mercy of an irresistible force pushing her towards the mega-star destiny that a New Age clairvoyant of some reputation among the brainless had predicted.

– 'You'll make it in a big way', the latter had pronounced with the reassuring smile of someone in the know. 'You'll be a success.'

After a year-long course in acting, Peter Ustinov selected her for one of his historical documentaries and agents gave her a role in some sit-coms. This was not, however, enough and Chloe left eventually for LA, the film industry's Mecca. Among others, she met there Jan Dunn who gave her a substantial role in her 2005 film *Gypo* next to Pauline McLynn and Paul McGann. Two years later she was in *Ruby Blue* with Bob Hoskins and Josiane Balasco and then in *The Calling* with Brenda Blethyn, Susannah York and Rita Tushingham.

During the same time she appeared in a few TV productions and was also given a small part in the 2006 Paul Greengrass film *United93*.

But by that time she had enough. She had her fun but she also realised that a successful film career was really out of reach.

Investing your life in it was equal to investing your life savings in the national lottery. Though very difficult for her, she changed, thus, direction, trained as a teacher and works now happily in a primary school in London.

The allure of a glamorous life can be as irresistible as saffron-robed Eosa's constant longing for young mortals – that, incidentally, was the result of a curse laid upon her by the goddess Aphrodite. Though full of sweet promises, it rarely, however, leads to happiness. Success in life can sometimes depend on something very simple.

As the central character in Pavlos Manesis' novel The Daughter. said:

–'I can see my eggs in the fridge. My pension, I can see that. I'm a success.'

Whatever, astrologers need to be aggressively avoided.

23

Our Borderless World

Winter in Skyros island serves as a reminder of what winter originally used to be.

Implacable hissing winds, vigorous as in Homer's times, take in their drift even the roaming spirits of the dead, and, derailed by their power, the rain whips uncompromisingly the face of the land. Unleashed, the elements enjoy their supremacy as if determined to demonstrate that, despite the electronics revolution and Justin Bieber and Lady Gaga, they are still the ones who run the show.

Snow comes occasionally, but in the winter's kingdom one can also come across some beautiful sunny days.

Whatever, the air carries around the scent of wood burning in the old fireplaces, the locals enjoy their wine in the tavernas, and politics, usually the honoured guest, all wet in the current corruption scandals' rain, dries up its socks in the corner of their daily concerns.

It was in this island that, together with another sixty or so guests of Skyros, I welcomed in the new millennium. The inclemency of the weather had given way to mild, pleasant days and the frantic celebratory spirit back home had ensured that one could reflect, if he or she wanted to, on Tony Blair's message to bottle and keep for ever the 'confidence and optimism' the arrival of the new millennium had generated.

I tried to bottle it, but with an enthusiasm disproportionate to Blair's expectations. In any case, doing so was not all that easy as among the sixty guests, there was a woman, skinny as an excuse, who on arrival let the staff know that she had come to Skyros in order to kill herself.

Obviously, she had no intention of bottling anything.

The choice was to send her back to Athens, where given the effervescence of the times she was bound to welcome in the new millennium in ways she would later on regret or keep her on the island and take responsibility for her life. We discussed the issue at the staff meeting.

– 'What on earth shall we do?', was the burning question.

Some suggested we send her back to Athens. My own preference was to keep her on the island, not forgetting, of course, all the extra publicity the *Sun*, the *News of the World* and the other facts-free tabloids would give us for free if something went terribly wrong.

Eventually, we did keep her there, but anxiety started blowing its nose very noisily disturbing the village's tranquillity.

The woman, of an age which had placed her already out of the evolutionary game, needed supervision 24 hours a day. That was the job of the six members of the staff. To make matters worse, she also decided to come out and, in a state of controlled hysteria, she also refused help from the males of the group. Totally exhausted after a few days, the females of the staff asked the female guests for help, which was generously offered.

But the problems persisted one way or another.

Despite being guarded, the woman often, for example, would walk out of her room into the village at 3.00 or 4.00 am and disappear in its labyrinthine streets, the island's Bermuda Triangle.

The whole staff and several guests, summoned from their beds and pale as a lemon that had just heard bad news, had no choice but to start searching for her everywhere they could go.

At the end, all went as well as one could hope for. She did not commit suicide, though several of us thought of doing so, and she returned home gleaming like a white stone in the rain! The letter she then sent us read:

– 'Thank you for the very good care you took of me.'

But, in the meantime, things at home started, just like the seasons, to change again and the same tired old fears reappeared to ruffle our days. The 'confidence and optimism' Blair had hailed was evaporating like boiling water in the pot over the burner.

The early signs of the coming trouble appeared in 2000 when the Dot-Com bubble hit the US and unsettled the financial markets.

This time, the baby-boomers were genuinely worried. With each market bulletin showing the plummeting of the paper value of their assets on which they had invested their savings, their hopes for a comfortable retirement were receding further into the background. Economists called it dis-saving.

Soon after, in 2001, the Texas-based Enron Corporation, the giant energy, commodities and services company, went bankrupt. Enron was the embodiment of the 1990s fundamentalist neoliberal beliefs and this coupled with institutionalised fraud and corruption made it the age's symbol of crony capitalism. Its collapse provided testimony to the limitless greed that can flood the people's brain even when they are rich beyond their wildest dreams.

It was also a fitting epitaph to the bubble decade of the 1990s and an appropriate introduction to the 21st century's schemes of institutionalised irresponsibility and corruption into which people seemed to slip as easily as in their bedroom slippers.

But Enron was not the only company to go under. The financial industry – savings institutions, banks and insurance companies – was plagued with problems that with the arrival of the new millennium trapped them all into a nightmare.

Early on the decade had still, however, a smile on its face, albeit Napoleon's smile in which the teeth are shown, but the eyes do not smile.

Still Ben Bernanke, the US Federal Reserve chairman, was happy to re-assure people in 2004 that in the 'bold new economic era, volatility had been permanently eradicated'. A smiling Gordon Brown in 2007, just before he became the UK's prime minister, did also reassure everybody that the world had just entered:

– 'An era that history will record as the beginning of a new Golden Age.'

The seething juice of his vision had obviously filled his head with its intoxicating fumes. His delusion's flattering smile had won him over. Or, perhaps, just like prime minister Tony Blair, who was happy to knight just about every scoundrel in the City, he believed in it with all the essential sincerity of hope.

The clock, meanwhile, was ticking but nobody could see the time. The financial system was just content to swim blissfully in its mathematically ordered universe. The gypsy girls were dancing in the City.

Superficially, in any case, it all seemed to go the 'right' way. The removal of trade and investment barriers, the growth of domestic markets, the artificially low currencies or the offshore outsourcing of jobs to Third World countries, which kept significantly increasing, were all helping to induce some sort of a languorous drowsiness, which is inimical to thinking. After all, as Labour grandee Peter Mandelson had said, one should feel:

– 'Immensely relaxed about people getting filthy rich.'

Except that nobody becomes 'filthy rich' in a 9 to 5 job.

The culture of dangerous greed and excessive risk-taking had by now taken deep roots extinguishing the moral instinct. But nobody seemed to care.

Meanwhile, in 1999 the euro, the biggest achievement in Europe's post-war history, was launched, and in 2002 most EU members joined it officially, tying their currencies to each other's. Despite warnings about the country's economy, Greece joined it on the 1st of January 2001. The old currencies were phased out. The continent's yellowing old teeth had been replaced by a glittering brand new set.

Bright red and yellow kites hung high in the blue sky in celebration.

The resolute ambivalence about it all, so evident in the UK, had not at the time reached me. My own innate feeling was, instead, relief as Europe had at last managed to bring to an end the era of turbulence, bridge its differences and look forward to a future holding promises for all. The hope that something better would emerge from it all had settled into our living space. The dangers of the euro deal, still not featuring in our radars, were, thus, inevitably left outside our daily concerns.

Like James Joyce and Marcel Proust, who, when they met, discussed not the ache of modern literature but the merits of dark chocolate truffles, all we were talking about was the value of the euroculture.

All the rest was left in the basement of our thinking and fed garlic so that it could be found easily even in the dark, if and when we needed to take a better look at it.

Two years later, the EU undertook a major eastward enlargement, admitting ten new member states. The euro has since become the second largest reserve currency and the second most traded currency in the world after the US$.

The importance of this momentous event was nevertheless overshadowed by the 2003 Iraq war, an adventure of heinous deceit, which the mighty opposition to it, of which I did not fail to be a part, failed abysmally to prevent. The Blair government had made a mockery of democracy and, even worse, destroyed completely the remaining faith in the institutions.

Faith, of course, does not take you far, but its absence takes you nowhere. Still the feeling of despondency this failure generated was overwhelming.

As unsettling, however, was the realisation that the world was changing irreversibly and too fast for its own good. To begin with, the accumulation of too much power in the hands of too few people had empowered these few with what was, in effect, a weapon of mass destruction. Its effectiveness was tested when it exploded 'accidentally' in their own back yard in 2008 – an explosion that gave the world the colour of last year's seaweed.

Yet, all this power was still not good enough. Like Theodora, the wife of Byzantine Emperor Justinian, who regretted that God had not endowed her with more orifices to give more pleasure to more people at the same time, the all too powerful conglomerates were, as they still are, looking for new openings.

As I mentioned in my book In Bed with Madness, the first part of my Trilogy, just one of these conglomerates, General Motors, had an annual revenue which matched the combined GDP of Ireland, New Zealand, Uruguay, Sri Lanka, Kenya, Namibia, Nicaragua and Chad. Though only 153rd in the 2006 league of the billion dollar brands, a long way after Exon Mobil, HSBC, IBM, Nestlé, Coca Cola, Boeing, Sony or Disney, McDonald's alone was financially stronger than the economies of Tanzania, Ethiopia and Sudan put together.

Oligopolistic tendencies were and still are clear in several key areas – pharmaceuticals and healthcare, financial services and banking, software, defence and telecommunications, oil, car and airplane manufacturing, shipping, industrial components, entertainment and the media.

In eight sectors of the economy just the top five corporations controlled fifty per cent of the global market in a way which enabled them to dictate policies to world bodies, including the EU.

Wal-Mart, the world's largest retailer, Charles Fishman said in his book The Wal-Mart Effect, is not even subject to market forces 'because it's creating them'.

Imperceptibly, the world economy has turned into the hostage of the oligopolies with the consumer, their prisoner, safely kept behind high walls. Crucial utilities – water, power, heating, internet and telephone – are supplied by a few dominant groups with baffling contracts damping out any competition and disempowering the consumer.

Only two companies, says Cambridge university professor Peter Nolan, were in 2009 globally dominant in the manufacture of large commercial aircraft and carbonated drinks, only three in mobile telecommunications, only four in beer, elevators, heavy-duty trucks and personal computers, only six in digital cameras, and only ten in motor vehicles and pharmaceuticals. Similar degrees of concentration appear in several other sectors.

Reduced to an almost meaningless political and economic unit, and largely unable to control their development, the nation state is simply overwhelmed by the forces it helped to unleash.

Indeed, the 'mega-institutions', consolidated further through mergers and acquisitions, are beyond the ability of anyone to control, tax or even regulate. Corporate finance makes sure no official opposition to its power can develop.

The politicians with a voice, as Orwell would say, nearly as silent as a voice can be while still remaining a voice, have neither the guts nor the motivation to act. Moreover, those investing in the stock market, often ordinary householders who live their lives with no blame and no praise, prefer to shut their eyes and enjoy the benefits of their corporate investments in the form of rising share prices. And international institutions, the World Trade Organisation, the International Monetary Fund and the World Bank, are ever ready to offer protection to the multinationals if the going gets rough.

Yet the consequences of the unchallenged dominance of the industrial and financial conglomerates are very far reaching.

The planet is ruthlessly exploited and botched, the consumer has to pay the cost of their high profits, producers of goods and components see their prices dictated and their margins squeezed and the labour force is coerced into submission. Further, extreme outsourcing sets supplier against supplier, worker against worker, and nation against nation.

As the servant of big business, all governments can do is provide the technological infrastructure, human resources and what is euphemistically called a 'flexible market', which stimulates the erogenous zones of the multinational investors.

Competing thereby for the goodwill of the wealthy, they antagonise their own nationals, whose allegiance is nevertheless bought by the promise of improved living standards through globally-induced economic growth. At the same time, increasingly dependent on corporations for solutions in all spheres of the public domain, people see their traditional policy-making structures constantly undermined, marginalised, even ridiculed.

AOL's Gerald Levine made clear the latter point.

– 'The global media', he asserted, 'is becoming more important than governments, NGOs or educational institutions'.

So have the banks and the corporations which have turned democracy into a victim of neoliberal cosmopolitanism. Governments, linked to financial institutions so closely that they can take an aspirin for each other's headache, are no longer free to determine their course of action.

The 1 per cent that controls the West's national wealth is, thus, able to allocate the 99 per cent of the population just 1 per cent democracy.

The civic society, fragmented and dysfunctional, structurally weak and ideologically disarmed, cannot stand up to the power of the mighty forces of capitalism – Google, Apple, Monsanto, News Corporation, Nike, Wal–Mart, GlaxoSmithKline, Phizer, Shell, Microsoft or McDonald's, all metaphors for a global economic system gone awry. It cannot influence the decisions of the economic and political élites, whether national or international.

In fact, even political élites are not free to make their own decisions. Elected representatives and their regulators are all just outclassed by a financial system whose power, almost infinite, often outsizes their power and leaves people at the mercy of pitiless external forces.

'The regulators', as Campbell Macfarlane, the Shanklin local carpenter, said, 'have been captured by the regulatees'. The latter have become 'untouchable'.

He then smiled as if he expected payment for his witticism.

This global leviathan system, supported by unregulated hedge funds, networked computer systems, advanced telecommunications, fast transportation systems for people, goods and services, and an incredible information processing capacity to manage its complexities, has eliminated physical distances. It has turned the entire world into its playground.

The exponential growth of new electronic communication and information technologies is changing even our personal realities faster than we can blink.

Almost every week a new gadget appears and captures the public's imagination. PlayStation, iPod, BlackBerry, Xbox, iPhone, MP3 players and Twitter, Facebook, Instagram and MySpace have turned into the new social world which absorbed us like dry earth absorbs rain water. It has taken us into a different dimension in the cyberspace.

Mobile phones are now smaller and smarter, TV screens bigger and thinner, information circulates faster and high definition television and digital cameras is now the norm. It was not too long ago when we were reading books on paper and newspapers delivered at our home, playing video games with our friends and heading down to the shops to buy music albums or to the market place to buy food or furniture. The internet had in no time made possible the downloading of books, music and videos or online shopping at the click of a mouse.

Books may well have been fully replaced in about twenty years time. Already, on the train to Portsmouth, I did not see a single person reading a book or even a newspaper. Most, including the man seated opposite me, someone who looked very much like Richard Attenborough, seemed to be endlessly busy with their smartphones.

By doing so, I do not think they had surrendered to the pleasures of it all. It was more like having submitted to the force of a habit.

Like the habit of sitting down.

Responding to trivial minutiae is, however, time not spent on enjoying what really matters including the pleasures of face-to-face interaction and learning new things. Internet searches are not a substitute for fully understanding a subject which only a book can offer. Even Eric Schmidt, chairman of Google, acknowledged that reading a book is

– 'The best way to really learn something'.

Online gaming, like the family-friendly Nintendo Wii, performing as well as Hollywood movies, were embraced by wider age groups and demographics. Computing going mobile meant we could work now on the train, the beach, at the dentist's waiting room or at home.

– At any rate, 'working at home', Simon Stevens, a half-Jewish friend cheekily said, 'is better than doing nothing or sitting with the wife'.

I wondered which half of his was Jewish.

Laptops, netbooks, notebooks, smartbooks or whatever their name fit in a handbag, email became a standard form of interpersonal written communication and road maps were binned as the Global Positioning System took over.

As importantly, our favoured TV programme cannot be missed because we can now click pause, go to the loo and watch the programme later or arrange its recording ahead of time.

Television, in any case, is not the sport of the millennians, those born between 1980 and 2000. For them there is not such a thing as a must-see TV. The nineties were the last decade of television as a live medium, and, perhaps, also the last decade of shared interests discussed in the office the next day. The future choice of viewing will be downloadable any odd time, for a price: videos on demand via digital recorders, web streams or mobile phones.

All we will at the end have in common is something everybody has: a belly button.

The electronic revolution has, meanwhile, reinforced social atomisation. There is now less need to speak to anyone. The apps have eliminated everyday risks such as the potential discomfort of having an actual conversation with someone. With 'automatic' supermarket checkouts, you do not even need to speak to the cashier.

Millions of people live now their lives through social networking sites, draw attention to themselves with the chickens' self-advertising instinct through YouTube, promote themselves through MySpace and entertain themselves through YouPorn.

The social media, providing the means to document our life online, can now turn us all into celebrities. Involving the youngsters in the programming through stories or actual products sponsored or created by the marketers is what also creates the new trends. The culture of celebrity, nourished by the TV channels, continues, meanwhile, to create household names for reasons that have nothing to do with sporting, artistic, political or economic achievements.

The youngsters are, thus, denied the time and space to work out their thoughts and desires, communicate effectively with their colleagues and define their identity. They are, of course, thrilled.

Yet digital technologies are affecting not just thinking patterns and other cognitive skills, but also lifestyles, culture and personal aspirations.

The apps have further turned the users into readily sellable data in the hands of the commercial data-mining machines. The very large databases and techniques such as pattern recognition and network analysis have enabled Google, Amazon, Microsoft and other technology giants to know each one of us better than our own mother.

As the adage goes, Google knows more about you than yourself.

And we still do not know where this technology will take us as we are only at the beginning of the big data era. Samsung sort of highlighted it when it alerted the world to its 'sinister' SmartTV, a model which might end up transmitting private conversations to unknown third parties.

Internet-connected tools like smoke alarms or dishwashers may well one day do the same.

Having become a mainstay and being increasingly available worldwide, the internet has also strengthened the western world's cultural grip on the developing world.

Globalisation has, in fact, turned into a cultural bulldozer.

Politically and socially unaccountable, financial markets and transnationals make fundamental decisions about what we eat, what clothes we wear, what drugs we use, how we entertain ourselves, what corrupt regimes are to be supported with our money or how we treat the earth and its population.

The lifestyle of the entire world is the target of a commercial carpet-bombing that threatens to annihilate traditions that go back even thousands of years. The American way of life as portrayed in films and television has turned into a standardised, commodified and dehumanised model to be copied. Patrolling the unconscious, its values impose their imprint on a planetary scale.

299

Even on the small Greek island of Skyros the locals drink coca cola, entertain themselves with American films on video, and frequent bars and pubs rather than the old style tavernas and cafés. Innocently cheerful, young girls look as if they have just emerged from Harvey Nichols.

All this subliminally undermines the nature of the islanders' relation with their past and their values, with their environment, with themselves and with each other, and reshuffles their identity. The 'needs' of peoples beyond the island's own shores become their needs, and western values, anchored on accumulation, consumerism and ostentatious living, replace their time-honoured traditions.

Cultures are, thus, being swept away. Significantly, however, unlike universal truths, those denounced by postmodernism, their disappearance is irreversible. The six hundred languages lost in the last one hundred years can woefully testify to it.

Considering, however, that, as the Californian teacher told his Latin pupils in Isabel Allende's The Infinite Plan, English was all Christ needed to write the Bible, one could also argue that we have five hundred and ninety-nine languages too many.

Though we have many pasts, it looks as if now we all have just a single future whose history, written, has been safely deposited in the Domesday Book.

At least until the 2008 crisis, one thing, however, had not changed and this was the expectations of ever-expanding wealth. The consumption habits of the previous two decades remained unchanged.

People had to live in houses with more bedrooms than a family needs, turbo barbecues, his'n'hers matching four-wheel-drives, heavy 'it' handbags and statement heels. Despite the products' built-in obsolescence and the constant dissatisfaction manufactured by the industry, in a consumption frenzy, they were happy to buy anything they did not really need.

All this led, of course, to record personal credit card debt. But nobody seemed to bother about it, particularly as Intense Pulsed Light treatments, Dermal Fillers or Botox injections ensured that our middle age contemporaries look younger than their children.

Surrendering to the consumerist fantasy seemed to be the reasonable thing to do particularly as there was very little resistance to it. I wondered at some point whether that was an acquired taste or a 'handout' nature had carelessly furnished us with.

Prejudiced in favour of the aberrant, the Greeks went at the same time beyond all known limits in order to reach the outer space of their fantasies.

They ended up in no time beyond all known corners of reality.

24

The Looting of Greece

W ealth attracted now in Athens and beyond the same voracious, brazen, insolent looks seen in the eyes of males accustomed to undressing all females on the street with the power of their imagination. It became the opium of the masses. A cult.

Following Andreas Papandreou's death in January 1996, new elections were held and the 'socialists' were again in power. But something had in the meantime changed. The death also of Konstantinos Karamanlis later, in 1998, saw the end of an era marked by the overpowering presence of charismatic leaders and the beginning of the people's alienation from the political system.

– 'They, the politicians, are all the same', Athenians would often be heard saying.

Nothing like this would have happened in the mid-eighties, when the farcical accounts of the semi-Gods' political battles were the daily news diet of the Greeks.

The new 'socialist' government was headed by Costas Simitis, a moderate man with the equally moderate looks of my Golders Green accountant. Having met him in London, when he was the agriculture minister, I was somehow surprised by his modesty and restrained tone of voice which one could hardly associate with the 'socialists' of Andreas Papandreou.

Abandoning the previous populist policies of the party in favour of the Blairite 'Third Way', the new prime minister raised taxes, reduced public expenditure, extended the privatization of state enterprises and in 1998 he also depreciated the national currency, the drachma.

Despite a storm of reactions in all sectors of the economy, the country seemed, however, to have entered a period of stability and rapid growth.

The inflow of funds from the European Union, which in 1989 reached the 3.8 per cent of GNP, played an important role in this respect as did the inexpensive labour, provided in particular by the 800,000 immigrants from Albania, Romania, Bulgaria and other countries. GDP in 2000 increased by 4.4 per cent.

The positive climate that was created during the period 1998-2000 and, in particular, the growing affluence of urban professionals, saw the impressive growth of the Athens Stock Market.

Hundreds of thousands of Greeks rushed into buying and selling shares in the expectation of immediate fat returns. The race was joined even by housewives, students and pensioners several of whom borrowed money from the banks to finance their investment.

The picture of a young female employee in an Athens shop talking, like an expert, about the Dow Jones is still vivid in my mind.

Despite the continued poverty of the urban unemployed and rural farmers, Simitis was, thus, able to win also the 2000 elections.

But soon after Greece found itself in the arms of a new financial crisis. The stock market 'miracle' was nothing but a financial bubble. The price of the shares dropped, the stock market crashed and hundreds of thousands of Greeks lost their money.

Among the losers were the shareholders of the community-owned Skyros ferry, whose 'clever' investments had left the company stripped of its cash assets. It was a disaster that, among other things, embittered the community.

303

– 'You're idiots', one would say to his old friends with an implacable bitterness in his red eyes.

– 'You don't understand the markets', another would reply with the confidence of a Harvard graduate and the benefit of his inexperience.

A year later, in 2001, following the submission of inaccurate figures about its public finances on account of which the country later on was condemned by the European Commission, Greece entered the eurozone. The drachma was replaced by the euro. The 'inaccurate' figures, incidentally, had been worked out with the 'help' of Goldman Sachs and other investment banks in return for hefty fees which added considerably to the cost of loans.

They nevertheless allowed the Greek government to raise billions in loans which did not count as debt.

The Greek economy did also benefit from the euro-oil, i.e. the generous agricultural subsidies, the regional aid funds and also the broad access to cheap credit which, among other things, fuelled a boom in house building. Unemployment, meanwhile, remained high at 11 per cent as the 24 per cent of the workforce employed in the huge construction sector were underpaid immigrants. Prices of goods were pushed upwards, but despite it the nation's living standards soared.

Feelings of unbridled joy, often transformed into a money-led spiritual ecstasy, swept the country.

Trapped by their morbid love of the coarse sentiments of its calls, the expanded middle class in particular was now looking forward to the gratification of every whim beyond all known limits and experiences.

The emerging picture was a mixture of the pathetic, the obscene and the grotesque.

The fault lines below the surface could not be detected. Yet something, I felt, smelt like rotten fish and that something had more than anything else to do with attitudes. Rather than productively invest the income that grants and subsidies had generated, the Skyrians, for example, used it, instead, to buy property in Athens and consumer goods.

– 'That's not right', I kept telling a few people now and then. 'You've been given an unique opportunity to upgrade the local economy and export its produce – meat, cheese, yogurt, honey, fish, renewable energy or even the folklorist art Skyros island is famous for – and you're just wasting it.'

Once, in response to my constant comments, a Skyrian put his arm round my shoulders as if I was in need of sympathy, the kind of sympathy one would expect after a near-death experience following an Al-Qaeda terrorist attack.

– 'It's all OK', he reassured me. 'Don't worry'.

People seemed to have turned into walking miscalculations.

Farmers, for example, a visiting official working for the minister of agriculture told me in Skyros, exported fruits to Germany. But, she then added:

– 'They put in the boxes' top layer what foreign importers had paid for and underneath they place all the rubbish they should have thrown away.'

She was really so upset that I could almost see her sadness dripping invisibly into her coffee. She knew where all this was heading.

My unease was also being reinforced by the detachment shown by the locals every time I could hear them talking about corrupt deals made by other locals. It was as if everything was part of a preordained order which could neither be questioned nor challenged and from which everybody had or could in the future derive some 'well-deserved' benefits.

Rather than abhorrent, corruption seemed to exert an irresistible charm which, unlike sex, age could not disarm.

Many business people did not seem, however, to share my exasperation with it all.

– 'This is Greece', I was often being reminded with a certain lack of patience for my apparent obtuseness. 'You've been living abroad for too long and lost truck of our ways.'

They almost made me feel like a disinherited son of my tradition.

Or, as someone else put it:

– 'High-mindness is for the loaded. We, poor, can't afford it.'

The poor, one of the town clerks present in the conversation facetiously commented, value their lives as much as the rich.

What we did not know at the time was that corruption had hugely affected the Simitis regime itself and its 'socialist' supporters. The tectonic fault lines under the surface of the country's politics had escaped me partly because the appalling layers of corruption surfaced only later, when Greece was thrown into the crisis, and partly because I had fully distanced myself from everyday politics.

But something, I knew, was fundamentally wrong. There was just too much easy money around backed up by the irresponsible, misguided and even foolish policy of the EU institutions and particularly its banks.

To begin with, Greece had entered the eurozone without having met the Maastricht convergence criteria. But even if it had, this would not have prevented the problems leading to the subsequent deep distortions in the structure of its economy. Fundamentally, Greece, under the new conditions, could no longer use the adjustment mechanisms states employ to fight high inflation. Neither depreciation of the currency nor a rise of the interest rates was now possible. The value of the euro and the euro interest rates were now the business of Berlin.

Meanwhile, in 2003 Germany and France abandoned their opposition to 'excessive deficits'. Breaking the Stability and

Growth Pact was for many what had prefigured the Greek debt explosion and the subsequent crisis.

But the Germans did not seem to care about deficits as, following the agreement at the turn of the century between business and the German trade unions to restrict wage growth, they were able to ensure both high profits and low consumption that forced up the country's national savings rates. Their excessive savings could only be invested abroad.

The German banks were, thus, only too happy to start pouring nearly unlimited amounts of money into the euro-periphery at extremely low or even negative real interest rates. Their exporters of military hardware and consumer goods were, of course, delighted. The eurozone had turned out to be a rich pasture for German cows.

But all this only destabilised the Greek economy. On the one hand, German and Greek interest rates converged because of the common currency, but, on the other, as Greek inflation was higher than German, the real interest rate in Greece was lower than that of Germany. Unlimited credit at excessively low interest rates was, therefore, bound to ignite asset price bubbles and even more inflation.

The cost of those misjudgments was, however, paid not only by the Greeks and the other euro-periphery people, but also by the German workers and taxpayers who at the end were forced directly or indirectly to bail out their own banks. Winners eventually were only conglomerates and banks, mainly in Germany, whose profits were much higher during the last decade than they could possibly have been otherwise.

But at the time we did not have a clue as to where all this was leading us to. And when the inevitable occurred, the Germans were only too happy to blame just the Greeks for their misfortune.

Despite their 'success' story, the 'socialists' began, however, to lose ground. The electorate turned towards New Democracy, which, among other things, had promised the compensation of the shareholders who had lost their money when the market crashed.

The 'socialists' populist policies in response to the collective and undiminished sense of entitlement had now been endorsed by New Democracy under the leadership of Costas Karamanlis, a nephew of Konstantinos Karamanlis. In March 2004 Karamanlis won, thus, the national elections and was in charge of the country when the 2004 Olympic Games were held.

The Games, organised at a cost of €8.5bl, filled the Greeks with pride partly because the country had modernised considerably its infrastructure and partly because of the successful holding of the event. It was the same year that Greece won the European football championship. To top the cake, the following year it also won the eurovision song contest.

The fact that the cost of the Games went 97 per cent over budget or that the Games were financed with loans which fuelled the country's enormous debt did not seem to befog the distant landscape. Nor did the fiscal profligacy which increased Greece's debt from €168bn in 2004 to €262bn in 2008.

The over-lending was so widespread that at one point it drove down the yield differential between Greek and German bonds to just six basis points – a ridiculously low level for two countries that differ so fundamentally in terms of economic management and financial conditions.

But the Greeks, the ordinary Greeks, myself included, could not see we were on the path to annihilation.

Happiness in ignorance is, perhaps, as Oedipus discovered, preferable to unhappy knowledge.

In this irresponsible cross-border lending, suppliers of credit were, however, as guilty as users. Recklessly, the European banks pursued an aggressive expansion strategy without adequate risk controls, a poor safety culture and a slapdash attitude to checks and balances. In the subsequent frenzy, credit standards collapsed and, as optimism soared, consumption grew to unsustainable levels.

In this irresponsible cross-border lending, suppliers of credit were, however, as guilty as users. The absence of due intelligence and responsibility when lending to Greece led, thus, inevitably to the banking blunders which, together with the Greek blunders, led to Greece's economic, political and social meltdown.

But for the time being, the feel-good factor overwhelmed the country, and banks, manufacturers and service providers felt confident enough to start investing more than €3bn annually in neighbouring countries.

At the same time, however, the unfathomable corruption of the system reached new heights and, when laid bare, enraged everything with blood in its veins.

It was something I could not even imagine.

Mind-boggling revelations were continuously appearing in the equally corrupt media as constant reminders of how the rich, these 'shameless sods strutting about like little gods', to recall Palladas of Alexandria, were becoming richer.

Hitting Greece like a tsunami, these scandals inevitably destroyed completely the public's confidence in everything.

Corrupt practices were easy to pursue as several dozen powerful families which control critical sectors, including banking, shipping, energy, construction and also TV stations, influential websites and daily newspapers, enjoyed an incestuous and mutually beneficial relationship with politicians. The preferential treatment of a number of construction companies during the preparation of the Olympic Games that cost the state vast amounts gives part of the picture.

Despite the lack of transparency in public affairs, government ministers of both parties, the 'socialists' and the conservatives, were often caught in what the US Time magazine called 'the looting of Greece': embezzlement, kickbacks, false billing and double invoicing and bribery with banknotes stuffed into envelopes, bags, briefcases and suitcases.

The oligarchs' tight stranglehold over the political system ensured that high-level corruption cost the country about €20bn every year.

Massive bribes were given and received for awarding state contracts to business at overpriced rates and kickbacks during competition bids for the purchase of materials intended for state owned utilities and welfare purposes. All sectors were involved including defence equipment, telecommunications and health or anything else mutually beneficial to the cosy nexus between the Greek oligarchy and politicians.

They also included sweetheart loans and slush fund cash in exchange for favours resulting in useless public works. The marina constructed at great cost in Skyros island sometime in the 1980s was just one of them. It may, of course, be used one day but not before the island's stream water turns into wine.

Malpractice and mismanagement became even more pervasive as the depth of corruption corroded pretty fast the core of the 'socialist' party itself. Not just leading figures, but even prime minister Andreas Papandreou himself was implicated, too, in what was a force 12 scandal.

In 1989 Papandreou was actually indicted by parliament in connection with a US$200m Bank of Crete embezzlement scandal from which George Koskotas, its owner, said the prime minister had profited. Papandreou, who claimed the US government was trying to discredit him, was eventually cleared of any wrongdoing but only after a 7–6 vote in the specially convened High Court trial.

Menios Koutsogiorgas, the most powerful minister in Greece at the time and likely successor to the prime minister Andreas Papandreou, was, however, charged for his part in the scandal.

Part of the evidence against him was the deposit of $1.2m in a Swiss bank account made by a close associate of Koskotas which he returned as soon as it became public knowledge. Taped conversations made public purported to show that he was to receive a total of $2m for 'tailoring' the bank secrecy law to Koskotas' measures.

Koutsogiorgas, who had probably acted at the instigation of his wife, whom he much loved, died in 1991 while on trial by a special tribunal set up to examine the case.

Having met him a few times in London, I had never been taken by his vacant, premeditated, opportunistic smiles. Uninvited and unwelcome just like the TV commercials in a Poirot nail-biting murder story, they were always there to offer some sort of eternal reassurance.

Criminal activities were so widespread that no section of the economy remained unaffected. One example was given by George Papandreou himself, prime minister from 2009 to 2011. He told parliament that the country was the hostage to a pan-Balkan fuel smuggling operation which was losing Greece an estimated €3bn a year. He spelt out exactly how damaging such criminal activities had been, but he did not name the perpetrators, i.e. the Greek oil companies.

Speech is silver, the elders used to say, but silence is golden. It makes sure that whatever happens in the dark never sees the daylight.

– 'What else would you expect', Katerina Remoundos, an old university friend from Athens, said resignedly over the phone.

Her mother would have clapped her ear if she heard the forceful utterances which followed her opening comment.

Still the oil companies that broke the law so flagrantly and chose modestly to retain their anonymity, subsequently helped to ensure George Papandreou was driven out of office.

– 'Prominent bankers and industrialists', Papandreou himself said later, 'were amongst those determined to see me go'.

He was not the only one to encounter the opposition of Greek tycoons.

Constantinos Mitsotakis, the centre-right prime minister who was forced to resign in 1993, blamed for his fall Socrates Kokkalis, the founder of Intracom, a telecoms equipment producer who is listed in the Forbes 500 richest people in the world. Kokkalis was selling equipment worth billions of euros to OTE, Greece's state telecoms company, which Mitsotakis was planning to sell to a French group that would have used its own equipment supplier.

But, perhaps, the most nauseating case involved the 'socialist' powerful defence minister Akis Tsochatzopoulos, a symbol of the 'socialist' party's high-rolling lifestyle. In 2013 he was jailed for 20 years on account of the bribes worth millions of euros he had received during Greece's biggest ever defence procurement between 1998 and 2001. The contracts related to the purchase of German submarines and Russian missile systems for the Greek navy.

In his defence, Tsochatzopoulos threatened to reveal 'a culture of corruption' among the 'socialist' politicians. He never did. But the finance ministry confirmed that 32 senior Greek politicians from both parties were under investigation by the financial police for alleged corruption and money-laundering.

We never heard anything about it ever since.

Tsochatzopoulos, incidentally, whom I had met a few times in London when he was the defence minister, had never impressed me with his qualities. I was hit in the face by his arrogance behind which I could easily detect a false set of values and an emotional ruthlessness which is often called charisma.

Interviewing him once, together with George Yemenakis, the London correspondent of an Athens TV channel and a friend of long standing, I got so annoyed at his shamming attitude that I started shaking my glass full of ice cubes producing a continuous ringing tone that disrupted the recorded conversation.

He looked at me with those chilly eyes, which he took with him wherever he went, let his mouth hung slightly open as if about to say something and, perhaps understandably, said nothing.

Bribing by foreign companies did not, however, end with Tsochatzopoulos. Associated with the sale of submarines, tanks, fighter jets and missiles to Greece by German, French, Russian and other foreign manufacturers, these scandals emerged to the surface when Antonis Kantas, former Secretary General for Armaments of the Greek Ministry of Defence between 1997 and 2002, admitted that during the 'socialist' era he had received nearly €12m in bribes for contracts.

– 'Who bribed you?', the magistrate asked him.

– 'I've taken so many bribes that I've lost count', he responded.

Sweeteners offered by various foreign suppliers of goods and services to potential clients in various countries, had, as it emerged, become increasingly crucial to their winning lucrative contracts.

In another such case, the German firm Siemens was found guilty in Germany for using slush funds and paying billions of euros in bribes to cozy up its Greek interlocutors in order to secure overpriced contracts funded by the Greek taxpayer.

One of those who admitted taking money from Siemens, Transport Minister Tasos Mantelis, was given in Athens a three-year suspended sentence. Siemens was estimated to have made payoffs of €100m over a 17 year period to politicians from both the conservative and the 'socialist' parties, including bribes paid to install a secure communication system for the Athens summer Olympics in 2004. The Greek government claimed that bribes paid by the company from the late 1990s to 2007 cost taxpayers €2bn in overpriced hospital buildings and defence contracts.

Greek officials who brokered the contracts gained millions of euros in kickbacks, and an investigation named in the same context also fifteen Greek politicians.

None of them has been charged.

Prosecutors were left nearly helpless to investigate complex graft cases, including offshore accounts – they were not even allocated funds to make long-distance calls – and parliament was only too eager to pass legislation giving immunity to ever-larger numbers of potential corruption targets. Apart from a few high profile exceptions, the state has been unwilling or unable to instigate legal procedures against them and so were foreign governments when their companies were involved.

As much involved in corruption as the Germans was also the Swedish communication tech company Ericsson, which in 1999 paid €13m in bribes to Greek politicians and military officials to secure the sale to Greece of its airborne surveillance system, and also Saab which took over from Ericsson. So were the Russians who supplied Greece with Kornet missiles and launchers.

Among those bribed to the tune of €1.5m were at least ten members of Greece's armed forces, including a former chief of staff. Bribes were coming, among others, from Ulrich Grillo, president of the Federation of German Industries, who denied the allegations, and the German company Rheinmetall, which confirmed that bribes had been paid.

Kraus-Maffei Wegmann (KMW) was another German company that paid bribes to secure the sale of 24 self-propelled howitzers and 170 Leopard-2 tanks in a deal worth €2bn. Sueddeutsche Zeitung, the German newspaper, revealed subsequently that KMW had also bribed two German socialist former MPs with Greek connections. The payments they received were in excess of €5m.

Other Greeks associated with the government were also charged with involvement in corruption and bribery relating to the procurement of four German Type 214-class submarines. Or for pocketing €23m in bribes to secure a submarine deal with the German firm Ferrostaal.

Asked to estimate the total pocketed in bribes from Greek defence deals over the past 20 years, a government official shrugged and replied:

– 'I'll retire and I still won't know.'

Bribes were so widespread that even a lower-ranking defence ministry employee was found to have a private jet.

I understand he asked for mercy on the grounds he had never before in his life had a private jet to take his fantasies to candlelit dinners in historic country mansions.

Bribing had by that time become a sort of an Olympic sport. Ruthlessly, foreign companies bribed their way into the Greek market and equally ruthlessly unscrupulous politicians, cynical officials and voracious oligarchs had been all busy feathering through them their own nests.

Healthcare employees were among the latter, too. Unearthed this time by the US authorities, their deals involved the pharmaceutical companies Johnson&Johnson and Smith&Nephew. The latter oversaw a system than channelled more than $9m in bribes through a maze of offshore companies to persuade Greek surgeons to use its artificial hips and knees.

At least another dozen healthcare companies were at the same time under investigation for violations of the US Foreign Corrupt Practices Act. In the UK, likewise, De Puy, a Leeds-based company, was found guilty for bribing Greek surgeons to the tune of £4.5m to secure contacts worth nearly £20m. The surgeons had substantial influence in choosing which firms' products should be bought.

Their moral numbness in the execution of their duty was truly beyond belief.

Equally culpable for this corruption were, however, the German and other governments which, though fully informed of the widespread ineptitude, corruption and criminality, chose as a rule to turn a blind eye. As guilty for malpractice were also various overseas financial institutions.

Two of them, JP Morgan, the US investment bank, and North Asset Management, a UK hedge fund, sold to Greek pension funds, managed by government appointees, €1.5bl structured bonds at inflated prices. The fund managers enjoyed in the process, among other things, a few dinners with amorous birds of the night, but the pension funds lost €40m in this transaction. When the scandal broke out into the open, judicial procedures against fifty people, including bankers and government officials, were initiated in Greece.

JP Morgan and North Asset Management were forced to buy back the bonds at face value.

In full swing, the Liars market had reached all levels of society, from top to bottom and pervaded every corner of the day to day life. Though ruthless and unscrupulous politicians had hijacked the economy and orchestrated the workings of the Greek crony capitalism, not a single constituent part of society could escape unscathed by it. Each one of them had been guilty of misconduct.

Deceit and corruption, woven into the country's fabric and evident throughout the entire system, reached new and unprecedented levels.

Clientelism, the corrupt political practice by which politicians reward people for their votes with a cushy government job or favours outside the frame of the law, was just a part of it. The bargaining chip for both politicians and constituents alike, it was what made everything possible.

Well-connected, the party supporters were able to get not only jobs at the expense of the best qualified, but also the means to break the law as the law-enforcers were at the mercy of the politicians. The state apparatus was, indeed, so enfeebled, corrupt and inefficient that even parking tickets could 'disappear' as fast as you can wink your eyes.

Apart from this, many public servants were only too happy to break the spirit or even the letter of the law in exchange for a *fakelaki*, the 'little envelope' stuffed with banknotes. Six in ten Greeks, a research showed, expected public officials to abuse their position for personal gain. Greasing palms seemed to be the norm.

This kleptocracy infiltrated most, if not all, public services and made sure you get a bed in a public hospital, a driver's licence, a planning permission to build where building is not allowed, proof of residence if you happen to be an illegal immigrant or a clean record if you happen to have spent time in prison. You could also ensure that your tax collector would overlook your true net income.

Cash was expected even if your request was fully in tune with the requirements of the law.

I paid it as a student to get the army certificate I needed in order to get a passport. Had I not paid, I would have, I was told, to wait until the officials had the time to look at it, i.e. the end of our geological period.

Incidentally, corruption at a daily, ordinary level is part of the British culture, too, as I have witnessed many times myself on the Isle of Wight.

People often choose to enjoy their unemployment benefits rather than get a job. Alternatively, they are willing to work but for cash so as not to lose these benefits. And fraud within the National Health Service costs something like £5bn a year due to the non-payment of prescription charges by patients, medical professionals claiming for work they have not done and overcharging by contractors.

But nothing compares to the sea of ordinary corruption in which Greece was drowning, the fraud that summed up pointedly and also most alarmingly the collapse of all values across all social strata.

The island of Zakynthos, 'the island of the blind', made the case most disturbingly. About 1.8 per cent of its population, i.e.

about 600 people including a taxi driver and a bird hunter, were able to receive blindness benefits on the back of fraudulent certificates supplied by doctors and local politicians.

'Blindness' did not prevent them, of course, to count very accurately the €2m a year paid to them by the taxpayer.

But Zakynthos was hardly alone as fraudulent claims were a problem across the nation costing the government hundreds of millions of euros every year. In another instance, as a friend was telling me, his auntie had been receiving a pension on account of her 'resistance' activities during the German occupation of the country. She had not only failed to join the resistance, he added. She had actually opposed it.

– 'Local politicians', he reflected with a sadness in plain clothes, 'had issued a false certificate'.

In Heraklion, Crete, likewise, out of the 489 people receiving social benefits, 73 were dead. The number of dead people receiving a pension in Greece numbered actually in their thousands, 9,000 of whom were more than 100 years old.

The applicants probably did not know they were dead.

Fraudulent claimants included farmers who drew billions of euros from the European Union on the strength of false subsidy claims or women who enjoyed multiple maternity benefits though they had never had any children.

– 'In effect', as my friend Nicos Papadakis, the Greek embassy's press attaché in London and a confident of prime minister Costas Simitis, put it, 'almost all Greeks, from media barons to shop keepers on islands and to municipal clerks in villages, were in one way or another part of it all.'

Greece had come to a dead end and the Greeks somehow knew it.

Corruption was, indeed, one of the chief causes of both the disgust felt by every Greek I knew and of the December 2008 resulting riots that shocked the entire Greek world.

'Institutionalised greed', I wrote in the *Financial Times* on the 12th of December 2008, 'has eroded traditional values and so has the ensuing lack of concern for anything outside the flow of money or the violence, hidden or otherwise, inherent in the actions of all those invested with power. Wealth and power are the only things that matter. People, particularly the vulnerable groups including old-age pensioners, hospital patients, prisoners, immigrants, petitioners, the unemployed or protesters, end up in despair, while those whose voices can be heard conveniently evade the issues.

'The latter', I emphasised, 'includes the Greek Left, both 'socialists' and communists, who have exploited the riots in the interests of party politics.'

The issue was no longer political. The nefarious, multifaceted fraudulent activities were not out of line with the traditions and the culture of the country.

'The issue', I said, 'is social, and as such it cannot be dealt with without a cultural revolution that will regenerate the collective morality in all areas, political, social and economic and will change the ethos of the country and the people's attitudes to life. What is needed is a new perspective which neither the conservative government nor the 'socialists' or even the communists can offer. The country is, unfortunately, deadlocked.

– 'It helps, however', I concluded, 'if the Greeks can just acknowledge it because acknowledgement is the first step towards the solution of the problems.'

Acceptance of the worst in ourselves, as Henry Miller said, may be the only sure way of transforming it.

When the moment of truth arrived later, the country started to wobble. The mood entered a downward spiral and the Greeks screamed like a hare caught in a gin. But still rather than acknowledge their own mistakes, they blamed the calamity on, originally, the 'politicians' and later on the 'foreigners', whether Germans, the ECB, the IMF or the leading financial institutions.

The focus shifted to the tragically ill-conceived and also cruel and inhuman terms attached to the bailout that, on the one hand, saved a few European banks from bankruptcy, but, on the other, stifled the Greek economy and drained the country of its blood.

Yet the crisis that hit the country in 2009 was not the result of the subsequent bailout. It was its cause.

Whatever happened after 2009 is, therefore, one story. What happened before it is another.

But this was not something one could easily discuss in Greece. Whenever I did, I found myself into a minority of one, a position that denied me by definition the intellectual supremacy held by the majority.

– 'The political and financial élite', I was informed by, among others, the niece of former prime minister Elias Tsirimokos, 'is corrupt to the bone and responsible for our fate'.

This as if all the others had been nice and innocent bystanders, familiar only with sports, food, sitcoms and children.

25

Work 'Powerfully Charged'

Looking for something with quietness on all its four windows, in 2004 I settled together with Christine Schulz, my affectionate, vivacious partner, in the Isle of Wight.

The island was, at first glance, an unlikely place for me to settle. But it appealed partly because as an island it defined my own state of mind at that stage of my life, and partly because it reflects an unconfessed aspect of myself: that which still inhabits the old world.

Perhaps, if I were still young and ambitious, I would still be in London whose stimulating environment I often recall with affection – the times when walking down Hampstead High Street, I would be meeting people asking me if I had read their latest novel, listened to their latest symphony or watched their latest play. It was that interaction that often burst the framework of the daily realities and reinforced my incentive to be creative myself and go, if possible, beyond the confines of my boundaries.

The beauty of it is that once you have made it in London, you have made it in the whole world.

I remember *The Guardian* once writing about Mikis Theodorakis, the composer, who, it said, if British, would be as well known worldwide as the Beatles. I would have no argument with it. Mikis is a genius of the very first order, the Beethoven of our time.

Moving to the Isle of Wight served a practical purpose, too. Most of the people going to Skyros lived either in London or the South-East. The facility to reconnect with the Skyros spirit after their return home ought, therefore, to be in that part of the UK, in close proximity to, and easily accessible from, their home and ideally on an island. The Isle of Wight perfectly fitted the bill.

The Isle is extraordinarily beautiful, tropical-looking in many places. Part of the old world which has completely crumbled in the UK's metropolitan centres, it is in the arms of a sublime uneventfullness and at peace with itself. Faithful to its history, unpretentious and unembellished, it maintains its traditional character.

Walking in its old towns is like walking into a fairy tale or, at least, in the back streets of yesterday, the times when, as George Burns, the comedian, said, the air was clean and sex was dirty. That was the time before we turned into something which is still waiting for a name. That was also the time we could remember what the future looked like.

The New World does not look here so new. The old weekly sewing parties have, of course, gone out of fashion and people, I am sure, do not sew gold coins into their old clothes. But the locals do not seem to pay high fees to modern living. Many cannot even hear the messages sent out by the metropolitan centres and others just blank them out.

So charmingly back in time, the Isle has not even come fully to terms with the presence on its shores of those foreigners who pollute the environment with their incomprehensible languages. A middle-aged female Shanklin shopkeeper whose sex life, I could bet, had gone stale since the death of princess Di, hearing two women talking in a foreign language, even reprimanded them for their audacity.

– 'You're in England, dear. You have to speak English.'

The women were talking in Welsh.

Interestingly enough, the island is largely unknown to the British, more familiar with the back streets of Kathmandu than with their own back yard. Hence their questions over the phone:

– 'Do I need a passport to visit the island?' 'Which side of the road do you drive in your part of the world?' 'What currency do you use?'

A woman who took a cab from Ryde to Shanklin expressed, likewise, her astonishment at 'how good the English of the taxi driver was'.

I wondered where she thought she was. In Jamaica?

Helped by John Wigham, the outlandish Skyros facilitator, the right place – The Grange in Shanklin – was eventually found and, though independent, became the British offshoot of Skyros.

The building is a magnificent 1820s mansion, part of the old Shanklin village and close to all shopping facilities. Yet its front faces a rapacious forest and a voluptuous sea neither of which care much about super high resolution 4K TVs or PlayStation Now. It is an extraordinary place.

Hence it won instantly, among others, the heart of my son, Ari, who in 2004 had here his wedding party. Nearly two hundred guests, mainly from London, danced to the frenzied tunes of the local bands and sung until the morning before, exhausted, they took their elevated spirits to bed for a few hours' rest.

Ari and his wife, Susie, live now in Switzerland together with their three kids, Leonardo, Alexander and Emelie.

The Grange, a B&B in which Skyros-type weekend courses are run, opened its gates in the summer of 2004. Christine was in charge of it. Dina at the same time took over the management of the Skyros London office, which was relocated to the Isle of Wight later, in 2008.

For a few years I was, thus, left with enough time and plenty of ink and paper to finish my Trilogy. Despite all changes, my energy had not gone. There was enough of it to light up a street.

There was also enough to deal with my mundane realities necessary to keep the show on the road, do, in other words, things like locking all doors at midnight or answering the phone when nobody else to answer it was there.

Having enough time, I did , thus, manage to finish my Trilogy which was handed over to the publisher, Imprint Academic, in September 2007. The moment it was published, in March 2008, was the moment that counterbalanced all my life's failures.

Perhaps, if I had handed it over a year later, when the financial crisis, responding to the bankers' invitation, arrived unceremoniously in the UK, it might have never been published.

The Trilogy went under the following titles:

– In Bed with Madness: Trying to Make Sense in a World that Doesn't

– The Greek Inheritance: Ancient Greek Wisdom for the Digital Era

– The Future of the Past: From the Culture of Profit to the Culture of Joy

Following their publication, people were not spotted reading the books greedily on the train to Guildford, the benches of Hampstead Heath or the libraries of Kensington. Sales failed to reach the 150 million copies of JRR Tolklen's The Lord of the Rings or the 107 million copies of JK Rowling's Harry Potter and the Philosopher's Stone.

But still the Trilogy, though I had forgotten to attach free vouchers for a night in Richard Branson's state-of-the-art Virgin Hotel, went into a second edition, and attracted some very flattering comments.

'This is tangible, compelling, driven and heartfelt writing at its best', wrote Kathryn Adams for Leonardo Online, the International Society for the Arts, Sciences and Technology. The books were 'powerfully charged'.

An Amazon reviewer did also find them 'the most thought-provoking books I've read' and for another one, Rodger Kibble, they offered 'a breath-taking whistle-stop intellectual and cultural history of the Western world'. The Writers' News also reviewed them in similar tones and also presented, in addition, my short biographical note.

Crysse Morrison, the author, found the Trilogy 'full of sound bites that snap at the heels of your conscience'. The books offer, she wrote while sipping her chilled Chardonnay, 'a well-argued, powerful, profound indictment of contemporary culture, that end paradoxically with hope'.

For another reviewer, Oliver W. Davies, the trilogy was 'impressive' and 'outperforms De Botton by streets. It was also written and closely argued as anything of Comte-Sponville'. 'Erudite and provocative', another reviewer said, 'these books are ultimately hopeful and help open up a new dialogue that potentially expands our human capacity'.

Antti Kuusela of Metapsychology did also view the books as 'a thought provoking work written with good style'. She cherished the idea that all is not necessarily lost, and she quoted a sentence from my book according to which 'the challenge is not practical... It is primarily spiritual and cultural. It is a challenge for our psyche. To meet it, we need to rediscover who and what we are -- indeed, what is the essence of being human'.

But, as many have pointed out, if people learned from books, libraries would be closed to the public.

I do not even know what I have learned myself from the books I have written. Like Faust, I feel 'no wiser than I was before'.

But, meanwhile, as time was ruthlessly advancing without reference to my requirements, I had started to feel increasingly challenged by developments beyond my control.

Without my agreement, the world, eager to reach its destiny as quickly as possible, was now running twice as fast as before. While anything but certain about the tincture of its coveted 'destiny', I was, however, in no doubt about my own disinclination to enter the race. The incentives were missing.

That would not be the case if I were in tune with our reality as it was re-defining itself. But I was not. The terrain had gradually started to look increasingly devoid of the naturalness I had been used to. The feeling of being at home in it was no longer what it used to be.

Fundamentally, I still preferred involvement with people rather than digital gadgets, meaningful rather than superficial cyber relations and a society engaged in the opening of the future's door rather than looking for the lost key to it. I did not need any new and great innovations to enjoy my life.

The major contribution to minor needs made by the digital technology had never caused waves of intoxicating uproar in my head. I could not see why I needed smart watches to provide me with data about my pulse, pupil dilation or stress hormones.

Such innovations, Pablo Neruda might have said again, 'don't do what the spring does with the cherry trees'.

Even worse, whatever its benefits, the 'bright' new age had also given me a feeling of discomfort originating in the knowledge that, irrespective of my efforts to keep up with the latest, I knew less and less every day. The idea of adventure, which in the past meant swimming in the womb of mystery, was now embodied in the act of ordering a book online.

Successfully done, it entitled me, or so I felt, to nothing less than a standing ovation.

Resentment, which Aristotle would have reminded me is beneath a magnanimous man, started gradually to build up. Rather than learning new things in order to improve myself, I now had to do so just in order to keep my head above water. The future suddenly seemed to me to be a cause of irritation rather than sanguineness.

Nostalgia for my father's time engulfed me in its arms. He had learnt what he needed to know by the age of 16, and that was enough to get him through until the day he laid down his fork and knife.

I only hope that the day we will demand a referendum on whether we want more new things may, perhaps, not be too far away.

And indeed, if we eventually comprehend fully what professor Stephen Hawking, one of Britain's pre-eminent scientists, has said about artificial intelligence, it may not be. When fully developed, he predicted, 'it could spell the end of the human race'. Or when we fully come to terms with other issues such as genetic engineering.

But there is a 'but' to all this, often inevitable as the interest the bank charges on your overdraft. This 'but' is enveloped in that new and ever-present condition of thought which has become almost a part of the eternal requirements. Whatever we feel about them, we just cannot do without all things with which the new world has endowed us.

I became fully aware of it the day my connection to the internet was interrupted for 48 hours. The world suddenly seemed to have come to an end. The internet, I realised at that moment, was now as indispensable to my existence as the air I breathe. And who knows what the future has in store.

Perhaps, Mama Mia, our Shanklin local restaurant, may well one day email me the pizza pepperoni I had ordered rather than deliver it by car. It would certainly save time and money.

Frustration had inevitably increased for an additional reason. When I started writing this book my intention was to follow developments using the personal tone I have done so far to describe events right up to the present day. To do so I needed, however, to be in London where I would be able to associate with many of the leading stars of the current Greek drama. But as a resident of this gentle island reality where developments occur beyond one's personal experiences I could not do that. Apart from the everyday essentials, anything beyond this looks as distant as the falling stars.

People can talk about the financial crisis, technology, globalisation or institutional corruption but, if one is not directly involved with the processes, he or she may well end up as detached from it as from the church's after life promises.

Living on the island was, of course, the result of a free rather than an enforced choice. But the reason behind this decision had less to do with the beauty of the island and more to do with something else that I was not too eager to acknowledge.

Something in all this was certainly sending me a message, perhaps in smoke signals: 'You're getting old.'

But I am not good at reading smoke signals.

Though at a conscious level unaware of it all, having finished my Trilogy but still unable to sit down and just watch myself growing old, in 2014 I wrote this book. It was only after I had finished it that I realised that my journey to the past, to a world I had never really left behind, was anything but accidental.

The feeling, as a result, was that time had turned the corner without me. I could still hear its footsteps, but I could no longer see its face.

In any case, going back several decades was a pleasure, albeit not an undiluted one. It was not exactly like opening the door to let the garden walk in.

Among other things, it made me wonder what happened to all those kids who sat together with me in the same class of the 10th boys school of Athens, behind the Panathinaikos FC stadium, listening to George Doukas, our classics teacher, who was trying, albeit without much success, to introduce us to the spirit of Pericles' Funeral Oration.

But I do not have the answer as I have lost track of them.

Walking in Athens I no longer recognise anybody. Even people I know from the age I started knowing are difficult to identify. Bellies grow, hair goes, backs are hunched by time and faces are marked by the wrinkles of the heart. Several of them must surely have passed the time when people are proud to be old.

In the process, I also often wondered what I managed to achieve after all those years. Nothing much, of course. My wisdom is not going to be the source of inspiration to the future generations. And success seems to have eluded me. A successful man, I always thought, is the one who does what he chooses to do and not what he has to.

This is a stage I have not reached and I do not think I ever will.

On the other hand, the past reviewed has left me with nothing to regret apart from my fundamental defects which, as Virginia Woolf said, no wise man regrets.

More seriously, however, going back in time makes me wonder if life has given me the ultimate prize: the fulfilment and happiness one can hope for. Sitting in a bit of space time occasionally provides, I address my inquiries to the stars which, unfortunately, just like God, have nothing to say in response.

Once, while enjoying a pint of prawns on the terrace of the Steamer Inn, a Shanklin pub on the seafront, I watched all those around me, simple, normal people trying to conquer a mountain masquerading as a hamburger, reprimanding their children for teasing the dog or exchanging jokes while leaking their ice cream cones.

They all seemed content and as much at home with the moment as a candle in the local church of Saint Blasius.

Even if sometimes it lasts no longer than an orgasm, happiness, I thought, is not something unattainable.

People could, just like me, choose the flavour of the ice cream they fancy: vanilla, pistachio, strawberry, chocolate or even bacon or garlic. The industry is ready to satisfy every trifling taste. And they look happy. Or, at least, content. Life, you are then convinced, is a gift we should be grateful for. Except that nothing is ever so simple.

From the moment we evacuate our mother's zone of influence, happiness demands something more substantial than an ice cream. It demands primarily the absence of fear, anxiety, stress or pain. It then rests on the satisfaction of our physical needs, some basic comforts, good health, loving relationships, a few good friends, acres of sea, snow or sunshine and, I believe, a clear conscience.

A challenging activity, a sense of purpose and a meaningful job into which we can put our heart is always a source of satisfaction. So is the pursuit of attainable goals. Bridget Jones certainly thought so though, unfortunately, she never managed to accomplish her own goal – a slim figure.

Goals are important, but for Aristotle, whose Nicomachean Ethics influenced decisively western philosophy, whatever they are, they can never be ends in themselves. They are only a means to an end: the attainment of happiness, eudaemonia.

Defining happiness in Aristotle's terms is a very challenging task, which inevitably took me for a walk into his mind. The pleasure of it turned in no time into a spiritual joy.

Eudaemonia is reached if life is lived in accordance with areté. Somehow inexact and uncertain and also poorly translated as virtue, the latter involves the active exercise of the soul's faculties in the pursuit of moral, intellectual and physical excellence. In this it is guided by Logos.

Again poorly translated in English as Reason, Logos is the voice of everything, visible and invisible, finite and infinite, ephemeral and eternal. Rooted in the subconscious, it is accessible through our intellect, instinct, feelings and intuition.

Happiness in the Aristotelian sense is, thus, a state of inner fulfillment reached in the pursuit of perfection. It is the affinity of what Heraclitus called the 'soul-fire' with the cosmic fire outside in the context of something larger than ourselves and also in tune with Logos, the voice of the universe. Thomas Acquinas understood it as the pure bliss of union with God.

As such, dependent neither on particular things nor on circumstances, eudaemonia is a steady and constant state in which we are happy even when misfortune hits our door. In that state we will be able to bear adversity with serenity, dignity and even pride.

A virtuous person, Cicero said, 'will be happy even on the torture rack'. The same was the meaning of Wittgenstein's last words – 'tell them it was wonderful', uttered after a life of more pain than most people experience.

This is exactly what is evident in the life of so many people from Rosa Luxemburg, Martin Luther King and Mother Teresa to millions of others whose names history, too busy with the chronicling of crimes, just failed to record.

It follows that without access to the commands of our better selves, the most we can expect in life is contentment provided, hopefully, through a succession of little infusions of pleasurable activities: a hot bath, a shopping expedition, a nice dinner, a ménage à trois, a drinking spree or just a good film on our TV screen.

All these may give us pleasure, but pleasure is not identical to happiness. Happiness cannot be bought. And choosing pleasure over happiness, Aristotle said, is certainly a very poor choice.

Riding on the back of an endless wealth creation and constant demand designed to satisfy the needs the advertising industry tells us we have, poor choices reflecting such poor values lead further and inevitably to dissatisfaction, discontent and an aggressiveness that seems to feed on bulls' testicles pies.

They force us to work harder, lose sight of our humanity and experience at the end a spiritual emptiness from which drugs or alcohol provide no escape. They only trap people in an inferno of vice.

Hence all the chill of our invisible realities that have entered inaudibly and irrevocably into our lives and the ensuing unhappiness which wealth can adorn in Karl Lagerfeld's latest Spring Couture collection but cannot eradicate.

Rather than a gift, life turns then ineluctably into a cross, which, Jesus warned us, we have to carry. 'Whosoever doth not bear his cross', he said, 'cannot be my disciple'.

At a personal level, things are not too bad. Though professional routines are still wearing me down, at least I do not have to worry where the next meal would be coming from. The soul-disfiguring consumerism has not touched me, nature in all its beauty is part of my universe and my creativity, the source of my energy and optimism, is still unscathed.

Perhaps, one day I will also write a novel, produce a few more songs or sculpt on stone my dreams.

Though content, I still, however, cannot 'blank out the still sad music of humanity'.

Life is tough for so many people. This may have to do with their reduced circumstances due to unemployment or very low income, health problems, marital break ups, social alienation, broken relations, loneliness, uncertainties, unmet needs, desires or expectations, professional misery, anxieties and fears, obsessions and compulsive behaviour, frustrations, anger, depression, phobias, alcoholism, drug abuse, low self-respect, emotional vacuum or self-destructiveness.

Exploring their values, determining their goals or just working out what is the meaning and purpose of their lives becomes at the end a luxury most people cannot afford. People are doomed forever to seek but never to achieve happiness.

But if the dream of the good life becomes subsumed into the callousness of reality, in whose cage we have been born, this has less to do with the individual and more with our 'one-dimensional' world.

Taking inanity into its bed and sending critical thinking to the kennels, our economic, social and cultural realities are, as a result, determined not by us but by a market that is totally dominated by financial institutions, multinational conglomerates and media empires. None of them care for anything but themselves. And none can be challenged. Their global power is just breathtaking.

The fragrant dream of a better world does not, thus, seem able to fly on the wings of our desires. We are free to do anything except change the world.

– 'Powerless with a guitar' as Gunter Grass put it rather melancholically, we can only watch life go by, while, 'finely meshed and composed, power has its way'.

Cynicism verging on nihilism has, as a result, become the new global ideology which the financial crisis at the end of the decade has only reinforced. This is not, however, the world I want to live in.

Discussing all this in Athens with Nikos Ntokas, a cynical ex-colleague and friend, was, as one might expect, short of results. He leaned forward with his elbows resting on his knees and his hands clasped together and just said nothing.

Unfortunately, I thought later, I had raised the issue with him when he had just finished having a quarrel with his dishwasher.

– 'If nothing else', he said eventually in the balcony of his flat in the Athens suburb of Holargos under a sky ribbed with reddish bars of cloud, 'this will make sure that we'll have something to talk about for the rest of our lives'.

Sadly, he died next year and I was left with one friend less. It seems that the longer we live, the fewer the friends we end up with to meet up for a Metaxa.

Though immovably fixed in my thoughts like Delos, the floating island, which was immovably fixed in the sea when Apollo was born, I do, however, come across times that I do also wish that my seemingly inordinate expectations had a body I could push down the river. I would then feel much freer to read a novel, watch the Arsenal game on TV or go to the nearby theatre to have, as Margaret Atwood would say, a few relaxing hours of treachery, sadism, adultery and murder.

Beguiled by the serpent of the entertainment industry, I might even then go for something irresistible such as that video party game, Kiss the Midget, and indulge in all the ageless pleasures time has never failed to honour.

After all, pursuing distant things in the arms of ever-active thoughts does anything but guarantee satiety.

Yet, I have never tried to escape the infinite of a vision by fleeing into the infinite of the illusion the 'me, me, me' society heedlessly provides. The urge to keep going is unpacifiable. I cannot help thinking, that to justify the air I breathe I needed to offer the universe something in return – if nothing else, my time.

Forgivable means of escape are not in any case easily available.

And instincts do not rust.

26

A Cultural Revolution

hree people, Lord Palmerston, the mid-nineteenth century British prime minister, once quipped, knew the answer to the Schleswig-Holstein question. That was a complex issue relating to two Danish duchies in the 19th century. But one of them was dead, the other had gone mad, and he himself had forgotten all about it.

I do not blame him for it. I cannot even remember myself the time I first met my own mother.

Perhaps, at least three people must have the answer to the question I keep asking myself while the Shanklin Bay sea keeps shimmering boundlessly with the most radiant indifference. What can we do so that we end up with a world that makes sense?

But, unfortunately, not knowing who they are, we are left all alone in the struggle to find the answer. I hope one day we will.

And hope, as they say, is happiness.

Looking for a new beginning myself, I went for inspiration just like the German and British Romantics, back to the fluid and cheerful culture of classical Greece. The idea did, of course, look to many outlandish, the mad exteriorisation of my unrestrained misconceptions.

– 'It's a joke', one of them, Myriam Hale, a New Ager from a different planet, said in a moment she thought I was beyond her vocal reach. Astonished at the idea, she almost spilled her wine.

All the air-kisses we had exchanged earlier no longer needed to be treasured.

That was in a 5-star hotel in Elounda, Crete, where years ago, when you could still smoke on the upper decks of buses, I had gone to give a talk in a New Age conference.

The reception of my suggestion was not, at least at the beginning, any easier at the conference hall itself.

– 'You can't be serious', a young fellow with a Mohican haircut, a ring through one nostril and eyes full of sympathy for my mental confusion told me in hushed tones but as emphatically. 'Ancient Greece, a world that thrived on slavery and treated women as inferior human beings, can't teach us anything'.

Yet, though the position of women and the existence of slavery undermine the philosophical underpinning of my thesis, the assumptions on which life was built are still humanity's guiding light.

A return to the values of a bygone era is, of course, inconceivable.

The river cannot start flowing backwards. But the power of concepts which can provide inspiration to our contemporaries is there, calling for their re-appraisal, recognition and restoration.

As John Fowles put it in his mesmerising The Magus, not all powers have to be discovered. Some have to be regained.

People started to get more interested and I was asked to define the core message of my ideas. I gave them the same answer Athene had offered to the Athenians:

– 'Let your State hold Justice as its chiefest prize.'

The Greek perception of Justice had its roots, as I said in my Trilogy, in the belief that everything in the universe was interconnected within a whole. In that whole everything had its place and required respect. Just as winter could not appropriate the time allocated to spring, a citizen could not grab what belonged to his fellow-citizens, the desires of the flesh could not be allowed to control the whole person and a dictatorship could not be sanctioned as a system by which a city is run.

Taking it to its contemporary context, it means that 'we' respect the rights of 'them', whether 'them' is women, consumers, ethnic minorities or foreign cultures, that the rights of the Third World to get affordable medicines are not annulled by something the West calls protection of intellectual property, or that our seasides are respected rather than violated by the furious forces of development.

Committing an offence against the whole was hybris, and hybris, as Solon, the Athenian statesman, forewarned, was bound to be punished in 'the court of time'.

Punishment could come sooner rather than later if and when, for example, we fail to appreciate rest as a time for silence and contemplation rather than as a means for recuperation for more work on the production line.

Squinting slightly, putting one finger to the chin and looking upwards thoughtfully, another conference acquaintance proceeded to put on record his full agreement with it.

– 'More work doesn't have much to recommend itself for'.

Before retiring to his placidity, he looked at the members of the conference with a seemingly authentic smile.

The same sense of Justice underpinned the Greeks' commitment to proportion, balance and symmetry in everything they did in life. The goal was, on the one hand, the avoidance of excesses, and, on the other, to the all-rounded excellence of the individual.

Excellence was pursued not just in one field, football, fashion design or medicine, but in all fields: intellectual, moral, aesthetic, emotional and physical. A man had to be a committed citizen, an honourable person, a creative thinker and a lover of beauty in all its forms.

– 'Balance, proportion and symmetry are still honoured concepts', my friend Nicos Papadakis remarked while we were enjoying a coffee in West Hampstead.

– 'We take good care of our bank balance, are fully aware of the need for proportional returns and distribute symmetrically our investments'.

His sense of humour was good. But Nicos, unfortunately, died in London in 2013 after a long illness. His funeral was attended by a number of people I knew from the years we were all committed to the struggle against the Greek dictatorship.

Age had not been kind to them.

In the same spirit, arbitrary acts, the prerogative of the barbarians, could not be excused in cities of noblemen. The citizens had to refrain from criminal, unethical or even just indecorous acts. More than that, committed to their community rather than to their own selves, they had also to make a positive contribution towards the welfare of their polis.

Those who failed to live up to the polis' expectations and violated the common trust were, even if they did nothing illicit, named and shamed. Letting down your friends, partners and fellow citizens, resorting to unethical practices or trespassing on the rights of the community for personal gain was contemptible.

– 'Our contemporary tradition is obviously not infected by this kind of conviction', Elias Kavouriades, a student at the Athens Law School whom I had met at a party, said jestingly while we were taking about it in Stadiou Street under the marquee of a movie house to keep dry during a heavy rain.

It is certainly not.

The rain, incidentally, was quite unexpected. The sky had refused to comply with the instructions issued by the weatherman.

All citizens of Greece, 'when Greece was young', were entitled, not just to equal rights before the law as in our own society, but to the enjoyment of everything their society considered to be good. This did not mean that inequality was not accepted. Those with money had, however, to spend it in a way beneficial to the community rather than for the satisfaction of lecherous pursuits.

The offspring of their perceptions and the mother of their achievements, the polis summed up the greatness of the human spirit. Athenian democracy, in particular, involved literally each and every citizen in its public affairs, from trade policy to diplomatic relations, from military campaigns to law court decisions, from artistic projects to civic duties and legislative matters.

The citizen had direct access to power, shared its responsibility, was an integral and decisive part of the whole decision-making process. Fully involved, a master rather than a subject, he was, as a result, inspired, motivated, proud to belong, eager to contribute and willing to suffer. The polis was his polis. His were its successes and its failures.

It was what inspired the Occupy movement in Athens and beyond.

As such, Greek democracy, Josiah Ober, professor of history at Princeton University, stated in the 1990s, provides the departure point for all those who refuse to accept the ever-expanding, hierarchical power of governments and corporations as an inevitable and natural outgrowth of social complexity. Its anti-bureaucratic, anti-secretive and anti-hierarchical nature, which all modern democracy refuses to be, is an eternal source of inspiration.

So is its commitment to civic virtue.

The latter demanded just and honourable action irrespective of achievements in the pursuit of the right and the good. Sincerity, truth, honesty, fairness, authenticity, loyalty, courage or any other quality presumed 'good' were not means in search of ends. They were ends in themselves, inherently capable of giving life the meaning one looks in vain to find in the TV sitcoms, this contemporary temple of spiritual fulfilment.

No noble ends could, therefore, justify dishonourable means.

Light years away from utilitarianism, things, likewise, had an intrinsic value for what they were rather than for their benefits. I was reminded of it when talking to Mark Gunston, the Skyros windsurfing instructor, who, at the age of 59, decided to take a three-year course in filming.

My conditioned mind was the first to react in response.

– 'What do you reckon are the job opportunities after that', I asked thoughtfully without thinking.

He remained cool as the ginger beer in his glass.

– 'I don't do it for money', he replied. 'I do it just because I like it.'

– 'Oh, my', I gasped very impressed, my unconditioned mind having instantly recovered possession of itself. 'Well done.'

The red squirrel that was scurrying along the oak tree signified inaudibly his approval.

Rather than for the purpose they served things were enjoyed for what they were. This was for the Greeks the road leading to happiness, which as Aristotle held, is associated only with what we choose for itself. The thing itself was excellence, the leading of a just and honourable life and the pursuit of beauty as demanded by the Greeks' irresistible impulse.

Beauty as an aesthetic concept signified love of the beautiful in its aesthetic, moral, intellectual and physical form. It also manifested itself in a person's character, the culture of the time or the foreign policy of the state.

But at the same time, the same Greek culture valued simplicity, a virtue, it was believed, only the unwise would not possess. Simplicity was its own ticket to admission into their sophisticated world.

Man, in any case, did not need much to live on. As in today's world, the best things in life cost nothing. Wealth was contemptuously dismissed because of its corrupting influence, and consumption was despicable.

Drawing a line between man's limited 'natural' and his unlimited 'unnatural' needs, the Greek culture placed the emphasis on one's ability to control his appetites, curb his desires for material goods and focus, instead, on the development of his potential.

– 'Become who you are', Pindar, the lyric poet who was nourished with honey instead of milk, said, meaning that the potential is within us in seed form the moment we are born.

Michael Eales, this perspicacious man long associated with Skyros, was in full agreement with this view. 'Absorbed in the pursuit of success as it is conventionally perceived, we rarely explore our true potential', he added when we were talking about it in Skyros island.

Laughing thunderously in his usual manner, he then reminded me of someone we both knew who had made a fortune as a banker and had come to Skyros looking for the soul he had when a baby. Having sold the one he had and living effortlessly on its proceeds did not, however, make his task as easy as he thought.

The emphasis was on character rather than personality, substance rather than image, doing rather than having, creating rather than consuming and becoming rather than being.

Rather than enrichment, consumption, showbiz, flat screen TV sets, miniature MP3 players or top-class lingerie, the ideal was self-realisation, the development of the individual's potential to the full, and immortality through one's oeuvre in life. Pleasure was not allowed to interfere with the pursuit of higher goals.

But at the same time work ought never to turn people into slaves. Doing so would preclude the pursuit of a beautiful life.

Having conquered their freedom from necessity, the necessity to work long hours to buy things they did not need, the Greeks were, thus, able to master their time and devote their energies to the attainment of all the personal qualities that a man *kalos k' agathos* was associated with.

The Greeks, Michel Foucault, the French social theorist who influenced decisively the thinking of our postmodernist era, said, had discovered 'the art of existence'.

Greece's influence can be seen in Marx, too, whose 'guiding model', Hannah Arendt who shared his views on the subject, said, was 'doubtless the Athens of Pericles', except that in the communist society 'the privileges of the free citizens were to be extended to all'.

These ideas, incidentally, which have an endangered species appeal, form the backbone of the Skyros concept, which, as the years progressed, developed and influenced a good number of people. Skyros had not just inspired them. More than that, it enabled them to travel beyond current realities and gave them what many have called 'a life-changing experience'.

The whole, which the Greeks associated with life itself, is, of course, no longer. Their impregnable belief in the intrinsic value of all things in life has been extirpated. The flag of Reason has turned grey. All that matters now is mastery of the world associated with the clout of depravity, Bangkok by night, as the added bonus.

But going back to the time when the dawn opened its petals and the day came to consciousness, is, I believe, a move to the front line of the conflict against conglomerates, bureaucracies and experts. It is the salient point in the battle against the ethos of the free market and the culture of apathy, disengagement and greed.

It will enable us, American sociology professor George E. McCarthy said:

– 'To look more deeply into ourselves and our society, into contemporary institutions and crises, psychological repression and linguistic distortions, and political legitimation and capital accumulation.'

It is what may provide the inspiration needed to make another effort towards the revitalisation of civil society. Hence the journey to the Greek past is a journey to the future which can give us back the sanity we have expelled from our lives, re-radicalise our thinking and help us to look forward with the fearless philosophical earnestness of the early years.

Going back to the earlier times would certainly be quite useful as after all, the recent financial crisis was triggered not only by miscalculation and greed but also by the loss of values in a basic sense. Successfully taken, such a step may also give again the contemporary Greeks the spirited eyes of pride.

– 'Interesting', a friend sharing a table in the basement of a taverna in Athens' Plaka district told me just as he had finished his gigantes plaki. 'But it's not do-able'.

– 'Perhaps you're right', I answered a glass of wine later. 'But we still need to look both inwards, into our own selves that keep pulling us apart from community and nature, and outwards into the culture and the socio-political institutions that express but also fortify our disengagement from the world of values. The journey inwards is necessary as undependable individuals can never contribute to a meaningful change.'

To me this is of major importance as, irrespective of our intentions, we just fail to live up even to our own expectations.

– 'I've seen people', I carried on, 'committed to democracy, and paying at times an exorbitant price for it, only to betray their ideals because of their own control-freak inner selves. I've associated with others contributing generously to noble causes and yet eaten up by ambition, envy, selfishness, greed, intemperance, bitterness, callousness, negativity or pretension. I've also met socialists, arrogant, devoid of any human feelings, radiantly indifferent to pain unless pain can be translated into the language of ideology.'

Inner and outer are not two sovereign republics. They are part of the One, in constant dialogue with each other, affecting each other even when the dialogue seems to be conducted between the deaf.

Inner awakening through self-scanning is thought to be the business of specialised agencies such as the Church or psychoanalysis whose founders did, admittedly, try to make a difference. It ought, however, to be the business of the civil society through a mass movement not affiliated to political parties so that it can act as the conscience of the nation.

– 'What I have in mind is something perhaps like the CND in the sixties or the Friends of Earth in the seventies and beyond', I told back in the early eighties my newspaper colleague Aristeidis Manolakos, a decent man who later on was elected president of the Greek NUJ.

While skilfully avoiding an oncoming car in Piraeus Street, Aristeidis listened, gave me a look of tolerant amusement and then smiled, I presume, at my naivety.

He was obviously certain that some things are never going to change.

The key-word to describe the essence of such a movement is Justice which, however, is open to as many interpretations as Damien Hirst's work.

It requires as far as I am concerned the recognition of everyone's right to live in peace in life's wintry streets, free from fear, domination, manipulation, abasement and exploitation. It is about security of existence, protection against avoidable risks, the development of the individual's potential and a person's freedom to enjoy all the simple pleasures of life.

Even if, to quote Italian filmmaker Pier Paolo Pasolini, as poor as a cat in the Colosseum, we all have a right to clean air and water, respect for who and what we are, active membership in the human club, a voice in the way our common affairs are run, and a friendly smile.

Everything that is not 'us', if 'us' is humans, males, Europeans, the young or the able-bodied is still part of 'us', even when it does

344

not have a voice to express its anguish, and even when we, blindly, at home with our misery, fail to see it and identify with it.

For inside 'their' distress lies a portion of our own.

This means that whatever is not 'us' is not a means to increase 'our' wealth and power, but something with intrinsic value worthy of our protection. The sun shines for all without discrimination.

Morality, after all, has nothing to do with a person's sexuality which is what the theocratic, heteronomous and, by definition, anti-humanist Judaeo-Christian dogma has decided. It relates only to our dealing fairly with everyone and everything: the members of our family and our friends, our employers or employees, suppliers and customers, leaders and supporters, nature, our community or the future generations.

This, which of course cannot be legislated, demands personal attributes – fair-mindedness, honesty and courage, in rather short supply in our time – and now and then a glass of wisdom. Or, perhaps, two.

Costas Raptopoulos, the civil engineer, conveyed instantly his unqualified agreement, but Mihalis Petralias, the solicitor in Halkida, just nodded slowly while trying desperately to swallow back a yawn.

As the embodiment of the hopes and prelapsarian aspirations of the whole of humanity rather than those reflecting class, gender, race or other interests, morality as a universal concept is not, of course, easily defined. The concept is as vague as the advice offered by the pythoness to Podalirius, the son of Asclepius.

He had consulted the Delphian oracle about the best place for himself to live safely only to be advised:

– 'Look for safety wherever you would suffer no harm even if the skies were to fall.'

Talking about morality, one does have to make allowances for the 'context'. But whatever the context, if asked, seagulls will never agree to die on oil-polluted beaches, monkeys will never acquiesce to ending their lives painfully in laboratories, forests will never permit their destruction by man. No person loves living in fear, no hungry, homeless, destitute people will ever concur with their condition, no repressed individuals, minorities or nations will salute their repression.

Likewise, no homosexual man or woman will accept his or her being bullied, no one will endorse his or her being racially discriminated against, no person will ever forego his or her right to be, and no culture or language will ever commit suicide. Nonetheless, people and situations are forced to submit to a power which places no limits on itself, coerced to accept what they do not want to accept and even consent to their exploitation, repression or destruction.

To me, this defines the universality of injustice, recognised, as Aristotle said, like the unsound condition of the body. As such, it sets the parameters within which universal Justice can be explored, and humanism, as the 'actual appropriation of the human essence' according to Marx or the 'endeavour to render man free for – and to find dignity in – his humanity' according to Heidegger, can be given flesh.

Even so, universally shared values to which the citizens of the world and all sexes will be invited to subscribe are not on display. There is not, for example, an authoritative answer to questions such as euthanasia, abortion, the cloning of human embryos for research purposes or the death penalty.

Likewise, there is nothing to guide us as to the desirable level of taxation, the powers of the EU or the nationalisation of assets, and there is not just one voice when it comes to issues such as genetically modified crops, the single currency or nuclear power. Though it remains the supreme guiding principle, equality has furthermore the looks of a blasted tree.

Full and equal distribution of everything – wealth, honours, dignity, in the name of social justice – has, of course, as much a chance to make it as a snowball in the seventh circle of hell. Fundamentally, the concept has its own internal limitations, for nature, refusing to progress or regress like her subjects, cannot, or is unwilling to, distribute her favours equally to everybody. And merit, as Aristotle said, has to be rewarded.

Even restricted, distributive justice is, however, anathema to those addicted to selfish calculation, the free marketers.

It is offered by the market but only as negative equality, i.e. one which treats humanity like a herd and feeds it cotton balls soaked in grease. Rather than being equal in strength, individuals are equal in their weakness and rather than being equal as distinct individuals, with their own diacritical marks, they are equal in their sameness. Likewise, rather than being equal in joy, they are equal in misery.

Searching for the essentials which will enable us to reconnect with the generous, benevolent and noble part of ourselves is bound to look like a journey to the other side of eternity. Yet this is the journey which can break through all barriers of the self and take us back on the road to some sort of original purity.

But man, as Zeus decreed some time ago, must suffer to be wise. Stupidity, ambition, greed or envy, the demands of an Ego, the governing part of our personality not controlled by the law, make sure of it. Nobody but one's own self can force a person to accept internal checks and balances, act with self-restraint, acknowledge the rights of the 'Other' and put in place a set of useful self-limitations.

The issue, though personal, is at the same time political because whole systems are built on the same 'precious us' mentality.

The individual, as Aristotle pointed out, has to be good, for the polis depends on it. At the same time, the goodness of all is necessary for the goodness of each. Hence individual goodness was not the task of the individual alone. The polis itself, breathing concern about its own destiny, had to ensure that a man becomes and also remains a good man.

But those pursuing structural changes, too full of self-importance, deal condescendingly with those on the path of inner transformation.

Those engaged in inner work, on the other hand, cannot often even grasp the importance of reaching out to what is commonly called reality. Yet without working at both levels, the inner and the outer, the personal and the political, the individual and his or her culture, the road to change will remain blocked like gutters choked in the winter with dead leaves.

The 'good life', Aristotle could have said again, is neither a life spent on the golf course nor in front of the television set, but a life committed to the pursuit of higher goals in the context of the polis.

In such a context, people reach their potential like water does its level.

As if inscribed upon the ebony of the night, the Left will not, however, easily see this truth. Its drive is towards policy choices dictated by a sense of social justice, which nevertheless cannot be achieved in a society consisting of self-seeking individuals, full of themselves and as guilty for the unseemliness and tribulations of life as the system itself.

Cambridge University Professor John Dunn reminded us of it in his book The Cunning of Unreason. 'If the purposes which govern state power... are to become wiser, less myopic or more austere', he pointed out, 'it is we who must change, not the states to which we belong'.

Words of wisdom do not, however, seem to take us all that far particularly at times when, chained down by the new world order, it is difficult to envisage a very different world. Of concern to most becomes then not the long term prospect, but survival from one day to another.

– 'You don't understand', someone whose complexion had been weathered from his pain told me in his house in Nea Smyrni, an Athens suburb, while he was watching on television an old

Greek film with Vasilis Logothetidis. 'I've got a law degree and two young children, we all live in my parents small flat, and often we can't afford to buy even a packet of crisps. If you want to help, tell me something that will make a difference in our lives.'

I could not blame him. Though oozing fine feelings, my words had offered no deliverance. Not a ray of light in them nor a promise of coming grace in the midst of a tragedy. I did not need a detector to spot the translucent stain despair had left on his heart.

Rather than being drawn into the jaws of the argument, I, thus, backed down. Distraught, soon after I took a car and went to Phaleron Bay, where, on the beach, I started throwing pebbles into the sea, which at the time, content with itself, was sighing as one turning in a deep sleep. Two young girls holding hands looked at me and suppressed a smile.

In the process, it occurred to me that, perhaps, opening holes in the water is what we all end up doing in our lives.

I was quite unhappy, but my stressed state of mind, I thought again, rather than a drawback might well be an asset. After all, the most promising time to go for the seemingly impossible is not when you are as happy as the young girl who takes her first gulp of champagne, but when you fall into the arms of despair.

For, as André Gide said, in destitution lies salvation.

Myself, I do not expect that one day I will 'hang out the washing on the Siegfried Line', as the First War song goes. And, perhaps, all I am doing amounts to nothing more than articulate a few useless thoughts in times devoid of any meaning.

The question posed by our need to live in a world that makes sense does not seem to have an answer. It is, indeed, bound to remain unanswerable for ever. Residing within our own selves, the forces mitigating against the Right and the Good are beyond the limits of our power.

'The world turns and the world changes', T.S. Eliot said, 'but one thing does not change: the perpetual struggle of Good and Evil'.

Even though historical events fly off towards the horizon line in succession like an endless row of cranes, the battle for the Right and the Good is, therefore, bound to continue until apocalypse changes the script.

Hence Heraclitus' understanding of Justice had nothing to do with 'love'.

– 'Justice', he said, 'is strife', 'war', so that all things end in tune 'with what they must be'.

Wars and battles may have been terrible ever since Claucus of Chios discovered the art of welding, but, as Porphyry, the Neoplatonist philosopher, explaining Heraclitus' views said, 'they all contribute to the harmony of the universe'.

And this dialectic made headlines in my thinking even when I felt all my plain labours had been in vain.

It still continues to dominate my thinking now that the global financial crisis has badly hit the eurozone and, more vicious than the earthquake that toppled the Colossus of Rhodes in 226 BC, has devastated Greece.

Life in Athens turned into a pale reflection of the previous vibrant era and people just stared at it like zombies lost in traffic. They still do so six years after the blow.

Europe, in its infinite wisdom, turned Greece into a prisoner like water imprisoned in water tanks and forced it to keep paying with sweat, blood and tears not only for its own but also for the European institutions' corrupt practices, mistakes and excesses.

It all has an explanation, short or long, which I would associate first and foremost with stupidity and greed. Yet, whatever the explanation, the fact remains that this tragic misadventure highlights only the madness in whose tuneless music we love to dance.

Madness has been and still is a conditional term in our judgment of everything.

Born in 1939, Yannis Andricopoulos spent the formative years of his life in Athens – years scarred by wars, deprivation and political repression. 'We managed to survive', he says, 'but only on grains of hope'.

With a BA in Politics, he joined the Athens daily *Avghi* in 1964 and in January 1967 he was sent to 'swinging London' as its correspondent. The appointment was, however, short-lived as the Greek dictatorship closed *Avghi* down in April 1967 and deprived him of his passport. His actions, the colonels claimed, were 'detrimental to the national interests of Greece'.

While a political exile, he earned a Ph.D. in History from London University. He was also elected as the head of the Greek National Union of Students (EFEE in exile). The latter's activities caused, among other things, his expulsion from a number of East European countries.

In 1974 he resumed his career as a London-based correspondent first for *Avghi* and then for *Eleftherotypia,* another Athens daily. In the same year, he also published his first book, *1944, Κρίσιμη Χρονια* (1944, A Critical Year), an edited version of prime minister Churchill's personal papers on 1944 Greece. He has since published three more books on 20th century Greek and European history and as a journalist he has reported from various trouble spots of the world.

In 1979 he co-founded, together with psychotherapist Dina Glouberman, Skyros Holidays, described by *The Guardian* in 2008 *as* 'the first and still the best' alternative holiday. He still co-directs it. Ten years later, from 1989 to 1994, he also edited *i-to-i,* an alternative London publication, which attracted contributions from numerous established journalists and authors.

His trilogy – *In Bed with Madness, The Greek Inheritance* and *The Future of the Past* – was published by Imprint Academic in both the UK and the US in 2008. Inspired by his involvement in the truculent world of politics and the graceful, personal world of Skyros, the Trilogy takes a critical view of contemporary politics and culture.